EDEN Annual Conference 2025

Shaping the Future of Education in the Age of AI: Empowering Inclusion, Innovation and Ethical Growth

Concise and Other Papers

Bologna, Italy
15 - 17 June 2025

Editor:

Elena Trepulė

ISBN: 979-8-3313-2646-3

Printed from e-media with permission by:

Curran Associates, Inc.
57 Morehouse Lane
Red Hook, NY 12571

Some format issues inherent in the e-media version may also appear in this print version.

European Distance and E-Learning Network (EDEN)
Budapest University of Technology & Economics
H-1111 Budapest, Egry J. u.1.
Hungary

Phone: +36 1 463 1628
Fax: +36 1 463 1858

secretariat@eden-online.org

Additional copies of this publication are available from:

Curran Associates, Inc.
57 Morehouse Lane
Red Hook, NY 12571 USA
Phone: 845-758-0400
Fax: 845-758-2633
Email: curran@proceedings.com
Web: www.proceedings.com

EDEN Annual Conference Proceedings

Shaping the Future of Education in the Age of AI: Empowering Inclusion, Innovation and Ethical Growth

EDEN 2025 Annual Conference

hosted by

University of Bologna, Bologna, Italy

15-17 June 2025

Edited by

Elena Trepulė

on behalf of EDEN Digital Learning Europe

EDEN Annual Conference Proceedings

2025 Annual Conference | Bologna, 15-17 June 2025

ISSN: 2707-2819

Published by EDEN Digital Learning Europe

Editor:

Elena Trepulė

Editorial co-ordination:

Gabija Morozovienė

EDEN DLE Secretariat

Kuklase tn 16-12, 13423, Tallinn, Estonia

E-mail: secretariat@eden-europe.eu

https://eden-europe.eu/

Co-funded by the European Union

Funded by the European Union. Views and opinions expressed are however those of the author(s) only and do not necessarily reflect those of the European Union or the European Education and Culture Executive Agency (EACEA). Neither the European Union nor EACEA can be held responsible for them.

Acknowledgement and thanks are given to the Conference Scientific Committee:

Wim E.A. Van Petegem, EDEN President, Belgium; Chair

Antonella Poce, EDEN DLE Management Board, Italy; Chair

Pier Cesare Rivoltella, Bologna University, Italy; Chair

Airina Volungevičienė, Lithuania

Alfredo Soeiro, Portugal

Chiara Panciroli, Bologna University, Italy

Denise Whitelock, The Open University, UK

Elena Trepulė, EDEN / Vytautas Magnus University, Lithuania

Giuliana Benvenuti, Bologna University, Italy

Josep M. Duart, UOC, Spain

Mart Laanpere, Tallinn University, Estonia

Maurizio Gabbrielli, Bologna University, Italy

Maurizio Sobrero, Bologna University, Italy

Polona Baloh Kremavc, Slovenia

Rebecca Montanari, Bologna University, Italy

Roberto Vecchi, Bologna University, Italy

Sandra Kučina Softić, University of Zagreb University Computing Centre, Croatia

Simone Martini, Bologna University, Italy

Simona Tondelli, Bologna University, Italy

Vlad Mihăescu, UPT, Romania

TABLE OF CONTENTS

Personalized learning

Assessment and micro-credentials

CONCISE PAPERS

Collaborating with Heritage Institutions is Essential to Your AI-Enhanced Teaching Practices in the Humanities

Deborah Seid Howes

President, Howes Studio, USA, deb@howesstudio.com

Correspondence: Deborah Howes: deb@howesstudio.com

Abstract:

A core practice of museums, heritage sites and other authorized collections of cultural materials is maintaining comprehensive digital archives for public benefit. Their professional staffs also produce educational programs and materials that augment public understanding of these collections as well as humanities more broadly. EdTech organizations developing AI tools for learning will maximize their impact by both integrating these digital resources into tool training and collaborating with humanities professionals on tool design. Here are three essential ways these partnerships can invigorate studies in the humanities:

Authority and accuracy: Large language models LLMs acquire information largely from the Internet and subsequently need extensive training to distinguish between factual from inaccurate content. Agents trained on these LLMs are known to "hallucinate" by inventing nonexistent citations, links, or facts. By contrast, retrieval-augmented generation (RAG) models are trained using pre-identified, authoritative sources. Imagine building AI agents on top of RAG systems dedicated to trusted sources such as museum-developed databases of collection images, object labels, media documentation, or digital catalogues. Not only would these RAG-based AI agents be valued by students and teachers for their trustworthy and verifiable outputs, but they would also be more energy efficient as they analyze a contained, high-quality dataset.

Equity: Prompts sent to LLMs can return culturally-biased results, for example, displaying images of white European males over individuals from the Global South. Many museums and heritage collections are broadening their holdings and research to reflect more diverse cultures and perspectives. Recent exhibitions—such as *Foreigners Everywhere* featured during the 2023 Venice Art Biennale—highlight underrepresented cultures, materials and practices. Cross-sector collaborations between cultural institutions, educators, and EdTech innovators can co-develop AI-enabled applications that support equity-forward learning experiences.

Experience: Early AI-based applications attempted to bring past events and figures "to life" via chatbots that "converse" as historical figures. However, increasing student proficiency in the humanities requires skill-building that goes beyond acquiring and memorizing facts. Humanities professionals are experts in fostering critical thinking skills–including observation, comparison, evaluation, experimentation, debate, and discussion. Museum staff regularly mentor emerging professionals, such as interns, to excel in these critical functions. Heritage educators can help train AI agents to guide students along an exploratory, self-directed learning path, mirroring the guidance they provide on public tours or when training classroom teachers on informal learning pedagogies. Multidisciplinary teams creating AI-enabled tools can expand learning goals to include the more elusive "how" and "why" of the humanities alongside the standard "who" and "what."

Keywords: artificial intelligence (AI), retrieval-augmentation generation (RAG), large language models (LLM), museum, heritage, humanities,

References

EDEN Digital Europe #OEW (2024) *The future of AI in formal and informal education context: inclusion, ethics and new perspectives*. [Webinar]. YouTube. https://youtu.be/Py-kq_kuqTY?si=-JxdVt9wi2B52i4s

Howes Studio (2023): *Museums and Artificial Intelligence.* HowesStudio.com

National Gallery of Art. (2024). *Teaching complex thinking through art with the National Gallery of Art*: https://www.nga.gov/learn/teachers/online-courses.html

From ADDIE to EDI: A Design Process for Instructional Chatbots

Eran Barak-Medina

Holon Institute of Technology, Israel, Faculty of Instructional Technologies; eranba@hit.ac.il

Correspondence: Eran Barak-Medina; eranba@hit.ac.il

Abstract:

Generative Artificial Intelligence (GenAI) paved the way for the rise of Instructional Chatbots. This type of instructional product has the potential to design performance support solutions that are just-in-time, engaging, and seamlessly integrated into the workflow. No more knowledge transference issues, Instructional Designers can now provide a solution that enhances performance and impacts real work processes in real-time.

Such an instructional solution requires instructional designers to examine and reframe the development framework to accommodate unique requirements and understanding of the features of this rising instructional tool.

For this purpose, we propose the EDI framework, which blends traditional Instructional Design elements with the unique decisions that instructional and performance-supporting chatbots require:

1. Empathy: Includes the "Why?" (what problem or challenge needs to be met), studying the learners and creating learner personas, researching the current workflow, and analyzing Use-Cases.
2. Design: Includes the organizing idea of the solution (or "the pitch"), designing the transformative knowledge structure of the chatbot (knowledge and prompting), and writing the script.
3. Iterate: Creating Use-Tests, first by the developers and then piloting with users, and adjusting the chatbot's design to optimize performance.

The EDI framework has been developed and tried with instructional technology students, and this experience has helped validate and refine it. The insights from applying this framework in developing instructional chatbots will be shared.

Keywords: Generative AI; Instructional Design; Chatbots.

References

Maheswari, B., & Nagarajan, R. (2024). EduChatbot: Implementing educational Chatbot for assisting the teaching-learning process by NLP-based hybrid heuristic adopted deep learning framework. *Kybernetes*.

Manohara, H. T., Gummadi, A., Santosh, K., Vaitheeshwari, S., Mary, S. S. C., & Bala, B. K. (2024, March). Human Centric Explainable AI for Personalized Educational Chatbots. In *2024 10th International Conference on Advanced Computing and Communication Systems (ICACCS)* (Vol. 1, pp. 328-334). IEEE.

Nguyen, H., Le, T. T., Nguyen, H., Nguyen, L. D., Dinh, D., Pham, V. T., & Nguyen, H. D. (2024). Design a Knowledge Chatbot System in Education Based on Ontology Approach. In *New Trends in Intelligent Software Methodologies, Tools and Techniques* (pp. 15-28). IOS Press.

Peterson, C. (2003). Bringing ADDIE to Life: Instructional Design at Its Best. *Journal of Educational Multimedia and Hypermedia, 12*(3), 227-241. Norfolk, VA: Association for the Advancement of Computing in Education

(AACE).

Ramandanis, D., & Xinogalos, S. (2023). Designing a chatbot for contemporary education: A systematic literature review. *Information*, *14*(9), 503.

Ruamsuk, Y., Mingkhwan, A., & Unger, H. (2024, February). Designing and Implementing Chatbot Dialogues for Effective Knowledge Exchange: A Methodological Approach. In *2024 IEEE International Conference on Big Data and Smart Computing (BigComp)* (pp. 464-469). IEEE.

Enhancing Computational Thinking Through Genai-Driven Educational Robotics

Noga Reznik[1], Maya Usher[2], Dan Kohen-Vacs[3]

[1] Faculty of Instructional Technologies, Holon Institute of Technology, Israel; Nogal@hit.ac.il

[2] Faculty of Instructional Technologies, Holon Institute of Technology, Israel; Mayau@hit.ac.il

[3] Faculty of Instructional Technologies, Holon Institute of Technology, Israel; mrkohen@hit.ac.il

Correspondence: Noga Reznik: Nogal@hit.ac.il

Abstract:

For over two decades, Computational Thinking (CT) has played a vital role in preparing students for the modern labor market. CT promotes systematic problem-solving by breaking down challenges, identifying patterns, and designing solutions (Wing, 2006). Recent advancements in Generative Artificial Intelligence (GenAI) have expanded the scope of CT education across various domains and educational levels (Kohen-Vacs et al., 2024; Kurtz et al., 2024). This study presents the development of a technological learning environment that integrates a humanoid robot (HR) enhanced with GenAI capabilities. Using a Visual Computer Language (VCL), students can program the robot to perform action sequences either on a physical robot or through a virtual, animated simulation (Figure 1).

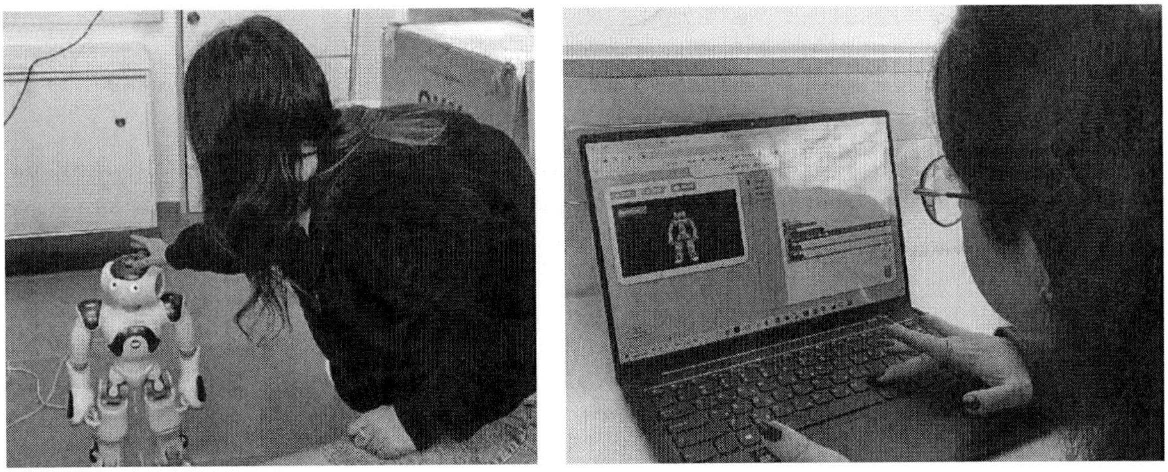

Figure 1: Students interactions with the tangible form and virtual representation of the HR

The environment includes a user interface (VCL UI) where students engage in block-based programming, execute their code on the robot, and receive formative feedback (see Figure 2).

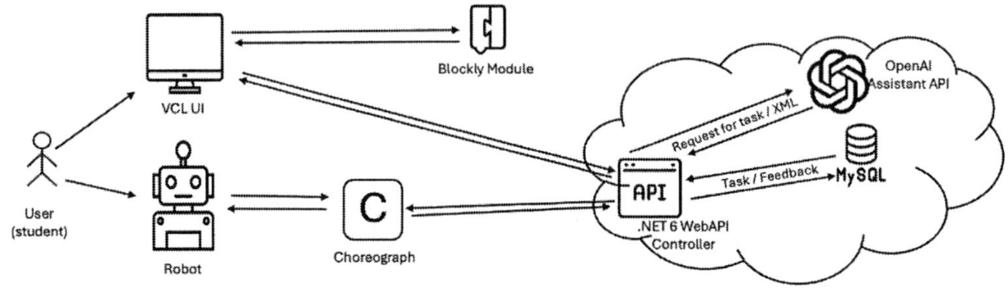

Figure 2. Overview of our developed environment

Students begin by answering three diagnostic questions prepared by the course instructor to assess their CT proficiency. Based on their responses, the system classifies each student into one of three difficulty levels. The GenAI module then generates a personalized CT task tailored to that level. Students complete the task using the VCL UI. Upon completion, students can view the results of their programming through two distinct modes. In the Tangible Mode, the solution is executed on a physical humanoid robot, offering real-time, hands-on feedback. This is enabled by the Choregraphe software, which translates the programmed block sequences into actions performed by the robot. A dedicated web controller serves as an interface between the Choregraphe software and the programming environment. Alternatively, in the Virtual Mode, the robot's actions are simulated within the VCL user interface, allowing students to visualize the outcome even when the physical robot is unavailable.

Both modes offer formative feedback to enrich the learning experience. All activities—including task generation, code execution, and student feedback—are logged in a MySQL database, enabling instructors to monitor student progress and adapt their teaching strategies. This personalized, adaptive learning environment—driven by GenAI and supported by tangible and virtual robotics—aims to enhance student engagement, foster problem-solving skills, and develop computational thinking in a dynamic, interactive setting.

Preliminary feedback from students highlights the system's ease of use, the appeal of block-based programming, and the value of immediate feedback and visualization features, all of which contributed to a more meaningful and enjoyable learning experience.

Keywords: Computational Thinking (CT), Generative Artificial Intelligence (GenAI), Visual Computer Language (VCL), Humanoid Robot, NAO, Educational Technology

References

Kohen-Vacs, D., Amzalag, M., Weigelt-Marom, H., Gal, L., Kahana, O., Raz-Fogel, N., Ben-Aharon, O., Reznik, N., Elnekave, M. & Usher, M. (2024). Towards a call for transformative practices in academia enhanced by generative AI. *European Journal of Open, Distance and E-Learning*, 26(1), 35-50. https://doi.org/10.2478/eurodl-2024-0006

Kurtz G, Amzalag M, Shaked N, Zaguri Y, Kohen-Vacs D, Gal E, Zailer G, Barak-Medina E. (2024). Strategies for Integrating Generative AI into Higher Education: Navigating Challenges and Leveraging Opportunities. *Education Sciences*, 14(5), 503.

Wing, J.M., 2006. Computational thinking. *Communications of the ACM* 49, 33–35.

Wing, J.M., 2006. Computational thinking. *Communications of the ACM* 49, 33–35.

Trust Under Test: Evaluating Students' Detection of AI-Generated APA Records and Its Impact on AI Trust

Lilach Gal[1], Netta Soreq[2]

[1] Faculty of Instructional Technologies, Holon Institute of Technology, Israel; Lilachg@hit.ac.il
[2] Faculty of Instructional Technologies, Holon Institute of Technology, Israel; Nettas@hit.ac.il

Correspondence: Lilach Gal: Lilachg@hit.ac.il

Abstract:

In the era of artificial intelligence, the proliferation of AI-generated academic content poses significant challenges to academic integrity and information literacy. User trust in AI-enabled systems is a critical determinant of their adoption and effective utilization in academic environments, particularly influencing how students and educators integrate these tools into their scholarly work (Kurtz et al., 2024). Research suggests that trust is shaped by user characteristics, system transparency, and ethical considerations (Bach et al., 2024). However, concerns regarding AI-generated misinformation and decision-making processes can foster skepticism and distrust (Scharowski et al., 2024).The aim of this study was to examine students' ability to evaluate the reliability of academic sources generated by Generative AI (GenAI) systems, as well as to investigate how exposure to unreliable information affects students' trust in AI as an academic tool.

Custom GPTs are specialized versions of OpenAI's ChatGPT, allowing users to modify model behavior through specific instructions, embedded knowledge, and enhanced capabilities (Zhao et al., 2024). These customizations enable domain-specific applications, including academic research, cybersecurity, and automated content generation.

Leveraging these capabilities, the present study initially aimed to investigate students' ability to detect AI-generated citations through an experimental design involving approximately 90 second-year undergraduate students from the Faculty of Instructional Technologies. Participants were divided into three groups, each exposed to different types of APA (Academic Publication Attribution) records: completely fabricated sources, sources with minor distortions, and reliable citations [see Figure 1]. To support this design, three custom GPTs were developed to generate experimental materials with varying levels of accuracy. Data collection was conducted within the mandatory "Information Science and Internet Literacy" course (2 credits), which focuses on developing critical digital literacy skills, including the evaluation of information sources, advanced search strategies, and understanding the implications of AI in academic writing.

Completely fabricated APA record:

• Wachs, S., Jiskrova, G. K., Vazsonyi, A. T., & Wright, M. F. (2019). **Protective factors against bullying and cyberbullying: A meta-analytic review.** Aggression and Violent Behavior, 45, 94-112.

APA record with minor distortions:

• Zych, I., Farrington, D. P., & Ttofi, M. M. (2019). Protective factors against bullying and cyberbullying: A systematic review of meta-analyses. *Aggression and Violent Behavior, 45*, 4-19.

Reliable APA record:

• Zych, I., Farrington, D. P., & Ttofi, M. M. (2018). Protective factors against bullying and cyberbullying: A systematic review of meta-analyses. *Aggression and Violent Behavior, 45*, 4-19.

Figure 1. Examples of APA Records by Level of Authenticity

While the original hypothesis posited that significant differences would emerge between groups in their ability to identify unreliable APA records, technical issues with the custom GPTs compromised the functioning of the experimental intervention, preventing it from operating as intended and thereby limiting the ability to assess the differential outcomes. Nevertheless, the research process itself yielded important insights into students' interactions with AI-generated academic content. These insights are crucial for refining future experimental designs and for informing subsequent studies on students' critical evaluation skills in the era of AI-driven content creation.

Keywords: Generative AI, Information Literacy, Information Literacy, Information Literacy, Information Literacy, ChatGPT

References

Bach, T. A., Khan, A., Hallock, H., Beltrão, G., & Sousa, S. (2024). A Systematic Literature Review of User Trust in AI-Enabled Systems: An HCI Perspective. *International Journal of Human-Computer Interaction*, *40*(5), 1251–1266. https://doi.org/10.1080/10447318.2022.2138826

Kurtz, G., Amzalag, M., Shaked, N., Zaguri, Y., Kohen-Vacs, D., Gal, E., Zailer, G., & Barak-Medina, E. (2024). Strategies for Integrating Generative AI into Higher Education: Navigating Challenges and Leveraging Opportunities. *Education Sciences*, *14*(5), 503. https://doi.org/10.3390/educsci14050503

Scharowski, N., Perrig, S. A. C., Aeschbach, L. F., von Felten, N., Opwis, K., Wintersberger, P., & Brühlmann, F. (2024). To Trust or Distrust Trust Measures: Validating Questionnaires for Trust in AI. *XXX*, *1*(1), 1–22. http://arxiv.org/abs/2403.00582

Zhao, B. Z. H., Ikram, M., & Kaafar, M. A. (2024). GPTs Window Shopping: An analysis of the Landscape of Custom ChatGPT Models. In *Proceedings of ACM Conference (Conference'17)* (Vol. 1, Issue 1). Association for Computing Machinery. http://arxiv.org/abs/2405.10547

Insights on Using GenAI: Through the Lens of an Assessment for Inclusion Framework

Geraldine O'Neill[1], Leigh Graves Wolf[2], Sheena Hyland[3]

[1] UCD Teaching & Learning, University College Dublin, Ireland; geraldine.m.oneill@ucd.ie
[2] UCD Teaching & Learning, University College Dublin, Ireland; leigh.wolf@ucd.ie
[3] UCD Teaching & Learning, University College Dublin, Ireland; sheena.hyland@ucd.ie

Correspondence: Geraldine O'Neill : geraldine.m.oneill@ucd.ie

Abstract:

The use of GenAI in assessment in higher education online, hybrid and in-person curricula is giving rise to challenges and opportunities for both staff and students (Xia et al, 2024). In parallel, higher education is striving to be more inclusive in its assessment and feedback practices (Ajjawi et al, 2023; Bain, 2023; Tai et al. 2023). The term 'assessment for inclusion' (AfI) is beginning to be used to describe the approaches that aim to give all students the opportunity to succeed (Ajjawi et al, 2023). This leads to the question: *How does the use of GenAI align with or conflict with our goals for inclusive assessment practices?*

This paper explores the use of GenAI through the lens of AfI. It draws on GenAI and assessment literature (i.e. Xia et al, 2024, Smolansky et al., 2023), the experiences of the authors as educational developers, and reflections on its use in a recent GenAI research study on students in a professional University Teaching Qualification programme (who were also staff) in a large research intensive University in Ireland. It critiques the use of GenAI using a new 'Assessment for Inclusion Framework', in particular through the lens of the framework's design principles, i.e. to be diverse across a programme; be authentic; be flexible; be manageable; be scaffolded; support active citizenship (UCD T&L, 2025).

Some insights include:

- Findings on the 'manageability' of assessment present a contradiction: while some studies suggest GenAI can save time during assessment tasks (Lee & Moore, 2024), this inquiry found students emphasised the significant time investment required to effectively learn and utilise GenAI tools as an increased burden.
- GenAI has the potential to help many students who struggle with writing to 'scaffold' their assignments and is one of the recognised value of its use with students (Perkins et al, 2024).
- GenAI can be weaker on 'authenticity' in assessment as it sources from more generic data. As a consequence, more 'authentic' assessments are being used as a means of deterring GenAI use, a more inclusive approach (Smolansky et al., 2023).
- The different technologies used in GenAI in assessment are vast; however, many institutions are financially restricted to a limited choice of technologies that all their students can access. Inequality in the accessibility of some students to the more powerful tools pulls against the overarching aim of 'equity' in assessment for inclusion (UCD T&L, 2025).

- Both the GenAI research on assessment (Xia et al, 2024) and assessment for inclusion research (Bain, 2023) advocate for more diverse approaches to assessment.
- GenAI has the ability to easily create rubrics for staff to use with their assessment. This can support the 'transparency' of assessment for students, a key design principle in AfI.

This concise paper presentation will further explore these and other AfI tensions around the use of GenAI. The critique of a GenAI use, through an AfI lens, is critical to ensure that we remain committed in higher education to the opportunity for all to succeed.

Keywords: Assessment, Inclusion, GenAI, Design Principles, Framework, Student Success

References

Ajjawi, R., Tai, J., Boud, D., & Jorre de St Jorre, T. (2023). *Assessment for inclusion in higher education: Promoting equity and social justice in assessment*. Routledge. https://doi.org/10.4324/9781003293101

Bain, K. (2023). Inclusive assessment in higher education: What does the literature tell us on how to define and design inclusive assessments? *Journal of Learning Development in Higher Education*, (27). https://doi.org/10.47408/jldhe.vi27.1014

Crawford, J., Cowling, M., & Allen, K. A. (2023). Leadership is needed for ethical ChatGPT: Character, assessment, and learning using artificial intelligence (AI). *Journal of University Teaching and Learning Practice*, *20*(3). https://doi.org/10.53761/1.20.3.02

Lee, S. S., & Moore, R. L. (2024). Harnessing generative AI (GenAI) for automated feedback in higher education: A systematic review. *Online Learning*, *28*(3) https://doi.org/10.24059/olj.v28i3.4593

Perkins, M., Furze, L., Roe, J., & MacVaugh, J. (2024). The Artificial Intelligence Assessment Scale (AIAS): A framework for ethical integration of generative AI in educational assessment. *Journal of University Teaching and Learning Practice*, *21*(6). https://doi.org/10.53761/q3azde36

Smolansky, A., Cram, A., Raduescu, C., Zeivots, S., Huber, E., & Kizilcec, R. F. (2023). *Educator and student perspectives on the impact of generative AI on assessments in higher education.* In L@S 2023 - Proceedings of the 10th ACM Conference on Learning @ Scale.

Tai, J., Dollinger, M., Ajjawi, R., Jorre de St Jorre, T., Krattli, S., McCarthy, D., & Prezioso, D. (2023). Designing assessment for inclusion: An exploration of diverse students' assessment experience. *Assessment & Evaluation in Higher Education*, *48*(3), 403-417. https://doi.org/10.1080/02602938.2022.2082373

UCD Teaching & Learning (2025). *UCD Assessment for Inclusion framework.* UCD Dublin. (https://www.ucd.ie/teaching/resources/inclusiveandinterculturallearning/ucdassessmentforinclusionframework/)

Xia, Q., Weng, X., Ouyang, Lin, T. J., & Chiu, T. K. F. (2024). A scoping review on how generative artificial intelligence transforms assessment in higher education. *International Journal of Educational Technology in Higher Education*, *21* (40). https://doi.org/10.1186/s41239-024-00468-z

GenAI in the Classroom: The Interplay of Teachers' Pedagogical Beliefs and Perceptions of the Technology

Omri Hadar[1] Meital Amzalag[2], Gila Kurtz[3], Yifat Ben-David Kolikant[4]

[1]The Hebrew University of Jerusalem, Jerusalem, Israel; omri.hadar@mail.huji.ac.il

[2]Holon Institute of Technology, Israel; meitalam@hit.ac.il

[3]Holon Institute of Technology, Israel; gilaku@hit.ac.il

[4]The Hebrew University of Jerusalem, Jerusalem, Israel; yifat.kolikant@mail.huji.ac.il

Correspondence: Omri Hadar: omri.hadar@mail.huji.ac.il

Abstract:

Generative Artificial Intelligence (GenAI) enables human-machine interaction in ways that differ significantly from previous information technologies. It can generate new knowledge, sustain coherent discussions, and evaluate ideas (Jovanovic and Campbell, 2022). Genai presents opportunities to transform teaching and learning, potentially fostering knowledge construction, critical analysis, and learner autonomy (Luckin 2024). However, this also raises concerns regarding ethics, data privacy, and algorithmic bias (Grassini, 2023).

Existing research on GenAI in education has focused mainly on its classroom integration, often assuming that such adoption is both inevitable and beneficial (Cheng & Wang, 2023; Pörn et al., 2024). This perspective aligns with broader narratives about education's adaptation to 21st-century needs. However, empirical studies suggest that teachers may hold different views on how schools should respond to technological change (Kolikant, 2019). Their perspectives shape not only how they engage with new tools but also how they negotiate educational priorities regarding new technological tools.

This study adopts a sociocultural perspective, viewing teachers' pedagogical choices as being mediated by psychological and technological tools. Moving beyond questions of GenAI integration, we examine how teachers perceive changes in their teaching due to technology availability, as well as the evolving context of their work within schools and the education system. To explore these perspectives, we conducted and thematically analyzed semi-structured interviews with 24 middle-school teachers in Israel (20 women, 4 men) from various subject areas. The interviews conducted during the summer break of 2024 focused on teachers' perceptions of GenAI and its relevance to their work, their views on the education system's readiness, and their strategies for adapting teaching practices.

Our main findings indicate that all teachers distinguish between using GenAI for lesson preparation and using it with students. While most teachers are open to using GenAI themselves, they remain hesitant regarding its use by students. Their willingness to incorporate GenAI aligns with their pedagogical orientations and perceptions of its affordances and limitations. For example, teachers who prioritize content delivery and perceive GenAI as an unreliable information source avoid using it in practice. In addition, teachers who value student thinking and view GenAI as undermining cognitive effort tend to restrict their use in student learning while using it themselves.

Assessment is a prominent theme. Teachers were concerned about the students' unethical use of technology. Some have explained that GenAI may deprive the essential tasks of the mental effort required. Teachers concentrated on blocking student use, preferring classroom work over homework and tests over projects and term papers.

This study supports previous research indicating that teachers' pedagogical beliefs shape their use of technology (Tondeur et al., 2020; Tondeur et al., 2017). Our findings contribute new insights by showing that teachers' engagement with GenAI is not only influenced by their pedagogical beliefs, but also by their understanding of technology's capabilities and limitations. Although this study is based on a small sample, it provides an empirical foundation for understanding teachers' perspectives on GenAI. Future research will expand these findings through quantitative analysis in a larger national study.

References

Ben-David Kolikant, Y. (2019). Adapting School to the Twenty-First Century: Educators' Perspectives. *Technology, Pedagogy and Education*, *28*(3), 287–299. https://doi.org/10.1080/1475939X.2019.1584580

Cheng, E. C. K., & Wang, T. (2023). Leading digital transformation and eliminating barriers for teachers to incorporate artificial intelligence into basic education in Hong Kong. *Computers and Education: Artificial Intelligence*, *5*, 100171. https://doi.org/10.1016/j.caeai.2023.100171

Grassini, S. (2023). Shaping the Future of Education: Exploring the Potential and Consequences of AI and ChatGPT in Educational Settings. *Education Sciences*, *13*(7), 692. https://doi.org/10.3390/educsci13070692

Jovanovic, M., & Campbell, M. (2022). Generative Artificial Intelligence: Trends and Prospects. *Computer*, *55*(10), 107–112. https://doi.org/10.1109/MC.2022.3192720

Kopcha, T. J., Neumann, K. L., Ottenbreit-Leftwich, A., & Pitman, E. (2020). Process over product: The next evolution of our quest for technology integration. *Educational Technology Research and Development*, *68*(2), 729–749. https://doi.org/10.1007/s11423-020-09735-y

Luckin, R. (2024). Nurturing human intelligence in the age of AI: Rethinking education for the future. *Development and Learning in Organizations: An International Journal*. https://doi.org/10.1108/DLO-04-2024-0108

Pörn, R., Braskén, M., Wingren, M., & Andersson, S. (2024). Attitudes towards and expectations of the role of artificial intelligence in the classroom among digitally skilled Finnish K-12 mathematics teachers. *LUMAT: International Journal on Math, Science and Technology Education*, *12*(3). https://doi.org/10.31129/LUMAT.12.3.2102

Tondeur, J., Van Braak, J., & Ertmer, P. A., & Ottenbreit-Leftwich, A. (2017). Understanding the relationship between teachers' pedagogical beliefs and technology use in education: A systematic review of qualitative evidence. *Educational Technology Research and Development*, *65*(3), 555–575. https://doi.org/10.1007/s11423-016- 9481-2

Co-designing Playful Learning with AI for Multiliteracy Education

Marjaana Kangas[1], Outi Kallionpää[2]

[1] University of Lapland, Faculty of Education, Finland; Marjaana.Kangas@ulapland.fi
[2] University of Lapland, Faculty of Education, Finland; Outi.Kallionpaa@ulapland.fi

Correspondence: Marjaana Kangas: Marjaana.Kangas@ulapland.fi

Abstract:

Playful learning approaches provide numerous opportunities for motivating students and giving them possibilities to use their creativity and imagination in learning. AI can be seen as an important tool and companion for playing with ideas, fostering inspiration in designing playful pedagogies, and promoting students' AI literacy in higher education (HE). In this study, 82 HE students participated in the course "Didactics of Finnish language and literature" (6ECT). They were asked to use AI in their pedagogical design process to explore the potential of AI in designing teaching for multiliteracy learning. The research data consists of the students' pedagogical plans and reflective diaries that were collected at the end of the course. Data was thematically analyzed. The findings indicate that AI supports creative co-design processes of the students when planning broader pedagogical plans of playful learning for multiliteracy learning. Most of the suggestions and ideas provided by AI, however, required critical evaluation by the students. In this process, students' knowledge of the curriculum, subject-specific pedagogical expertise, and understanding of the context of primary school played a central role. The results show that the playful learning approach can support HE students' learning and innovative design of teaching in playful multiliteracy education.

Keywords: Playful learning, AI, multiliteracy, higher education

Introduction

Playful learning approaches provide numerous opportunities for motivating students and giving them possibilities to use their creativity and imagination in learning. AI can be seen as an important tool and companion to play with ideas and for promoting inspiration in designing playful pedagogies in higher education (HE) (Kangas & Heljakka, 2024). Playful learning approaches can also be seen to play a key role in multiliteracy education supporting the goals of creativity, collaboration and knowledge co-creation (Ollonen & Kangas, 2024; Warner, 2024). Playful learning can positively influence learners' motivation, academic performance, willingness to take risks and learn from failure, and promote the development of key competencies, including problem-solving, creative thinking, innovation, and digital literacies (Bateson & Martin, 2013; Ollonen & Kangas, 2024; Whitton, 2022) Although generative AI is widely studied, it has primarily been examined through the lens of technology rather than as part of playful learning (Kangas & Heljakka, 2024), or the teaching of a specific subject. In this research, AI is used in co-designing playful learning for multiliteracy education in higher education, specifically in the context of teacher education.

Playful learning is understood as learning activities embedded with playful engagement and exploration, where creativity, emotions, collaboration, narrativity, embodiment and meaningful technologies are recognized as essential elements of learning (Kangas, 2010). Multiliteracy education is here referred to an expanded view of literacy education that goes beyond the traditional focus on reading and writing skills to encompass a broad set of abilities, including the use of diverse information sources, understanding of texts, production of multimodal content, and critical evaluation of information across various social, cultural, and technological contexts (Gee, 2008; Lankshear & Knobel, 2011; Rasi, Kangas & Ruokamo, 2019). Today, multiliteracy education needs to be promoted at all school levels of education from early childhood education to higher education (HE).

In our study, HE students co-designed playful learning processes for primary school pupils using AI and engaged in their own playful learning as part of their university studies. In this paper, we are interested in HE students' experiences on the co-design of playful learning process with AI. The study targeted the following research questions:

1. How do HE students perceive pedagogical planning with AI when the goal is to increase primary pupils' multiliteracy and interest in literature through playful learning?
2. How does playful learning support HE students' pedagogical planning with AI?

Methodologies

In this study, 82 higher education (HE) students from teacher education, University of Lapland, participated in the course "Didactics of Finnish language and literature" (6ECT). One of the goals in the course was to promote students' AI literacy skills (Ng et al, 2021) and design playful learning and teaching as part of university studies. The students' task was in small groups to co-design pedagogical plans based on playful learning and literacy education for primary school pupils by using AI. They were asked to use AI in their pedagogical design process, and this way to get familiar with the potential of AI in design teaching. First, the students were introduced to the pedagogical goals of literature education and then to the playful learning pedagogy. After this, they started to co-design a teaching module based on playful learning in interaction with AI. The research data consists of the students' pedagogical plans and reflective diaries (N=82) that were collected at the end of the course. All data was thematically analyzed.

Findings and Conclusions

The findings indicate that the students perceived AI as supporting their creative co-design processes when creating broader pedagogical plans of playful learning for multiliteracy education. This aligns with recent research on the use of AI in higher education; AI can serve as a tutor or companion, providing ideas and inspiration for the planning and co-creation process (Kangas & Heljakka, 2024; Wang et al., 2023). However, most of the suggestions and ideas provided by AI required critical evaluation by the students. In this process, students' knowledge of the curriculum, subject-specific pedagogical expertise, and understanding of the context of primary school played a central role. The results also show that the playful learning approach can support HE students' AI literacy and innovative design of teaching in playful multiliteracy education. As Long and Magerko (2020) note, AI literacy refers to a set of competencies that enable individuals to critically evaluate AI technologies, communicate and collaborate effectively with AI, and use AI as a tool.

The findings suggest that integrating AI into teacher education can enhance students' creative and pedagogical design skills, especially when emphasizing the use of imagination and the meaning of supporting motivation of the learner in the process. The study highlights the potential of combining playful learning and AI to support students' pedagogical thinking, creativity, and multiliteracy competence. Engaging with AI through playful approaches can offer a meaningful opportunity for learning how to use AI as a tool in pedagogical planning. However, AI use in multiliteracy education must be grounded in students' curriculum knowledge, subject didactics, and contextual understanding of school practice.

Ethics and consent

The study followed the ethical principles for scientific research established by the Finnish National Board of Research Integrity (https://www.tenk.fi), the Data Protection Act, and informed consent was obtained from the participants.

Funding Information

This study is part of the research activities of TRANSPEDA project, funded by Media Industry Research Foundation of Finland.

References

Bateson, P. P. G., & Martin, P. (2013). *Play, playfulness, creativity and innovation.* Cambridge University Press.

Kangas, M. (2010). Creative and Playful Learning: Learning through Game Co- Creation and Games in a Playful Learning Environment. *Thinking Skills and Creativity*, 5(1), 1–15.

Kangas, M. & Heljakka, K. (2024). AI Play in Higher Education: Students' perceptions of play and co-creation of knowledge with generative AI. In T. Ahram & W. Karwowski (Eds.). *Human Factors in Design, Engineering, and Computing*. AHFE (2024) International Conference. AHFE Open Access, vol 159. AHFE International, USA. http://doi.org/10.54941/ahfe1005571

Lankshear, C., & Knobel, M. (2011). *New Literacies: Everyday Practices and Social Learning* (3rd ed.). McGraw-Hill Education / Open University Press.

Long, D. & Magerko, B. (2020). *What is AI Literacy? Competencies and Design Considerations*. CHI 2020, April 25–30, 2020, Honolulu, HI, USA.

Ng, T., Leung, J., Chu, S., Qiao, M. (2021). Conceptualizing AI literacy: An exploratory review. *Computers and Education: Artificial Intelligence*, 2, 100041.

Ollonen, B., & Kangas, M. (2024). Teacher motivational scaffolding and preschoolers' motivational triggers in the context of playful learning of multiliteracy and digital skills. *Early Childhood Education Journal*, 1-15.

Rasi, P., M. Kangas, and H. Ruokamo. (2019). Promoting Multiliteracy in the Finnish Educational System. In M. Paksuniemi & P. Keskitalo (Eds.), *Introduction to Finnish Educational System* (pp. 97–111). Brill/Sense Publishers.

Wang, T., Lund, B. D., Marengo, A., Pagano, A., Mannuru, N. R., Teel, Z. A., & Pange, J. (2023). Exploring the potential impact of artificial intelligence (AI) on international students in higher education: Generative AI, chatbots, analytics, and international student success. *Applied Sciences*, 13(6716). https://doi.org/10.3390/app13116716

Warner, C. (2024). *Multiliteracy Play: Designs and Desires in the Second Language Classroom*.

Whitton, N. (2022). *Play and learning in adulthood. Reimagining pedagogy and the politics of education.* Palgrave. Macmillan.

The Classroom of the Future: From Digital Competencies During the Pandemic to Artificial Intelligence as a Pedagogical Aid

Paola Espejo[1]

[1]Universidad de Las Américas Chile, Universitat Oberta de Catalunya, Spain; pespejo@udla.cl

Correspondence: Paola Espejo: pespejo@udla.cl

Abstract:

The COVID-19 pandemic had a profound impact on education, disrupting school systems globally and forcing the massive adoption of digital technologies as the primary means of communication and instruction. Distance and hybrid learning models, initially deployed as emergency solutions, proved to hold significant potential for transforming the future of teaching and learning (Azevedo et al., 2021). Amid this urgency, teachers were compelled to rapidly adapt their pedagogical practices, incorporating multimedia resources, promoting autonomous learning, and receiving training in digital tools—often in combination with traditional technologies (Bozkurt et al., 2020; García Aretio, 2021; UNESCO, 2020).

Despite the challenges, this transition opened important avenues for educational innovation. It fostered global collaboration, broadened access to Open Educational Resources (OER), and promoted more inclusive teaching practices. The crisis also highlighted the importance of an open, equitable, and student-centered pedagogy, grounded in digital competencies and the ability to respond to uncertainty with adaptability and creativity.

Within this context, the program *"The Classroom of the Future: Integrating Active Methodologies, Emerging Technologies, and Artificial Intelligence in Education"* was created. This free initiative was designed to provide teachers with a comprehensive and updated perspective on the pedagogical potential of educational technologies. Its purpose is to equip educators with tools, resources, competencies, attitudes, and critical knowledge to help them not only adapt to the changing educational landscape but also become active leaders in the creation of meaningful and engaging learning environments through active methodologies. The program was conceptualized and implemented by the Viña del Mar Campus of Universidad de las Américas in Chile, launching in August 2020 with the training of more than 600 teachers. The initiative was carried out with the official support of the Regional Office of the Ministry of Education (Secretaría Ministerial de Educación) in the Valparaíso Region, Chile. By 2024, the program has trained over 1,200 teachers across urban and rural areas of the region, and it is set to continue in 2025.

Data collected through a structured instrument revealed that most participating teachers—regardless of whether they worked in highly urban or rural settings—were familiar with and actively using AI tools in their professional contexts. Their general emotional response toward AI was characterized by enthusiasm and curiosity rather than fear or resistance. Furthermore, the experience of the pandemic significantly changed teachers' perceptions of educational technologies, reinforcing their pedagogical value. However, unequal access to reliable internet connections continues to be the main obstacle to broader implementation and equity in digital education.

This experience demonstrates the transformative potential of combining active pedagogies, digital competencies, and artificial intelligence in teacher training, especially when framed within a human-centered and inclusive approach.

Keywords: Educación postpandemia; Metodologías activas; Inteligencia Artificial en educación; Formación docente; Brecha digital.

References

Albadarin, Y., Saqr, M., Pope, N., & Tukiainen, M. (2024). A systematic literature review of empirical research on ChatGPT in education. *Discover Education, 3*(1), artículo 60. :10.1007/s44217-024-00138-2

Atkinson-Abutridy, J. (2024). *Grandes Modelos de Lenguaje. Conceptos, técnicas y aplicaciones*. Alfaomega.

Azevedo, J., Rogers, F., Carroll, S., Cloutier, M., Chakroun, B., Chang, G., Mizunoya, S., Reuge, N., Brossard, M. & Bergmann, J. (2021). *El estado de la crisis educative mundial: un camino hacia la recuperación (Vol. 2). Resumen Ejecutivo.* Banco Internacional de Reconstrucción y Fomento / Banco Mundial, UNESCO y UNICEF. http://documents.worldbank.org/curated/en/402111638769366449/Executive-Summary

Bozkurt, A., Jung, I., Xiao, J., Vladimirschi, V., Schuwer, R., Egorov, G., Lambert, S., Al-Freih, M., Pete, J., Olcott, Jr., D., Rodes, V., Aranciaga, I., Bali, M., Alvarez, A. J., Roberts, J., Pazurek, A., Raffaghelli, J. E., Panagiotou, N., de Coëtlogon, P., Shahadu, S., Brown, M., Asino, T. I., Tumwesige, J., Ramírez Reyes, T., Barrios Ipenza, E., Ossiannilsson, E., Bond, M., Belhamel, K., Irvine, V., Sharma, R. C., Adam, T., Janssen, B., Sklyarova, T., Olcott, N., Ambrosino, A., Lazou, C., Mocquet, B., Mano, M., & Paskevicius, M. (2020). A global outlook to the interruption of education due to COVID-19 pandemic: Navigating in a time of uncertainty and crisis. *Asian Journal of Distance Education, 15*(1), 1-126. :10.5281/zenodo.3878572

García Aretio, L. (2021). COVID-19 y educación a distancia digital: preconfinamiento, confinamiento y posconfinamiento. *RIED. Revista Iberoamericana de Educación a Distancia, 24*(1), 09-32. :10.5944/ried.24.1.28080

UNESCO Instituto Internacional de Planeamiento de la Educación. (2020). *Sistematización de respuestas de los sistemas educativos de América Latina a la crisis de la COVID-19.* https://siteal.iiep.unesco.org/respuestas_educativas_covid_19

Perspectives on AI Use in Higher Education: A Qualitative Study of Students and Teachers

Meden Ema[1] , Radovan Marko[2], Košmerl Tadej[3], Makovec Radovan Danijela[4], Strel Karmen[5]

[1] Faculty of Arts - Department of Educational Sciences, University of Ljubljana, Slovenia; ema.meden@ff.uni-lj.com
[2] Faculty of Arts - Department of Educational Sciences, University of Ljubljana, Slovenia; marko.radovan@ff.uni-lj.com
[3] Faculty of Arts - Department of Educational Sciences, University of Ljubljana, Slovenia; tadej.kosmerl@ff.uni-lj.com
[4] Faculty of Arts - Department of Educational Sciences, University of Ljubljana, Slovenia; danijela.makovecradovan@ff.uni-lj.com
[5] Faculty of Arts - Department of Educational Sciences, University of Ljubljana, Slovenia; karmen.strel@ff.uni-lj.com

Correspondence: Ema Meden: ema.meden@ff.uni-lj.si

Abstract:

This qualitative study explores the integration of generative artificial intelligence (Gen-AI) into higher education, examining experiences and perspectives of students and teachers from Slovenia's three public universities with the pedagogical dimension of AI integration (Chan, 2023). Two focus groups were conducted: one with seven teachers and one with ten students, both representing all three universities. The study investigates (1) the ways and pedagogical processes in which Gen-AI tools are used, (2) the perceived benefits of Gen-AI regarding efficiency, innovation, and personalization, and (3) the key technical, organizational, didactic, and ethical barriers to broader implementation, along with possible solutions.

Our research indicates a pedagogical shift from traditional lectures toward active, problem-based learning that fosters independent thinking and creativity. Educators integrate Gen-AI to design learning activities, develop materials, and adopt student-centred approaches. To ensure meaningful engagement and verify learning outcomes, they adopt new assessment strategies, including oral defences, systematic monitoring of project development, and phased evaluation of assignments. Diverse assessment methods are a key strategy for successful AI integration, aligning with findings in the field (Xia et al., 2024). Teachers also use Gen-AI to address ethical concerns such as copyright issues, source fabrication, and critical evaluation of AI-generated content.

Students use Gen-AI across various academic tasks, including creating learning materials, conducting literature searches, analysing data, enhancing language proficiency, and supporting programming activities. Gen-AI assists them in drafting seminar papers, structuring research projects, generating summaries, and developing presentations. Students are encouraged to critically assess AI-generated outputs, focusing on content accuracy, source reliability, and conceptual coherence. Using frameworks such as the SAMR model (Substitution, Augmentation, Modification, Redefinition), they reflect on the pedagogical value of Gen-AI and its ethical and practical limitations.

Participants identified key benefits and challenges of Gen-AI, echoing findings from other studies (Roschanei et al., 2023). AI enhances efficiency by automating routine tasks, fosters innovation through creative teaching and learning strategies, and enables personalized learning tailored to individual needs. Gen-AI also improves access to academic support, especially for students lacking other resources.

Among the challenges, participants noted Gen-AI's tendency to generate inaccurate or false information. Organizationally, educators emphasized a lack of sufficient training, tools, and institutional support. Didactically, participants expressed concerns that over-reliance on AI could hinder the development of critical thinking and independent learning skills. Ethically, both groups raised issues regarding authorship, plagiarism, and algorithmic bias. Teachers and students alike stressed the urgent need for responsible, critical, and ethical use of Gen-AI, supported by clear institutional guidelines.

This study shows that while the integration of Gen-AI offers considerable potential, it also demands careful management. To ensure positive outcomes, institutions must establish responsible frameworks, promote AI literacy, and balance technological advantages with the cultivation of critical academic skills. Strengthening assessment practices and enforcing ethical standards are essential for maintaining academic integrity. The future of Gen-AI in higher education depends on its thoughtful integration as a supportive tool that enhances, rather than replaces, essential academic competencies.

The data was collected in the project Generative Artificial Intelligence in Education (project code NRP: 3350-24-3502), funded by the European Union - NextGenerationEU and the Republic of Slovenia, Ministry of Education.

Keywords: Gen-AI, Higher Education, AI integration

References

Chan, C. K. Y. (2023). A comprehensive AI policy education framework for university teaching and learning. International Journal of Educational Technology in Higher Education, 20(1), 38. https://doi.org/10.1186/s41239-023-00408-3

Roshanaei, M. , Olivares, H. and Lopez, R. (2023) Harnessing AI to Foster Equity in Education: Opportunities, Challenges, and Emerging Strategies. *Journal of Intelligent Learning Systems and Applications*, 15, 123-143. https://doi.org/10.4236/jilsa.2023.154009

Xia, Q., Weng, X., Ouyang, F. et al. A scoping review on how generative artificial intelligence transforms assessment in higher education. *International Journal of Educational Technology in Higher Education,* 21(1), 40 (2024). https://doi.org/10.1186/s41239-024-00468-z

Integrating AI Chatbots in Higher Education to Enhance Reflective Practice

Corinna Galliano[1]

[1]Strategy Innovation and Entrepreneurship, The University of Sydney Business School, Australia; corinna.galliano@sydney.edu.au

Correspondence: Corinna Galliano: corinna.galliano@sydney.edu.au

Abstract:

The rapid integration of artificial intelligence (AI) in both industry and academia necessitates a critical re-evaluation of educational strategies that not only prepare students for an AI-driven world but also foster ethical and responsible AI use. While existing research highlights benefits such as reduced speaking anxiety (Hapsari & Wu, 2022), increased autonomous learning (Martínez-Téllez & Camacho-Zuñiga, 2023), and improved cognitive flexibility (Chauncey & McKenna, 2023), much of the focus has been on instructional effectiveness. However, there is a significant gap in understanding how AI chatbots can systematically develop reflective skills and promote ethical AI engagement.

Reflective practice is a crucial shift away from traditional assessment methods, particularly in an era of generative AI. It fosters innovation by encouraging adaptability, responsiveness to learner needs, and critical interrogation of established norms (Schön, 2013). To advance this approach, I am developing an AI agent, using Cogniti[1]. The system prompt is designed for the AI chatbot to act as a mentor, guiding students through self-reflection. Using Kolb's Experiential Learning Cycle (1984), the chatbot helps students structure their weekly reflections following interactive workshops.

Chatbot-based interactions can extend the educator's role beyond the classroom, acting as a mentor that helps the student to elicit concrete experiences had in the workshops and fosters deeper reflective observation of these. Throughout this process the chatbot enhances abstract conceptualization of the learning emerging from those experiences and encourages the student to actively experiment with newly acquired knowledge. This process not only motivates meaningful engagement with AI tools but also cultivates critical AI literacy and responsible usage practice (Vallis et al., 2024), ensuring students use AI as a mentor that foster their critical thinking rather than mere task completion.

This study aims to explore how AI chatbots can be effectively integrated into higher education to actively engage students, enhance reflective skills, and promote ethical AI use. Currently, we are pilot testing the chatbot to be used in two postgraduate units within the Business School, both of which feature highly interactive workshops and experiential learning activities. Previously, students submitted weekly reflections via online logs, built using our SRES[2] .The logs were structured with guiding questions to help students structure their reflections. With the

---

[1] https://cogniti.ai/

[2] Student Relationship Engagement System

introduction of the AI agent, students will now submit their chatbot-facilitated reflections. These weekly reflections contribute towards to their final reflective portfolio assessment meeting the marking criteria sustained engagement throughout the unit, while offering students with 'raw material' to craft their final reflective portfolio.

To assess the impact of this agent in fostering student reflections, we will collect qualitative data through focus groups, open-ended surveys, and transcripts of chatbot interactions. By comparing these reflections with those from the previous log system, we aim to evaluate student engagement with the chatbot and the depth of their reflective thinking.

This study contributes to the growing discourse on transformational learning with AI, offering insights into the pedagogical potential of AI agents in fostering self-reflection, ethical AI literacy, and deeper learning engagement.

Keywords: AI chatbot as mentors, reflective practice, experiential learning, ethical AI use, critical thinking

---

References

Chauncey, S. A., & McKenna, H. P. (2023). A framework and exemplars for ethical and responsible use of AI Chatbot technology to support teaching and learning. Computers and Education: Artificial Intelligence, 5, 100182.

Hapsari, I. P., & Wu, T. T. (2022, August). AI chatbots learning model in English speaking skill: Alleviating speaking anxiety, boosting enjoyment, and fostering critical thinking. In International Conference on Innovative Technologies and Learning (pp. 444-453). Cham: Springer International Publishing.

Harvey, M., Coulson, D., Wisdom Journeys, & McMaugh, A. (2016). Towards a theory of the Ecology of Reflection: Reflective practice for experiential learning in higher education. Journal of University Teaching and Learning Practice, 13(2), 7–27.

Kolb, D. A., Boyatzis, R. E., & Mainemelis, C. (2014). Experiential learning theory: Previous research and new directions. In Perspectives on thinking, learning, and cognitive styles (pp. 227-247). Routledge.

Martínez-Téllez, R., & Camacho-Zuñiga, C. (2023, October). Enhancing mathematics education through ai chatbots in a flipped learning environment. In 2023 World Engineering Education Forum-Global Engineering Deans Council (WEEF-GEDC) (pp. 1-8). IEEE.

Schön, D. A. (2013). The reflective practitioner: how professionals think in action. Ashgate.

Vallis, C, Wilson, S., Gozman, D. et al. (2024). Student Perceptions of AI-Generated Avatars in Teaching Business Ethics: We Might not be Impressed. Postdigit Science and Education 6, 537–555. https://doi.org/10.1007/s42438-023-00407-7The following provides examples of referencing for the main kinds of publications.

Enhancing Personalized Formative Feedback in Higher Education: A GenAI-powered Tool Design and Implementation

Marcelo Maina[1], Nati Cabrera[2], David García-Solórzano[3], Carolina García-Londoño[4]

[1,2,3,4] Universitat Oberta de Catalunya, {mmaina; ncabrera; dgarciaso; dgarcialon}@uoc.edu

Correspondence: Marcelo Maina: mmaina@uoc.edu

Abstract:

The increasing demand for personalized, formative feedback in higher education requires innovative technological solutions that enhance efficiency while maintaining pedagogical quality. Despite extensive research on feedback practices, significant challenges persist for both faculty and students, including workload management and the quality of feedback provided (Henderson et al., 2019). This study explores the integration of an AI-powered tool—FeedSmart—to assist educators in delivering personalized, formative feedback, reducing workload, and improving pedagogical outcomes.

Recent advances in Generative AI (GenAI) present promising opportunities to support educators in crafting high-quality textual feedback with reduced effort (Lee and Moore, 2024). Research has demonstrated that systems employing large language models (LLMs) with generic prompts excel in linguistic correction and the structure of written feedback (Alghannam, 2024). In some cases, AI-generated feedback demonstrated superior readability compared to teacher-provided feedback and included more process-oriented guidance (Dai et al., 2023). However, these systems often lack in-depth content analysis, are prone to errors, and require augmentation with teachers' contextual understanding to achieve full effectiveness (Ouyang et al., 2024).

FeedSmart distinguishes itself by aiding the feedback delivery process while preserving the critical pedagogical role of faculty. Its design followed three key steps. First, it involves a collaborative process with teachers to develop a checklist that integrates evaluation criteria and learning objectives, ensuring alignment with course outcomes. Second, a detailed rubric was created based on these criteria, incorporating four feedback types—positive, negative, suggested resources, and examples. This rubric generates structured prompts that guide teachers in crafting final feedback messages. Third, FeedSmart employs a prompt aligned with established principles of effective feedback to ensure clarity, specificity, a motivational tone, and actionable guidance. Based on the teacher's evaluation through the rubric, FeedSmart facilitates the generation of structured and personalized feedback, helping students identify strengths and areas for improvement while promoting self-regulation.

The research employed a quasi-experimental design involving 11 faculty members from a Master's final project course. Teachers initially provided feedback using traditional methods and subsequently used FeedSmart to generate AI-assisted feedback. Data collection included questionnaires, analysis guides, and focus groups, enabling a comprehensive assessment of feedback quality, tool usability, and its impact on teaching workload.

Preliminary results indicate that FeedSmart significantly improves the quality of textual feedback by enhancing consistency, structure, specificity, and readability. Teachers positively evaluated its capacity to highlight strengths in students' tasks, with feedback aligning well with learning objectives and evaluation criteria. However, experiences regarding the tool's ability to provide actionable resources and improvement strategies varied. While FeedSmart shows promise in facilitating structured and motivational feedback, further refinements are necessary to enhance its ability to consistently offer meaningful, tailored guidance to students.

Keywords: Feedback, formative feedback, GenAI tool, Higher education, Faculty.

References

Alghannam, M. (2024). Artificial intelligence as a provider of feedback on EFL student compositions. *World Journal of English Language, 15*(2), 161. https://doi.org/10.5430/wjel.v15n2p161

Dai, W., Lin, J., Jin, H., Li, T., Tsai, Y. S., Gasevic, D., & Chen, G. (2023). *Can large language models provide feedback to students? A case study on ChatGPT*. In N.-S. Chen, G. Rudolph, D. G. Sampson, M. Chang, R. Kuo, & A. Tlili (Eds.), ICALT 2023 (pp. 323–325). IEEE. https://doi.org/10.1109/ICALT58122.2023.00100

Henderson, M., Ryan, T., & Phillips, M. (2019). The challenges of feedback in higher education. *Assessment & Evaluation in Higher Education, 44*(8), 1237–1252. https://doi.org/10.1080/02602938.2019.1599815

Lee, S. S., & Moore, R. L. (2024). Harnessing generative AI (GenAI) for automated feedback in higher education: A systematic review. *Online Learning, 28*(3), 82–104. https://doi.org/10.24059/olj.v28i3.4593

Ouyang, F., Guo, M., Zhang, N., Bai, X., & Jiao, P. (2024). Comparing the effects of instructor manual feedback and ChatGPT intelligent feedback on collaborative programming in China's higher education. *IEEE Transactions on Learning Technologies, 17*, 2227–2239. https://doi.org/10.1109/TLT.2024.3486749

AI-Assisted Grading in Online Degrees: Optimizing the Teaching and Learning Experience While Promoting Scale

Randall Fullington[1]

[1] Office of Academic and Learning Innovation, University of Colorado Boulder, United States; randall.fullington@colorado.edu

Correspondence: Randall Fullington: randall.fullington@colorado.edu

Abstract:

This paper explores how the University of Colorado Boulder (CU Boulder) successfully scaled graduate enrollments while enhancing interactions between students and university representatives. The case study highlights CU Boulder's implementation of structural features necessary for scale, including asynchronous, online, low-cost programs that are stackable and open to anyone who can demonstrate their ability to succeed. Since launching its first at-scale online master's degree in 2019, CU Boulder has enrolled 9,806 unique students across four graduate degree programs. Automation of course experiences, such as lecture videos, readings, student-led discussions, coding assignments, and multiple-choice quizzes, contributed to enrollment gains. However, peer review grading for qualitative assignments has proven less satisfactory. To address this, CU Boulder piloted AI-peer review grading in non-credit courses, yielding promising results with increased grading stringency and positive student feedback. Building on these outcomes, the university is now piloting AI-assisted grading in for-credit courses, with teaching assistants reviewing AI-suggested grades. This approach aims to provide a more reliable and efficient means of grading qualitative assignments at scale, ensuring accurate attainment of program learning outcomes and increasing course staff-to-student contact points.

Keywords: AI-Assisted Grading; Automation; Graduate Education; Online

Scaling graduate education requires implementing structural features that reduce university staff and faculty involvement while enabling student enrollment growth. This work in progress explains how the University of Colorado Boulder (CU Boulder) is scaling enrollments while increasing touch points between students and university representatives. The study shows that universities can scale enrollments, increase interactions between students and course staff, and provide measurable learning outcomes.

CU Boulder launched its first at-scale online master's degree in 2019. Over the next five years, it launched three more master's degrees and seven graduate certificates. Each program implements structural features necessary for scale: asynchronous, online, low-cost (relative to American graduate tuition), stackable, and open to anyone who can prove they can do the work. This last feature is key because it removes barriers such as submitting application materials, locating recommenders, paying for transcript delivery, and paying for professional testing.

Since 2019, CU Boulder has enrolled 9,806 unique students across the four graduate degree programs. In 2024 alone, it enrolled 4,800 unique students. To achieve these enrollments, the university automated most of the course experience, such as lecture videos, readings, student-led discussions, coding assignments, and multiple-choice quizzes. Students and staff are mostly satisfied with automation for these items. For qualitative assignments, the university implemented peer review grading. The results have been less satisfactory than other automations. Students frequently wait long periods to receive peer reviews, some students offer to give good grades to peers if they return the favor, and staff are often called in to grade assignments if reviews are not received by the end of the session deadline. The overall result is an unsatisfactory experience for students and staff alike.

To improve student and staff experiences while preserving the scalability of the degrees, CU Boulder piloted AI-peer review grading in its non-credit online courses. It was necessary to start the trial in non-credit courses due to anxiety from the university and students over AI-assisted grading for transcripted courses. The trial ran in 47 classes and included 30,140 graded submissions. The results are promising. From September to March, CU Boulder saw a 19% decrease in learners passing on their first attempt, suggesting that learners are being graded more appropriately. Moreover, only 6% of learners asked to opt out of AI-powered grading, and students who provided simple up/down feedback rated the experience positively 86% of the time. Finally, the AI-powered system successfully completed 90% of all assignment submissions, underscoring the reliability of the tool and student willingness to participate.

Building off these positive results, CU Boulder decided to pilot AI-assisted grading in five for-credit courses, with the key difference of having teaching assistants review the AI-suggested grades to confirm or adjust as needed. This pilot will run for multiple 8-week sessions to gather enough feedback and data to share with university administration and propose a formal move from student-led peer review to a more reliable and efficient means of grading qualitative assignments at scale while ensuring more accurate attainment of program learning outcomes and increasing course staff-to-student contact points.

Leveraging Virtual Reality and Artificial Intelligence to Enhance Employability Skills in Undergraduate Accounting: A Case Study from Ireland

Trevor Prendergast[1], Noëlle O`Connor[2]

[1]Head of Department of Accounting and Business Computing, Technological University of the Shannon, Ireland; trevor.prendergast@tus.ie
[2]Centre for Pedagogical Innovation and Development, Technological University of the Shannon, Ireland; noelle.oconnor@tus.ie

Correspondence: Trevor Prendergast: trevor.prendergast@tus.ie

Abstract:

Recent publications have added to the literature on immersive technologies in education, such as Yang et al. (2024) and Cooper et al. (2024), who focus on STEM; Liu et al. (2023), and Saab et al. (2023), who researched the use of VR in Nursing and Elsayed (2023), who explored student use of VR in Tourism-related disciplines. The present study adds to the literature by considering the use of such technologies in an undergraduate accounting context.

During the most recent cyclical review of an undergraduate bachelor's degree programme in accounting at the Technological University of Shannon (Ireland), part of the feedback from industry was a greater need to develop soft skills in graduates. A multi-pronged approach was implemented, one strand of which was a career-development 5 ECTS module titled "The Evolving Professional," created in Year 2 of the programme that preceded the year-long placement in Year 3 of the programme. A novel feature of the module was the utilisation of the Metaquest Virtual Reality (VR) headsets in conjunction with the Virtual Speech software and Artificial Intelligence (AI) agent to develop student interview skills. Each student (n = 26) was assigned a headset and a license to use the software, and a series of introductory sessions were held with the university's Teaching and Learning Unit to familiarise both staff and students with the use of the devices and the associated software. During class time, students undertook three 1-hour sessions of simulated interviews using the hardware and software, at the end of which feedback was provided by the AI agent. This information was saved to a student account and could be accessed outside of class time. Furthermore, students had the opportunity to borrow a headset from the library and, using the previously saved feedback, take additional simulated interview sessions with a view to improving competence. Student feedback was elicited by means of a focus group (n=26), with emerging data suggesting the novelty of the VR headsets was a significant factor in positive student perceptions of the technologies. The ability to access feedback from the AI agent outside of formal class time was deemed particularly useful by students and was considered a low-stakes opportunity to develop competence in interview techniques.

The integration of VR technology and AI agents in career development education presents a novel approach to enhancing graduate employability skills. Findings from the present study's implementation of VR in "The Evolving Professional" module suggest that immersive learning environments can significantly improve student engagement, skill acquisition, and confidence in professional settings. The ability to access AI-generated feedback and practice interviews in a low-stakes, self-directed manner contributed to students' perceived readiness for real-world employer interactions. This study aligns with growing literature on immersive technologies in education, expanding the discourse beyond STEM and healthcare fields to include business and career development. Future iterations of this module will explore refinements in content delivery, assessment methods, and industry collaboration, ensuring that VR and AI remain effective tools in bridging the gap between academic learning and professional success.

Keywords: Virtual Reality, Artificial Intelligence, undergraduate education, career development, soft skills

References

Cooper, G., Thong, L. P., & Tang, K. S. (2024). Transforming science education with virtual reality: An immersive representations model. Educational Media International, 61(3), 229-251.

Elsayed, K., & Daif, R. (2023). Tourism and Hospitality Edutainment: a Qualitative Study of Students' Perspectives on Integrating Virtual Reality Into Education. Journal of Southwest Jiaotong University, 58(4).

Liu, K., Zhang, W., Li, W., Wang, T., & Zheng, Y. (2023). Effectiveness of virtual reality in nursing education: a systematic review and meta-analysis. BMC Medical Education, 23(1), 710.

Saab, M. M., McCarthy, M., O'Mahony, B., Cooke, E., Hegarty, J., Murphy, D. and Noonan, B. (2023). Virtual reality simulation in nursing and midwifery education: A usability study. CIN: Computers, Informatics, Nursing, 41(10), 815-824.

Yang, C., Zhang, J., Hu, Y., Yang, X., Chen, M., Shan, M., & Li, L. (2024). The impact of virtual reality on practical skills for students in science and engineering education: a meta-analysis. International Journal of STEM Education, 11(1), 28.

AI vs. Human Role-Playing: Investigating Social Presence and Learning Outcomes

Carmen Winkel[1], Katharina Frosch[2], Friederike Lindauer[3]

[1] Brandenburg of University of Applied Science, Project ELI Incubator, Germany; carmen.winkel@th-brandenburg.de
[2] Brandenburg of University of Applied Science, Department of Business and Management, Germany; frosch@th-brandenburg.de
[3] Brandenburg of University of Applied Science, Department of Business and Management, Germany; lindauer@th-brandenburg.de

Correspondence: Carmen Winkel: carmen.winkel@th-brandenburg.de

Abstract:

Social presence is an important factor in creating engaging and effective communication, as it shapes the way individuals perceive and connect with others in digital environments. It refers to the extent to which a communication medium allows users to feel personally connected, experiencing interactions as authentic and engaging (Kreijns, Xu, & Weidlich, 2022). While some studies highlight the importance of social presence in chatbot interactions, particularly in contexts requiring trust and empathy—such as mental health support (Grub & Naab, 2025)—its role in educational settings remains largely underexplored, despite the increasing use of chatbots in education (Tang & Hanif, 2024). Although social presence has been identified as a key factor in user engagement with chatbots, research has predominantly focused on commercial applications rather than educational contexts (Jin & Youn, 2022).

A high degree of social presence is considered crucial for fostering acceptance, motivation, and positive learning outcomes in computer-mediated educational scenarios. This study investigates the role of perceived social presence within AI-powered role-playing scenarios and its impact on student learning outcomes and satisfaction.

The study addresses two central research questions: (1) What differences exist in perceived social presence between face-to-face interactions and online, chatbot-supported ("Talk-to-Transform", T2T) simulations, and (2) how does perceived social presence influence students' self-assessed learning outcomes and training satisfaction?

An experimental field design was employed, involving N=32 students. Participants experienced role-play interactions via the T2T chatbot and compared these interactions explicitly to traditional face-to-face conversations. Social presence was assessed using an adapted version of Gunawardena and Zittle's (1997) Social Presence Scale, alongside specific items evaluating the realism, emotional warmth, and functionality of interactions.

The empirical findings confirmed notable differences between online and face-to-face interactions. Specifically, chatbot-based interactions were rated significantly lower in emotional warmth and perceived realism but higher in perceived functional communication. Despite the lower realism, high social presence during interactions with the T2T simulator was strongly correlated with positive outcomes: notably, increased interest compared to traditional formats, greater perceived leadership skill improvement, higher willingness to recommend the training to peers and overall training satisfaction. The analyses further confirmed that participants experiencing higher levels of social presence reported significantly greater satisfaction and perceived effectiveness of training.

Overall, the findings demonstrate that while chatbot-mediated interactions might lack the emotional depth and authenticity of face-to-face communication, they provide significant functional benefits and positive impacts on learning outcomes and satisfaction when high social presence is established. These insights contribute to the ongoing discourse on effective design of AI-mediated educational interventions and underscore the need for further research to refine the measurement and enhancement of social presence in digital educational environments.

Keywords: social presence, AI-driven role-playing, supervisory leadership communication, workforce agility, computer-mediated communication (CMC), experiential learning design

References

Grub, M., & Naab, T. (2025). Empathie im digitalen Zeitalter: Vergleich der Nutzerwahrnehmung von menschlichen und KI-Chatoperatoren in der digitalen psychischen Gesundheitsversorgung. In *Book of Abstracts. Jahrestagung der Fachgruppe Rezeptions- und Wirkungsforschung in der Deutschen Gesellschaft für Publizistik- und Kommunikationswissenschaft (DGPuK), 22.–24. Januar 2025, Bamberg* (S. 197–206). Abgerufen von https://www.uni-bamberg.de/fileadmin/kowi/Tagung_FG_RezFo/Book_of_Abstracts.pdf

Gunawardena, Charlotte N.; Zittle, Frank J. (1997). Social presence as a predictor of satisfaction within a computer-mediated conferencing environment. *American Journal of Distance Education*, 11(3), 8–26. doi:10.1080/08923649709526970

Jin, S. V., & Youn, S. (2022). Social Presence and Imagery Processing as Predictors of Chatbot Continuance Intention in Human-AI-Interaction. *International Journal of Human–Computer Interaction, 39*(9), 1874–1886. https://doi.org/10.1080/10447318.2022.2129277

Kreijns, K., Xu, K., & Weidlich, J. (2022). Social presence: Conceptualization and measurement. *Educational Psychology Review, 34*(1), 139-170. https://doi.org/10.1007/s10648-021-09623-8

Yin, T. T., & Hanif, H. (2024). Enhancing Malaysian University English Test Reading Skills: Investigating ESL Students' Performance and Perspectives on MUETBot Intervention. *International Journal of Academic Research in Progressive Education and Development, 13*(1), 1528-1536. http://dx.doi.org/10.6007/IJARPED/v13-i1/20208

AI-Driven Simulations for Agile Communication: Exploring Strategies of Young Professionals in Workforce Transformation

Maria Paz Mormontoy Tacuri[1], Friederike Lindauer[2], Katharina Frosch[3], Carmen Winkel[4]

[1,2,3] Department of Business and Management, Brandenburg University of Applied Sciences, Germany
[4] Project ELI Incubator, Brandenburg University of Applied Sciences
[1] mormonto@th-brandenburg.de
[2] lindauer@th-brandenburg.de
[3] frosch@th-brandenburg.de
[4] winkel@th-brandenburg.de

Correspondence: Maria Paz Mormontoy Tacuri: mormonto@th-brandenburg.de

Abstract:

In an era of rapid organizational and technological change, communication agility is crucial for effective leadership. Although research underscores AI's role in professional learning, little is known about how young professionals navigate workplace communication challenges (Pavitra & Agnihotri, 2023). This study examines how AI-driven simulations offer training opportunities for young professionals to develop effective communication during leadership challenges. Immersing participants in realistic scenarios, these simulations reveal adaptive communication strategies beyond conventional training methods. By eliciting multiple agility dimensions, the simulations create a rich context for nuanced practices, highlighting subtle communication strategies employed in dynamic leadership environments.

This research addresses the gap in AI-driven training for managerial workforce agility by analyzing communicative patterns within the Talk2Transform (T2T) Simulator, a novel AI-powered chatbot that simulates employee-manager dialogues within a fictional organizational setting. This study investigates how young professionals incorporate key agility dimensions and the communication strategies used into staff communication. The T2T Simulator enables participants to engage in five distinct conversational scenarios, ranging from conflict resolution to performance reviews, within a fictional company undergoing transformational change toward agility. By situating each interaction in a unique transformation context, the research examines how participants approach workforce agility in leadership interactions, uncovering best practices and potential challenges.

This study employs qualitative content analysis to explore communication strategies used by young professionals in AI-driven professional training. Across 270 transcribed simulation rounds, participants' reflections on agility were documented, enabling us to both identify communication patterns and assess the frequency of the reported agility dimensions. This analysis is grounded in Petermann and Zacher's workforce agility framework (2022), ensuring a focused evaluation of agility-related dimensions. To further investigate how these dimensions manifest in communication, we will conduct a qualitative analysis on a selected subset of transcripts, examining recurring patterns of communication and their implications. Detailed findings will be given in the final presentation of the project.

In the AI-driven simulation, participants actively applied the top three agility dimensions: accepting changes, collaboration, and reflection. A frequency analysis of 270 simulation transcripts revealed that collaboration was referenced in 62% of cases, reflection in 44%, and accepting changes in 43%, while other dimensions (e.g., create transparency or learning) appeared in fewer than 30% of transcripts. This pattern underscores how the simulation's interactive design directly prompts these behaviors, offering valuable insights into agile communication strategies. These preliminary findings indicate that AI-based simulations can effectively reinforce adaptability, teamwork, and continuous learning, highlighting their potential as training interventions for developing agile teams that navigate rapid organizational change.

Keywords: AI-Driven Simulations, AI Leadership Training, Workforce Transformation, Communication Agility, Agile Communication Strategies, Managerial Communication

References

Petermann, M. K. H. & Zacher, H. (2022). *Workforce Agility: Development and Validation of a Multidimensional Measure.* Frontiers in Psychology, 13. https://doi.org/10.3389/fpsyg.2022.841862

Pavitra, K. H. & Agnihotri, A. (2023). *Artificial intelligence in Corporate learning and Development: Current trends and future possibilities.* In IEEE Xplore. https://ieeexplore.ieee.org/stamp/stamp.jsp?tp=&arnumber=10391698

Hybrid Decision Support for Higher Education: GenAI Chatbots as Transformative Tools for Academic Advising

Christian-Andreas Schumann[1], Emelie Schwill[2], Hannah Baumann[3], Isabell Mrotzek[4]

[1] University of Applied Sciences Zwickau, Germany, Christian.Schumann@fh-zwickau.de
[2] University of Applied Sciences Zwickau, Germany, Emelie.Schwill@fh-zwickau.de
[3] University of Applied Sciences Zwickau, Germany, Hannah.Baumann.ktu@fh-zwickau.de
[4] University of Applied Sciences Zwickau, Germany, Isabell.Mrotzek@fh-zwickau.de

Correspondence: Emelie Schwill, Emelie.schwill@fh-zwickau.de

Abstract:

This paper examines integrating Generative AI (GenAI) chatbots into higher education decision-making through a hybrid system combining AI and human expertise. A WHZ Zwickau case study highlights chatbots' role in enhancing accessibility, streamlining operations, and offering tailored guidance, while addressing challenges like data reliability, user acceptance, and complex queries. The research underscores the importance of inclusive, scalable, and sustainable AI systems that balance innovation with human-centered approaches.

Keywords: Decision support systems, Hybrid AI, Chatbots in Education, Administrative Efficiency, Student Support Systems, Transformative Education Tools

Introduction

Decision-making in higher education requires balancing student needs with institutional goals. Prospective students seek detailed program and career guidance, but administrative offices often face limitations in delivering personalized advice due to repetitive queries. Generative AI chatbots address these challenges by automating responses, offering tailored advice, and improving accessibility, thereby supporting inclusive education (Schumann et al., 2022). This paper examines hybrid decision-support systems, with a focus on GenAI chatbots, through a theoretical analysis and a case study at WHZ Zwickau.

Theoretical Background

AI-powered chatbots perform tasks requiring intelligence, leveraging generative AI to create new data, such as text, using machine learning (Kohne et al., 2020; Gimpel et al., 2023). Large language models (LLMs), a subset of generative AI, produce human-like text and integrate features like translation or image recognition (Kohne et al., 2020). Applied across customer service, marketing, and education, chatbots offer significant benefits but also pose risks, such as biased outputs, emphasizing the need for responsible use (Schön et al., 2023).

Methodology

Following Tranfield et al.'s (2003) systematic literature review method, 23 sources were analyzed from databases like EBSCO and Scopus, focusing on recent publications. A case study at WHZ Zwickau evaluated a chatbot's academic advising through user feedback and technical analysis, assessing its capabilities in handling FAQs and providing guidance.

Findings

Generative AI chatbots in education automate FAQs on admissions and registration, offering 24/7 responses and reducing administrative workloads, particularly for first-year students (Chukwuere, 2024; Nguyen et al., 2021; Santana et al., 2021). They support academic planning (Cunningham-Nelson et al., 2019) and personalized learning but may hinder critical thinking if overused (Fersch et al., 2023; Labadze et al., 2023). In counselling, chatbots improve access but lack nuance for complex cases, necessitating customization (Chan et al., 2018; Kuhail et al., 2023).

At WHZ, a chatbot using IBM Watson and DeepL automates multilingual FAQs, aiding international students and reducing staff workloads (Schumann et al., 2024). While praised for 24/7 availability, challenges include incomplete database integration and limited user acceptance. Planned enhancements aim to expand personalized guidance and learning support.

Summary and Discussion

Chatbots streamline operations, enhance administrative efficiency, and improve transparency (Chukwuere, 2024; Cunningham-Nelson et al., 2019). However, their focus on FAQs limits their potential for learning and counselling. By offering personalized feedback and tailored support, chatbots can better address diverse student needs (Chukwuere, 2024; Kuhail et al., 2023). Expanding functionalities at WHZ could align chatbot capabilities with research and maximize their institutional impact (Chan et al., 2018; Schumann et al., 2024).

This study highlights the transformative potential of generative AI chatbots while emphasizing areas for growth, ensuring their broader application in higher education.

References

Chan, C. H.; Lee, H. L.; Lo, W. K.; Lui, A. K. F., 2018, Developing a chatbot for college student programme advisement, In: International Symposium on Educational Technology.

Chukwuere, J. E., & Handoko, B. L. (2024). The future of generative AI chatbots in higher education. Journal of Emerging Technologies, 4(1), 36-44.

Cunningham-Nelson, S., Boles, W., Trouton, L., & Margerison, E. (2019). A review of chatbots in education: practical steps forward. In 30th annual conference for the australasian association for engineering education (AAEE 2019): educators becoming agents of change: innovate, integrate, motivate (pp. 299-306). Engineers Australia.

Fersch, M.-L.; Schacht, S.; Woldai, B., 2023, Exploring AI in Education: A Quantitative Study
for supporting the admission of universities, In: The 13th IEEE International Conference

Gimpel, H.; Hall, K.; Decker, S.; Eymann, T.; Lämmermann, L.; Maedche, A.; Röglinger, M.; Ruiner, C.; Schoch, M.; Schoop, M.; Urbach, N.; Vandirk, S., 2023, Unlocking the Power of Generative AI Models and Systems such as GPT-4 and ChatGPT for Higher Education. A Guide for Students and Lecturers, University of Hohenheim.

Kohne, A., Kleinmanns, P., Rolf, C., & Beck, M. (2020). Chatbots. Aufbau und Anwendungsmöglichkeiten von autonomen Sprachassistenten. Wiesbaden.

Kuhail, M. A., Al Katheeri, H., Negreiros, J., Seffah, A., & Alfandi, O. (2023). Engaging students with a chatbot-based academic advising system. International Journal of Human–Computer Interaction, 39(10), 2115-2141.

Labadze, L.; Grigolia M.; Machaidze L., 2023, Role of AI chatbots in education: systematic literature review, In: International Journal of Educational Technology in Higher Educati-on 20, 56, 2023.

Nguyen, M. T., Tran-Tien, M., Viet, A. P., Vu, H. T., & Nguyen, V. H. (2021, November). Building a chatbot for supporting the admission of universities. In 2021 13th International Conference on Knowledge and Systems Engineering (KSE) (pp. 1-6). IEEE.

Santana, R., Ferreira, S., Rolim, V., de Miranda, P. B., Nascimento, A. C., & Mello, R. F. (2021). A Chatbot to Support Basic Students Questions. In LALA (pp. 58-67).

Schei, O. M.; Møgelvang, A.; Ludvigsen, K., 2024, Perceptions and use of AI chatbots among students in higher education: A scoping review of empirical studies, In: Education Sci-ences, 14(922).

Schulz, A., & Dreher, M. (2020). Different counselors, many options: Career guidance and career plans in secondary schools. German Economic Review, 21(1), 65–106.

Schumann, C. A., Schwill, E., Mrotzek, I., Bahn, L., & Bahn, T. (2024, June). An AI-Supported Adaptive Study System for Individualized University Services. In The Learning Ideas Conference (pp. 168-175). Cham: Springer Nature Switzerland.

Schön, E. M., Neumann, M., Hofmann-Stölting, C., Baeza-Yates, R., & Rauschenberger, M. (2023). How are AI assistants changing higher education?. Frontiers in Computer Science, 5, 1208550.

Schumann, CA., Nitsche, AM., Tittmann, C., Reuther, K. (2022). Hybridx Higher Education – A Multidimensional Overlay of Hybrid Forms of Learning and Teaching. In: Guralnick, D., Auer, M.E., Poce, A. (eds) Innovations in Learning and Technology for the Workplace and Higher Education. TLIC 2021. Lecture Notes in Networks and Systems, vol 349. Springer, Cham. https://doi.org/10.1007/978-3-030-90677-1_31

Tranfield, D., Denyer, D., & Smart, P. (2003). Towards a methodology for developing evidence-informed management knowledge by means of systematic review. British journal of management, 14(3), 207-222.

Norma: An AI-Powered Chatbot for Legal Education

María Julia Martínez Candado[1], José R. Sepúlveda Sanchis[2]

[1] School of Social and Juridic Sciences, Universidad Internacional de Valencia, Spain; mjmartinezc@universidadviu.com
[2] Vice Chancelor of Technology, Universidad Internacional de Valencia, Spain; joseramon.sepulveda@unviersidadviu.com

Correspondence: José R. Sepúlveda Sanchis: joseramon.sepulveda@unviersidadviu.com

Abstract:

The increasing complexity of legal terminology presents a challenge for students, particularly those who are not specialized in law. To address this issue, we developed *Norma*, an AI-powered chatbot designed to assist students in understanding legal terms through interactive engagement. Norma provides personalized explanations at three different levels: an expert-level explanation for law students, an intermediate-level description, and a simplified version for non-experts. This feature aligns with the emerging trend of using clearer and more accessible legal language in law and professional settings.

Norma is built on Python with Flask and leverages the OpenAI API to generate responses- The front end is developed using JS Three.js. It integrates a structured database of legal terms tailored to the students' course materials while also accessing additional sources for enriched learning. Students interact with Norma via a text-based interface, where they type legal inquiries and receive responses in a dynamic text bubble. The chatbot serves as an engaging and interactive tool for reinforcing course content, fostering a more immersive learning experience.

The chatbot has been tested in the *Fundamentos del Derecho* course, part of the *Grado en Recursos Humanos y Relaciones Laborales (Human Resources and Labour Relations)* degree program. Over the course of a full semester, students actively used Norma to clarify doubts and reinforce their understanding of legal concepts. Feedback collected from students indicates a positive impact on both engagement and comprehension. Many students have expressed interest in implementing Norma in other courses, underscoring its potential as a scalable educational tool.

Looking ahead, we aim to expand Norma's capabilities beyond law courses, transforming it into a general-purpose tutor adaptable to different subjects and degrees. Future iterations will also integrate voice responses alongside text to enhance accessibility and interaction. Additionally, there are plans to extend Norma's use to faculties beyond the law school, making it a versatile and widely applicable learning tool.

This paper presents the development process, implementation, and student impact of Norma, highlighting the potential of AI-driven chatbots in legal education and beyond. By fostering a more interactive and accessible learning experience, Norma represents a step forward in using artificial intelligence to support academic success.

Keywords: AI Chatbot, Legal Education, Legal Terminology, Artificial Intelligence in Learning, Interactive Learning, Student Engagement, EdTech, Personalized Learnign.

References

Queudot, M., Charton, E., & Meurs, M.-J. (2023). Improving Access to Justice with Legal Chatbots. *Canadian Journal of Law and Technology*, 15(1), 23-40.

R A, K., S, K., & R, R. (2023). Legal Solutions - Intelligent Chatbot using Machine Learning. *International Journal of Legal Studies*, 10(4), 112-130

Savelka, J., Ashley, K. D., Gray, M., Westermann, H., & Xu, H. (2023). Explaining Legal Concepts with Augmented Large Language Models (GPT-4). *Legal Informatics Review*, 8(2), 78-95.

Savelka, J., & Ashley, K. D. (2023). The unreasonable effectiveness of large language models in zero-shot semantic annotation of legal texts. *Journal of Legal Technology*, 12(3), 45-67.

AI as a Companion for Self-Reflective Learning: Shaping Future Skills in Dialogue

Jörn Allmang[1], Ulf-Daniel Ehlers[2]

[1] Baden-Wuerttemberg Cooperative State University, Germany; joern.allmang@dhbw-karlsruhe.de
[2] Baden-Wuerttemberg Cooperative State University, Germany; ulf-daniel.ehlers@dhbw-karlsruhe.de

Correspondence: Jörn Allmang: joern.allmang@dhbw-karlsruhe.de

Abstract:

Dialogical learning in education has a long tradition as foundational for critical evaluation and learner empowerment (Freire, 1984), communicative action (Habermas, 1981) or in fostering learners' self-reflection and metacognitive skills (Konrad, 2004). With the ubiquitous availability of generative AI and the immense potential of dialogical engagement with an AI Companion (Giannakos et al., 2024; Lai, 2024), interactive dialogue processes are becoming more crucial to self-reflective learning processes. This form of self-reflection and examination of one's own development also provides a solid basis for the development of so-called Future Skills, competences that allow individuals to successfully act in emerging contexts (Ehlers, 2020) and are becoming increasingly important in the dynamic era of generative AI. This raises the challenge of how learners can reflect on, assess and concretize Future Skills as well as their own competence development.

This session will showcase a tool for dealing with one's own Future Skills development in higher education, with an AI-supported dialogue system that accompanies learners in their skills development by promoting self-reflective learning processes. Through a "Dialogical AI Assessment", students interact with the AI by describing personal learning situations and practical experiences, and reflecting on their Future Skills development on the basis of problem-centered key questions. The AI provides an initial analysis of which Future Skills are addressed in the experiences and formulates specific questions in order to further differentiate the learning experience. The aim is to provide in-depth reflection and feedback on the level at which the individual's competences have been developed. By enabling adaptive, reflective self-assessment through an AI-supported dialogue, this tool embodies innovative pedagogical techniques that bridge academic learning with situational, personalized experiences - a core challenge and opportunity in Higher Education.

Furthermore, the tool shows brief challenging situations from university, private or professional life that students can use as a basis for self-assessing their Future Skills. This design invites learners to put themselves in the role of the decision-maker and propose solutions or analyze the situation, mirroring real-world problem-solving and by not providing a simple answer, such vignettes encourage independent thinking and reflection in multiple perspectives (Jeffries & Maeder, 2005). An AI-Assistant, incorporated into the tool, optimally supports and automates the creation of these challenging action situations, creating a flexible system that is individually tailored to different target groups, perspectives and competence requirements, opening space for AI-assisted personalized learning. Teachers can select a parameter set (target group, study/training program, academic year, type of university/school) as well as a competence framework, on the basis of which the action situations are created. The session invites participants to discuss possible applications and the further development of the approach.

Keywords: Future Skills, competence-development, self-reflection, self-assessment, AI, Higher Education

References

Ehlers, U.-D. (2020). Future Skills. The Future of Learning and Higher Education.

Freire, P. (1970). Pedagogy of the oppressed (; M. B. Ramos, Trans.). Herder and Herder.

Giannakos, M., Azevedo, R., Brusilovsky, P., Cukurova, M., Dimitriadis, Y., Hernandez-Leo, D., Järvelä, S., Mavrikis, M., & Rienties, B. (2024). The promise and challenges of generative AI in education. Behaviour & Information Technology, 0(0), 1–27. https://doi.org/10.1080/0144929X.2024.2394886

Habermas, J. (1981). Theorie des kommunikativen Handelns. Bd. 1: Handlungsrationalität und gesellschaftliche Rationalisierung. Frankfurt/M.

Jeffries, C., & Maeder, D. W. (2005.). Using Vignettes To Build and Assess Teacher Understanding of Instructional Strategies.

Konrad, K. (2004). Förderung und Analyse von selbstgesteuertem Lernen in kooperativen Lernumgebungen: Bedingungen, Prozesse und Bedeutung kognitiver sowie metakognitiver Strategien für den Erwerb und Transfer konzeptuellen Wissens

Lai, J. W. (2024). Adapting Self-Regulated Learning in an Age of Generative Artificial Intelligence Chatbots. Future Internet, 16(6), 218. https://doi.org/10.3390/fi16060218

Personalising Learning with Custom GPTs in Higher Education: Practitioner Reflections on Design and Implementation

Palitha Edirisingha[1], Giasemi Vavoula[2], Terese Bird[3]

[1] School of Education, University of Leicester, UK; pe27@le.ac.uk
[2] Department of Museum Studies, University of Leicester, UK; g.vavoula@leicester.ac.uk
[3] Leicester Medical School, University of Leicester, UK; tmb10@leicester.ac.uk

Correspondence: Palitha Edirisingha: pe27@le.ac.uk

Abstract:

Generative Artificial Intelligence (GenAI) has made significant inroads in Education, and the Higher Education (HE) sector is no exception. Students are using these tools for academic tasks, and universities are catching up to develop policies and protocols to guide students in their ethical use of these technologies. While there are big questions about the potential for misuse of GenAI tools by students, prominent researchers in the field have pointed out the range of affordances of these technologies for supporting students' learning. Sharples (2024) envisioned the development of Social Generative AIs as well as suggested that GenAI can be incorporated into 40 innovative pedagogies (Sharples, 2019). Wegerif and Major (2024) proposed that new AI tools could be helpful dialogic partners for students, aligning with a dialogic theory of educational technology.

University teachers have a big responsibility for helping students' ethical and productive uses of GenAI tools, and increasing number of teachers are innovating in this area by creating customised chatbots such as custom GPTs. Some of the illustrative examples include custom GPTs developed for providing first-level feedback for undergraduate essays (Ankerstein 2024), in Anesthesia Practice (Fisher and Fisher, 2024) and in Sociology of Education (Fulgencio, 2024).

With support from our University's teaching development funding and following a practitioner research and 'expert reflections' approach (Ullmann et al, 2024), our presentation offers a work-in-progress report on the development and testing of three student-oriented custom GPTs in our departments: an Ethics GPT (Museum Studies), a Placement GPT (Medicine) and an Essay Planner GPT (Education). GPT-4 was used as the foundational model, and the knowledge bases of the GPTs were developed using internal documents, including those created by the academics in our departments. Buckingham Shum's (2024) advice was helpful in writing and refining prompts for the GPTs. Performance of these were evaluated in controlled conditions with groups of students while a panel of tutors with domain knowledge were involved in evaluating the responses generated from the custom GPTs. The conference presentation will cover the iterative development of the custom GPTs based on the insights from student and teacher evaluations, the research methodology, the work involved in developing students AI literacy skills, and plans for making the three GPTs available for students and wider rollout across the university including the involvement of the central services such as the library.

Keywords: Artificial Intelligence; Generative AI; Custom GPTs; Personalisation of Learning; AI Literacy Skills

References

Ankerstein, C. A. (2024) ChatGPT and Me: implementing and evaluating a custom GPT for written corrective feedback. *Ubiquity Proceedings, 4*(1): 32. https://doi.org/10.5334/uproc.154

Buckingham Shum, S. (2024) *Qreframer: a chatbot prompt that reveals your assumptions* [https://oercommons.org/courseware/lesson/114039/overview]

Fisher, A., & Fisher, G. (2024) Evaluating performance of custom GPT in Anesthesia Practice, *Journal of Clinical Anesthesia, 93,* 111371: 10.1016/j.jclinane.2023.111371

Fulgencio, S.-V. (2024) Developing Effective Educational Chatbots with GPT: Insights from a Pilot Study in a University Subject. *Trends High. Educ., 3:* 155–168. https://doi.org/10.3390/higheredu3010009

Sharples, M. (2024) *Social Generative AI: A Future for International Education, keynote speech at INTED2024, Valencia,* https://iated.org/talks/Sharples_AI [01.03.2025]

Sharples, M. (2019) P*ractical Pedagogy: 40 New Ways to Teach and Learn*, London: Routledge

Wegerif, R., & Major, L. (2024) *The Theory of Educational Technology: Towards a Dialogic Foundation for Design,* London: Routledge.

Operationalizing AI: Leveraging Effective Pedagogy and Communication Strategy to Integrate AI in Higher Education

Walker Winslow-Stephenson[1]

[1] UNC Global Affairs, University of North Carolina at Chapel Hill, United States; wwinslow@unc.edu

Correspondence: Walker Winslow-Stephenson: wwinslow@unc.edu

Abstract:

The integration of artificial intelligence in higher education often prioritizes classroom instruction and research applications, leaving administrative and support staff without clear guidance on how to effectively leverage AI in their work (Chhatwal et al., 2023). This gap represents a missed opportunity to enhance efficiency, foster interdisciplinary collaboration, and streamline global grant-seeking efforts. At UNC Global Affairs, adapting to emerging technologies and using them to identify new opportunities for collaboration is a central component of our mission. Compiling insights from staff interviews, training sessions, and recurring questions, this integration of AI into the administrative side of the higher education workplace offers a grounded, department-level case study that may be extrapolated to inform broader institutional strategies.

This case study examines the process of designing and implementing AI tools for university departments to enhance administrative workflows and support faculty in international grant applications. Through a series of interviews with staff and an analysis of existing operations, AI-driven solutions were integrated into various institutional processes to improve efficiency and accessibility.

Successful AI adoption by administrators and staff requires more than just technological proficiency; it necessitates a strategic approach rooted in theoretical frameworks. Using the Technology Acceptance Model as a foundation and applying two-way communication theory and complexity theory pedagogy, we positioned AI integration as a non-linear, adaptive process shaped by messaging, stakeholder interactions, and evolving staff needs (Davis, 1989; Theunissen & Rahman, 2010; Granić, 2022). Through continuous dialogue, ongoing training, and user-driven modifications, the implementation process enhanced both perceived usefulness and ease of use, fostering a culture of experimentation and adaptability that drove higher adoption rates and long-term buy-in (Hazaimeh & Al-Ansi, 2024).

This case study demonstrates how universities and departments can effectively implement AI and other emerging technologies by treating integration as an iterative, cyclical, and dialogic process. By intentionally utilizing two-way communication and embracing complexity-aware pedagogies, institutions can ensure AI adoption is inclusive, responsive, and impactful, leading to greater engagement and long-term success (Read, 2025).

Keywords: Artificial Intelligence, AI Pedagogy, Communication strategies, Technology Acceptance Model

References

Chhatwal, M., Garg, V., & Rajput, N. (2023). Role of AI in the education sector. Lloyd Business Review, 2(1), 1–7. https://doi.org/10.56595/lbr.v2i1.11

Davis, F. D. (1989). Perceived usefulness, perceived ease of use, and user acceptance of Information Technology. MIS Quarterly, 13(3), 319. https://doi.org/10.2307/249008

Granić, A. (2022). Educational technology adoption: A systematic review. Education and Information Technologies, 27(7), 9725–9744. https://doi.org/10.1007/s10639-022-10951-7

Hazaimeh, M., & Al-Ansi, A. M. (2024). Model of AI acceptance in Higher Education: Arguing teaching staff and students perspectives. The International Journal of Information and Learning Technology, 41(4), 371–393. https://doi.org/10.1108/ijilt-01-2024-0005

Kent, M. L., & Lane, A. (2021). Two-way communication, symmetry, negative spaces, and dialogue. Public Relations Review, 47(2), 102014. https://doi.org/10.1016/j.pubrev.2021.102014

Read, I. (2025, March 11). Balancing Innovation and Integrity: AI Integration in Liberal Arts College Administration. https://arxiv.org/html/2503.05747v1

Theunissen, P., & Rahman, K. (2010). Dialogue and two-way symmetrical communication in public relations theory and Practice. https://openrepository.aut.ac.nz/handle/10292/3360

Educator Competencies in the Age of AI

Jasmin Cowin[1]

[1] TESOL/Bilingual Department, Touro University, United States; jasmin.cowin@touro.edu

Correspondence: Jasmin Cowin: jasmin.cowin@touro.edu

Abstract:

The assertion by Fei-Fei Li (The Atlantic, 2023) that "The time has come to reevaluate the way AI is taught at every level. The practitioners of the coming years will need much more than technological expertise; they'll have to understand philosophy and ethics, and even law," signals a profound shift in the educational landscape. It posits that AI literacy, prompt fluency, and adaptive learning design are not merely beneficial but critical skill sets for both educator effectiveness and student success. The AI Index Report 2025 reveals a significant preparedness gap: while two-thirds of countries now offer or plan to offer K–12 computer science education, and 81% of K–12 CS teachers in the U.S. believe AI should be foundational to this education, less than half of these educators feel adequately equipped to teach it (Stanford Institute for Human-Centered Artificial Intelligence, 2025). This challenge is compounded by a lack of institutional readiness, with UNESCO (2023) reporting that few educational institutions have established formal guidance or policies on the use of generative AI. The Digital Education Action Plan 2021–2027 (European Commission, 2020) emphasizes digital competence as a core skill, thereby highlighting the pressing need to cultivate these advanced educator competencies.

The first of these essential competencies is AI literacy, a proficient operational knowledge of how these complex systems function, their inherent limitations, and their multifaceted impact on learning environments. This understanding is emphasized by both the European Commission (2024) and UNESCO (2023, p. 31). When educators possess robust AI literacy, AI can serve as a "force multiplier" for implementing effective, evidence-based teaching strategies (Mollick & Mollick, 2023, p. 2), such as rapidly generating diverse and contextually relevant instructional examples.

A second crucial competency is prompt fluency, the skill of crafting, adapting, and critically evaluating prompts directed at AI systems to achieve specific and desired educational outcomes. As Gattupalli, Maloy, and Edwards (2023, p.2) underscore, "Prompts are a common language between humans and AI systems... a set of instructions or questions that are given to a large language model (LLM) to guide its output." Effective prompt fluency extends to include bias-aware prompting. This is an iterative practice (European Schoolnet, 2024) vital for identifying and mitigating issues such as cultural misrepresentation or ingrained biases within AI-generated materials. Such advanced fluency empowers educators to intentionally direct AI tools, transforming their role from passive consumers of technology to critical, engaged users who can align AI outputs with pedagogical goals (Liu et al., 2023).

Finally, adaptive learning design competency involves the intentional and informed use of AI systems to create personalized learning pathways and instructional experiences. Educators must be able to interpret AI-generated insights and data appropriately, always considering crucial developmental and cultural contexts specific to their learners.

In conclusion, educators should not be seen as passive users of AI tools. Instead, they must be recognized as informed practitioners, content specialists, and co-creators of responsible, inclusive, and effective instructional design infused with loving kindness toward their students.

Keywords: AI Literacy, Prompt Fluency, Adaptive Learning Design, Educator Competencies

References

European Commission. (2020). *Digital education action plan 2021–2027: Resetting education and training for the digital age (COM 2020 624 final).* Publications Office of the European Union.https://education.ec.europa.eu/focus-topics/digital-education/action-plan

European Commission. (2024). *Regulation (EU 2024/1689) on harmonised rules on artificial intelligence (Artificial Intelligence Act).* https://eur-lex.europa.eu/eli/reg/2024/1689/oj

European Schoolnet. (2024). *AI4EDU: Final report on teacher capacity and ethical AI use.* https://www.eun.org

Gattupalli, S., Maloy, R. W., & Edwards, S. A. (2023). *Prompt literacy: A pivotal educational skill in the age of AI (College of Education Working Papers and Reports Series No. 6).* University of Massachusetts Amherst.

Li, F.-F. (2023, November 7). My north star for the future of AI. *The Atlantic.* https://www.theatlantic.com/author/fei-fei-li/

Liu, P., Yuan, W., Fu, J., Jiang, Z., Hayashi, H., & Neubig, G. (2023). Pre-train, prompt, and predict: A systematic survey of prompting methods in natural language processing. *ACM Computing Surveys, 55*(9), 1–35. https://dl.acm.org/doi/10.1145/3560815

Mollick, E. R., & Mollick, L. (2023, March 17). *Using AI to implement effective teaching strategies in classrooms: Five strategies, including prompts.* The Wharton School Research Paper. SSRN. https://ssrn.com/abstract=4391243

Stanford Institute for Human-Centered Artificial Intelligence. (2025). *AI index report 2025.* https://hai.stanford.edu/ai-index/2025-ai-index-report

UNESCO. (2023). *Guidance for generative AI in education and research.* https://unesdoc.unesco.org/ark:/48223/pf0000386693

Enhancing Communication Skills Through AI-Supported Roleplay

Asma Aydi[1], Santhiya Thangavelautham[2], Katharina Frosch[3], Carmen Winkel[4], Friederike Lindauer[5]

[1] Brandenburg University of Applied Sciences, Department of Business Management, Germany; aydi@th-brandenburg.de
[2] Brandenburg University of Applied Sciences, Department of Business and Management, Germany; thangave@th-brandenburg.de
[3] Brandenburg University of Applied Sciences, Department of Business and Management, Germany; frosch@th-brandenburg.de
[4] Brandenburg University of Applied Sciences, Project ELI Incubator, Germany; carmen.winkel@th-brandenburg.de
[5] Brandenburg University of Applied Sciences, Department of Business and Management, Germany; lindauer@th-brandenburg.de

Correspondence: Santhiya Thangavelautham: thangave@th-brandenburg.de

Abstract:

Developing effective communication skills remains a critical challenge for future leaders. Traditional teaching methods often fail to provide sufficient practical experience, while newer studies indicate that AI-based role-playing simulations offer promising opportunities for developing communication skills (Stampfl et al., 2024, p. 2244). However, empirical evidence on the effectiveness of AI-based role-playing is still limited (Bowers et al., 2024, p.39). In this context, effectiveness refers to whether learners can improve their communication skills while ensuring an engaging learning experience.

To address this gap, this study investigates two key aspects: (1) How does AI-assisted role-playing enhance communication skill development, and (2) how does the design of these simulations influence learner engagement.

We conducted a field experiment. The study participants (N=32) engaged in a role-playing scenario where they assumed the role of a supervisor interacting with a simulated dissatisfied employee (an AI chatbot). After all simulation rounds, participants reflected on their experience in a post-training evaluation survey (N=19). Each participant completed about eight simulation rounds. However, since not all participants completed every conversation, the final number of documented conversations is 279.

We assessed perceived enjoyment and difficulty based on participants' responses to reflection questions (N=246). However, only 19 participants completed the post-training evaluation survey, which served as the primary data source for analyzing self-reported improvements in communication skills. The questionnaire evaluates the training format, intensity and effectiveness using an adapted scale by Kron et al. (2017), which also includes self-assessment questions about improvements in communication skills. Another key aspect of our analysis is how perceived enjoyment and difficulty evolve over time and how they may be influenced by a) context and b) personas (i.e., the character and typical behaviors of the T2T chatbot).

Our results indicate that AI-assisted role-playing can be effective in improving the perceived communication skills of future leaders. Statistical analysis of the survey data shows notable self-reported improvements in communication skills following the post-data survey findings. However, these findings are specific to our application scenario and cannot be generalized beyond this context. Furthermore, our data indicates that the training format is engaging, meaning it is easy to use, realistic, clear, and enjoyable. Moreover, most participants stated that they prefer AI-supported simulations over traditional teaching methods, suggesting this approach offers better opportunities for developing communication skills.

Keywords: Communication Skill Development, AI-Supported Roleplay, Technology-Enhanced Learning Strategy, Simulated Conversations, Learning Outcomes, Field Experiment

References

Stampfl, R., Geyer, B., Deissl-O'Meara, M., & Ivkic, I. (2024). Revolutionising role-playing games with ChatGPT. Advances in Artificial Intelligence and Machine Learning, 4(2), 2244–2257. https://doi.org/10.54364/AAIML.2024.42129

Bowers, P., Graydon, K., Ryan, T., Lau, J. H., & Tomlin, D. (2024). Artificial intelligence-driven virtual patients for communication skill development in healthcare students: A scoping review. Australasian Journal of Educational Technology, 40(3), 39–57. https://doi.org/10.14742/ajet.9307

Experiences with the Use of Generative Feedback Combined with Failure At-Risk Detection

Pau Cortadas-Guasch[1], David Baneres[2], Anna Espasa[3], M. Elena Rodriguez[4], Montserrat Martinez-Melo[5], Ana Elena Guerrero-Roldán[6]

[1] Faculty of Economics and Business, Universitat Oberta de Catalunya, Spain; pcortadas@uoc.edu
[2] Faculty of Computer Science, Multimedia and Telecommunications, Universitat Oberta de Catalunya, Spain; dbaneres@uoc.edu
[3] Faculty of Psychology and Education Science, Universitat Oberta de Catalunya, Spain; aespasa@uoc.edu
[4] Faculty of Computer Science, Multimedia and Telecommunications, Universitat Oberta de Catalunya, Spain; mrodriguezgo@uoc.edu
[5] Faculty of Psychology and Education Science, Universitat Oberta de Catalunya, Spain; mmartinezmelo@uoc.edu
[6] Department of Applied Pedagogy, Universitat Autònoma de Barcelona, Spain; AnaElena.Guerrero@uab.cat

Correspondence: Pau Cortadas-Guasch: pcortadas@uoc.edu

Abstract:

Artificial Intelligence techniques offer different opportunities for teachers to provide better support to learners. On the one hand, predictive analytics can detect learners potentially at risk of failing (Baneres et al., 2019) or dropping out (Bañeres et al., 2023) a course. On the other hand, generative tools have emerged to deliver additional support. Among the multiple possibilities, such as chatbots (Khennouche et al., 2024) or personalised learning resources (Li & Li, 2024) that may reduce the overload in teachers' work for repetitive tasks, generative feedback can be a key factor in enhancing the quality of the learning process.

In previous work, we have explored how an early warning system (EWS) can improve support to learners by detecting at-risk failure for a course. We developed an EWS that, by using predictive models, can raise different alarms represented in a semaphore metaphor to notify teachers and learners about the potential risk of failure (Guerrero-Roldán et al., 2021). Such an alarm became the feedback that students received on each continuous assessment activity when it was graded. Additionally, the alarm was complemented with learning support information depending on the at-risk level, giving guidelines and recommendations to pass the course.

The motivation for this work is the convergence of the information related to both at-risk detection and learning support, which were provided by the teacher for the different continuous assessment activities and delivered to the learners in different messages. Such inconvenience produced some complaints since guidelines and recommendations were not aligned among messages in some cases.

This work aims to describe the experience of combining such information (i.e., at-risk detention and learning support) in a unique personalized feedback aided by a generative tool. Although there are multiple works where generative tools have already been used for feedback (Kusam et al., 2024; Lee & Moore, 2024; Tzirides et al., 2024), our contribution explores multiple ways for constructing such feedback, evaluating the teacher's efficiency and, in the end, combining with at-risk detection information for giving learners highly useful information to pass the course.

Keywords: Predictive analytics, early warning system, feedback, teacher's efficiency

References

Bañeres, D., Rodríguez-González, M. E., Guerrero-Roldán, A. E., & Cortadas, P. (2023). An early warning system to identify and intervene online dropout learners. International Journal of Educational Technology in Higher Education, 20(1). https://doi.org/10.1186/s41239-022-00371-5

Baneres, D., Rodríguez-Gonzalez, M. E., & Serra, M. (2019). An Early Feedback Prediction System for Learners At-Risk within a First-Year Higher Education Course. IEEE Transactions on Learning Technologies, 12(2), 249–263. https://doi.org/10.1109/TLT.2019.2912167

Guerrero-Roldán, A. E., Rodríguez-González, M. E., Bañeres, D., Elasri-Ejjaberi, A., & Cortadas, P. (2021). Experiences in the use of an adaptive intelligent system to enhance online learners' performance: a case study in Economics and Business courses. International Journal of Educational Technology in Higher Education, 18(1). https://doi.org/10.1186/s41239-021-00271-0

Khennouche, F., Elmir, Y., Himeur, Y., Djebari, N., & Amira, A. (2024). Revolutionizing generative pre-traineds: Insights and challenges in deploying ChatGPT and generative chatbots for FAQs. In Expert Systems with Applications (Vol. 246). https://doi.org/10.1016/j.eswa.2024.123224

Kusam, V. A., Moore, L., Shrestha, S., Song, Z., Lu, J., & Zhu, Q. (2024). Generative-AI Assisted Feedback Provisioning for Project-Based Learning in CS Courses. 2024 ASEE Annual Conference & Exposition.

Lee, S. S., & Moore, R. L. (2024). Harnessing Generative AI (GenAI) for Automated Feedback in Higher Education: A Systematic Review. Online Learning, 28(3), 82–106.

Li, R., & Li, K. (2024). Practical Research on Intelligent Evaluation of Generative Learning Resource Quality. 2024 13th International Conference on Educational and Information Technology (ICEIT), 57–60.

Tzirides, A., Zapata, G., Bolger, P., Cope, B., Kalantzis, M., & Searsmith, D. (2024). Exploring Instructors' Views on Fine-Tuned Generative AI Feedback in Higher Education. International Journal on E-Learning, 319–334.

Analysis of Digital Competence and Digital Teaching Competence Training Platform Designed by Five Valencian Universities

Anna Sánchez-Caballé[1], Francesc Esteve-Mon[1], MariaAngeles Llopis-Nebot[1]

[1] Department of Pedagogy and Didactics of Social Sciences, Language and Literature, Universitat Jaume I, Spain; acaballe@uji.es

Correspondence: Anna Sánchez-Caballé: acaballe@uji.es

Abstract:

The increasing integration of digital technologies in education has necessitated the development of digital competence (DC) and digital teaching competence (DTC) among educators (Paz & Gisbert, 2024). In response to this need, five universities from the Valencian region of Spain have collaborated to design a digital training platform aimed at enhancing these competencies. The platform offers more than 50 learning contents based on the DigComp (Vuorikari et al., 2022) and DigCompEdu (Redecker, 2017) frameworks, which serve as references for digital competence in general and for educators specifically. This study, which is part of a research project (Ref.: CIGE/2023/18), presents an analysis of the content of these courses to determine which areas of DC and DTC are most and least emphasized within the training materials.

A content analysis approach was employed to examine the courses available on the platform. The classification of the course content was conducted using the categories defined in the DigComp and DigCompEdu frameworks. The objective was to identify which areas were most frequently addressed and which were underrepresented. This analysis aimed to provide insights into the focus areas of the training and to highlight potential gaps that need to be addressed in future course development.

The initial findings indicate that the DigComp framework is the most extensively covered in the training platform. Within DigComp, the most emphasized area is "Communication and Collaboration," which includes skills related to digital interaction, information sharing, and online collaboration. Conversely, the least represented area is "Problem Solving," suggesting a lack of training focused on troubleshooting, innovation, and critical digital problem-solving skills. For the DigCompEdu framework, which focuses on DTC, the most frequently addressed area is "Teaching and Learning." This highlights a strong emphasis on integrating digital tools into instructional strategies and improving pedagogical approaches using technology. However, the least emphasized area is "Empowering Learners," indicating a gap in training related to fostering autonomy, differentiation, and personalized learning experiences through digital tools.

The findings of this study suggest that while the digital training platform provides a broad range of courses, certain areas within both the DigComp and DigCompEdu frameworks require further attention. The strong focus on Communication and Collaboration in DigComp is aligned with current digital transformation trends in education, where digital communication and teamwork are essential. However, the lack of emphasis on problem-solving may indicate a need for more training that fosters advanced digital skills, such as troubleshooting and innovative use of digital technologies. Similarly, the prominence of Teaching and Learning within DigCompEdu reflects a commitment to improving educators' ability to integrate technology into pedagogical practices. Nevertheless, the underrepresentation of Empowering Learners suggests that additional training efforts should be directed toward fostering student autonomy and digital empowerment.

These insights provide valuable guidance for the future development of training courses. Expanding content in underrepresented areas will help ensure a more balanced and comprehensive approach to developing digital competence among educators. Future research should explore the effectiveness of these courses in improving educators' digital skills and their impact on teaching practices.

Keywords: Digital Competence, Digital Teaching Competence, Spain, Online Course

References

Paz, L. E., & Gisbert, M. (2024). Competencia digital docente y uso de tecnologías digitales en la educación universitaria. *Revista Complutense de Educación, 35*(4).

Redecker, C. (2017). *European Framework for the Digital Competence of Educators: DigCompEdu* (Y. Punie, Ed.). Publications Office of the European Union.

Vuorikari, R., Kluzer, S., & Punie, Y. (2022). *DigComp 2.2: The Digital Competence Framework for Citizens – With new examples of knowledge, skills and attitudes*. Publications Office of the European Union.

A Framework for Developing Virtual Educational Escape Room in Teacher Training

Olena Beskorsa[1], Michael Reicho[2]

[1] Institute of Education Research and Teacher Education, University of Graz, Austria; olena.beskorsa@uni-graz.at
[2] Institute of Education Research and Teacher Education, University of Graz, Austria; michael.reicho@uni-graz.at

Correspondence: Olena Beskorsa, olena.beskorsa@uni-graz.at

Abstract:

Escape rooms are a form of game-based learning that can be used to promote critical thinking, problem-solving, collaboration, and communication skills (Veldkamp et al., 2020). While game-based learning is often associated with digital platforms and cutting-edge technologies, its pedagogical potential extends beyond technological aspects. To encourage a deeper discussion on the benefits of game-based learning, this paper presents the Virtual Educational Escape Room in Teacher Training (VEER2T) framework. The primary aim is to conceptualise the process of developing VEER2T and support educators in creating their own games for the purposes of education. VEER2T is a project developed by the lecturers at the University of Graz (Austria) for didactic purposes and implemented in teacher training courses.

Escape rooms, in their broadest sense, are live-action and team-based games in which players solve a series of challenges aimed at completing a mission or unravel a mystery within a limited time (Nicholson, 2015). Virtual Educational Escape Room represents the digital adaptation of traditional escape rooms, originally created for entertainment and later incorporated into educational settings. This adaptation requires the alignment of the game design elements (narrative development, puzzle construction, etc.) with pedagogical methodologies (Veldkamp al., 2020). The VEER2T Framework provides a structured methodology and serves as a guiding framework for educators to design their own virtual escape rooms. It consists of six key components: virtual environment, narrative design, participants, objectives, themes, and quizzes/materials.

The first step of the VEER2T Framework involves selecting an appropriate virtual *environment* for the activities. Immersive 3D virtual environments (metaverses) offer significant potential for fostering collaboration and meaningful interaction (Davis et al., 2009). Metaverse allows for building a space using physical objects in a way that is similar to reality and realising the storyline of the escape room. Realistically, participants, acting as avatars, are immersed in the narrative continuity of the virtual environment.

The second step focuses on developing a compelling *narrative* for the escape room experience. In VEER2T, real-life scenarios are produced through video-based storytelling, requiring students to respond to specific situations. The narrative encompasses who the characters are, what conflicts they are facing, and where this is all taking place. The narrative defines key elements such as characters, conflicts, and settings, providing context for problem-solving and interactive learning (Fotaris, & Mastoras, 2022).

The third step is to consider *participants* and conduct the analysis of their needs before designing content, materials and quizzes. This step mirrors best practices in both educational content development and game design, where understanding the target audience is crucial (Clarke et al., 2017). For VEER2T, factors such as participants' educational needs, content difficulty levels, cooperation modes (individual or group activities), and student numbers should be considered. This analysis ensures the development of an engaging and accessible learning experience.

The fourth step defines the *objectives* of VEER2T. Early established objectives align activities with learning outcomes and thematic elements. The objectives defined are the following: to add playfulness to learning and teaching, create a more inclusive learning environment, increase students' engagement and motivation, enhance digital skills, and show pre-service teachers possible alternatives to traditional teaching methods.

The fifth step is aimed at the consideration of the overall *theme* of the experience. Similar to physical escape rooms, virtual rooms follow the popular theme of detective mystery, kidnapping, prison breaks, spy games, etc. For VEER2T, the detective mystery is selected as an overall theme that is closely interlaced with the content of the academic course. The theme selection navigates the game experience using a range of decorations and props, puzzles and clues (Clarke et al., 2017). One of the options of the metaverse that has been extensively used is the right to edit and create content, as well as consume the content created by others. This allows creating materials and quizzes and incorporating them into the virtual space for organising further collaboration.

The sixth step involves designing *quizzes and materials* and integrating them into the virtual escape room. Materials, derived from the course subject matter, help students process information and take quizzes. The materials are presented through different media (audio, video, pictures, texts, etc.). This aligns with the goal of creating an inclusive environment for students through the multiple ways of representation that increase the accessibility of information (Matthews, Cavanaugh, & Wilson, 2023). The quizzes, which are carefully aligned with the topic and objectives, encourage students to critically engage with the content and develop problem-solving skills. Cognitive puzzles, designed to stimulate logical thinking, play a central role in the game. The final "meta-quiz" connects all previous challenges, serving as the ultimate key to escape. A variety of digital tools, such as online crosswords, jigsaw puzzles and Morse code generators, are used to create the quizzes.

The VEER2T framework provides a holistic approach to integrating technology-enhanced learning practices in higher education. By providing a structured methodology, it enables educators to design immersive, engaging, and pedagogically meaningful virtual escape rooms. The paper highlights how the VEER2T framework can serve as a valuable resource for developing contextually relevant and interactive learning experiences that can be adapted to various educational settings.

Keywords: virtual escape room, framework, teacher education, metaverse, innovative teaching, game-based learning

References

Clarke, S., Peel, D., Arnab, S., Morini, L., & Wood, O. (2017). EscapED: A framework for creating educational escape rooms and interactive games to for higher/further education. *International Journal of Serious Games, 4*(3), 73-86.

Davis, A., Murphy, J., Owens, D., Khazanchi, D., & Zigurs, I. (2009). Avatars, people, and virtual worlds: Foundations for research in metaverses. *Journal of the Association for Information Systems, 10*(2), 90-117. https://doi.org/10.17705/1jais.00183

Fotaris, P., & Mastoras, T. (2022). Room2Educ8: A Framework for Creating Educational Escape Rooms Based on Design Thinking Principles. *Education Sciences, 12*(11), 768. https://doi.org/10.3390/educsci12110768

Matthews, S., Cavanaugh, C., & Wilson, P. H. (2023). Multiple means of representation? A critical analysis of Universal Design for Learning checkpoint 1.2. *Policy Futures in Education, 21*(2), 190-204. https://doi.org/10.1177/14782103221097514

Nichols, R. (2014). *The video game business.* Basingstoke, Palgrave McMillian.

Veldkamp, A., Van De Grint, L., Knippels, M. C. P., & Van Joolingen, W. R. (2020). Escape education: A systematic review on escape rooms in education. *Educational Research Review, 31,* 100364. https://doi.org/10.1016/j.edurev.2020.100364

Enhancing Student Retention in AI-Driven Education: A Personalized Reward-Based Approach/System

Clifford Itumeleng Molefe[1]

[1] Department of Psychology, University of South Africa, South Africa, molefci@unisa.ac.za

Correspondence: Itumeleng Molefe: molefci@unisa.ac.za

Abstract:

The integration of Artificial Intelligence (AI) in education has revolutionized teaching and learning, particularly through online platforms. However, online education presents challenges such as low student engagement, poor attendance, and high dropout rates, particularly among first-year students (Siemens et al., 2020). One of the key issues is the lack of motivation to attend virtual classes, often resulting in reduced student retention (Brown & Green, 2021) and another issue is that students lack data bundle support and the technical know-how of the platforms. Additionally, many educators struggle with online teaching tools, further contributing to disengagement (Laurillard, 2019). This paper proposes a dual solution: a personalized reward-based learning system to incentivize student participation and targeted educator training programs to enhance digital teaching proficiency.

Online education provides flexibility but lacks the personal engagement found in traditional classrooms. Many students, particularly in their first year, face difficulties in staying motivated due to the absence of immediate reinforcement and social interactions (Garrison & Vaughan, 2021). The accessibility of course materials online can lead students to assume that live participation is unnecessary, and now access to AI tools, which give prompt answers quickly, lead to lower attendance rates because they get everything from AI tools. Additionally, some students disengage due to the technical challenges faced by educators, as many struggle to effectively utilize online teaching tools, leading to ineffective lesson delivery and further student disengagement (Means et al., 2020).

Student Retention Issues – High dropout rates due to a lack of engagement and motivation.

Limited Personalization – Traditional methods fail to cater to diverse learning styles.

Educator Preparedness - Many instructors lack training in AI-powered tools.

Keywords: AI in education, student retention, personalized learning, online learning challenges, educator training

References

Brown, A., & Green, T. (2021). *The essentials of instructional design: Connecting fundamental principles with process and practice* (4th ed.). Routledge.

Deci, E. L., & Ryan, R. M. (2000). *The "what" and "why" of goal pursuits: Human needs and the self-determination of behavior.* Psychological Inquiry, 11(4), 227-268.

Garrison, D. R., & Vaughan, N. D. (2021). *Blended learning in higher education: Framework, principles, and guidelines.* Wiley.

Kirkwood, A., & Price, L. (2014). *Technology-enhanced learning and teaching in higher education: What is 'enhanced' and how do we know?* A critical literature review. Learning, Media and Technology, 39(1), 6-36.

Laurillard, D. (2019). *Teaching as a design science: Building pedagogical patterns for learning and technology.* Routledge.

Luckin, R. (2018). *Machine learning and human intelligence: The future of education for the 21st century.* UCL Institute of Education Press.

Means, B., Bakia, M., & Murphy, R. (2020). *Learning online: What research tells us about whether, when and how.* Routledge.

Salmon, G. (2013). *E-tivities: The key to active online learning.* Routledge.

Siemens, G., Gašević, D., & Dawson, S. (2020). *Learning analytics: Theories, methods, and applications.* Springer.

Enhancing Healthcare Education Through AI-generated, Clinically Relevant Assessments

Hadar Arien-Zakay[1]

[1] The Faculty of Medicine, School of Pharmacy, Institute for Drug Research, The Hebrew University of Jerusalem, Jerusalem, Israel; hadar.az@mail.huji.ac.il

Correspondence: Hadar Arien-Zakay: hadar.az@mail.huji.ac.il

Introduction: Artificial intelligence (AI) is increasingly recognized as a transformative tool in medical and pharmacy education, (Nagi et al., 2023; Zhui et al., 2024), including assessment design (Mbakwe et al., 2023). This study builds upon our previous work (Author, 2024), which demonstrated that integrating question-based learning (QBL) within a blended pharmacology course significantly reduced failure rates and improved student performance across Bloom's Taxonomy (Giffin, 2002). Expanding on this foundation, we developed an AI-driven framework to generate pharmacology exam questions that ensure cognitive rigor, contextual relevance, and real-world clinical applicability. The primary objective is to support personalized learning while enhancing student engagement and self-assessment.

Methodology: This research defines a structured process for AI-assisted question generation to ensure alignment with course content, student knowledge levels, and clinical relevance. The AI model was trained using pharmacology course materials to contextualize content, student learning trajectories (specifically considering second-year nursing students' backgrounds, including their prior coursework in physiology, anatomy, and early clinical exposure), pre-existing assessment items classified by Bloom's Taxonomy, and guidelines from the National Board of Medical Examiners (NBME, 2021) for constructing written test questions. These elements ensure the generated questions remain within students' cognitive and experiential scope while upholding assessment validity.

The AI-assisted question development follows a five-step process. First, the system generates multiple-choice, open-ended, and case-based questions that incorporate clinical reasoning elements. Second, faculty members evaluate conceptual clarity and alignment with course objectives. Third, clinicians assess the accuracy and realism of clinical cases to maintain clinical validity. Fourth, an iterative refinement process ensures that questions not meeting the required standards are either revised manually or reprocessed using refined AI prompts. Finally, validated questions are categorized by cognitive complexity and clinical relevance, making them ready for integration into the course assessment framework.

Preliminary Findings and Future Directions: At this stage, the focus remains on optimizing AI-generated questions as precise and clinically relevant assessment tools. Ensuring coherence with course content and student preparedness is a key challenge and priority. The next phase will involve validating the questions embedded within our online self-assessment system, allowing students to interact with AI-generated assessments throughout the semester. This will facilitate an evaluation of student engagement in formative assessments, self-assessment performance trends across different cognitive categories, and final exam outcomes, comparing student success rates with prior cohorts. While this research focuses on second-year nursing students, the structured AI-driven question-generation paradigm can be adapted for various healthcare education settings, expanding its impact across multiple disciplines.

Conclusion: The integration of AI-generated, clinically relevant assessments represents a scalable and adaptive innovation in pre-clinical education. This approach not only enhances assessment efficiency but also ensures pedagogical soundness, clinical authenticity, and cognitive alignment. Future work will focus on assessing the educational impact of this model and expanding its implementation to broader healthcare education curricula, further refining AI's role in competency-based learning and adaptive assessment. Incorporating AI-driven assessments into pharmacology education also supports the Bologna Process framework, promoting standardized, student-centered, and clinically relevant medical training across institution.

Keywords: Artificial Intelligence in Education, Pharmacology Assessment, Question-Based Learning (QBL), Personalized Learning in Healthcare, AI-Generated Exam Questions, Competency-Based Medical Education

References

Author. (2024). Blended learning in nursing pharmacology: elevating cognitive skills, engagement and academic outcomes. Frontiers in Pharmacology, 15, 1361415.

Giffin, S. D. (2002). A Taxonomy of Internet Applications for Project Management Communication. Project Management Journal, 33(4), 39–47. https://doi.org/10.1177/875697280203300405

Mbakwe, A. B., Lourentzou, I., Celi, L. A., Mechanic, O. J., & Dagan, A. (2023). ChatGPT passing USMLE shines a spotlight on the flaws of medical education. PLOS Digital Health, 2(2), e0000205. https://doi.org/10.1371/journal.pdig.0000205

Nagi, F., Salih, R., Alzubaidi, M., Shah, H., Alam, T., Shah, Z., & Househ, M. (2023). Applications of Artificial Intelligence (AI) in Medical Education: A Scoping Review. Studies in Health Technology and Informatics, 305, 648–651. https://doi.org/10.3233/SHTI230581

Zhui, L., Fenghe, L., Xuehu, W., Qining, F., & Wei, R. (2024). Ethical Considerations and Fundamental Principles of Large Language Models in Medical Education: Viewpoint. Journal of Medical Internet Research, 26, e60083. https://doi.org/10.2196/60083

National Board of Medical Examiners. (2021). Constructing written test questions for the health sciences. Retrieved from https://www.nbme.org/sites/default/files/2021-02/NBME_Item%20Writing%20Guide_R_6.pdf

Personalized Learning: Learning Support Strategies in Higher Education Distance E-Learning

Madumetja Rodney Mabusela[1]

[1] University of South Africa, College of Human Sciences, South Africa; mabusmr@unisa.ac.za

Correspondence: Madumetja Rodney Mabusela: mabusmr@unisa.ac.za

Abstract:

The landscape of education is continually evolving, and open, flexible, and distance learning models and technologies are at the forefront of this transformation. This article explores the possible support structures to utilized to speak into distance learning. The key aspects of the future of education, especially student support, include personalized learning experiences, an early alert system, reward system. These factors will empower learners worldwide with accessible, engaging, and relevant educational opportunities, preparing them for success in the work market.

Firstly, when we speak of student personalised learning. The future of open, flexible, and distance learning will be characterized by personalized learning experiences tailored to individual needs. Technology will enable the collection and analysis of vast amounts of learner data, allowing educational institutions to design customized learning pathways. Adaptive learning algorithms will identify learners' strengths, weaknesses, and learning styles, delivering content and assessments accordingly. This approach will maximize learner engagement, retention, and overall academic success.

Secondly is the early alert system. The purpose of academic monitoring is to ensure that as many students as possible are successful in their studies, and it is the responsibility of both staff and students.

Staff participate in the task of choosing, admitting, and placing students wisely; providing exceptional coaching and evaluation; guaranteeing that students are afforded the chance and method to evaluate and examine their performance on a consistent basis; and providing suitable educational assistance to students. Students have the obligation of committing themselves entirely to their revision; observing their routine in their revision; and using all the existing resources (academic counselling, academic support and career and personal counselling) to effectively complete their lessons, preferably in the minimum time for their qualification and not exceeding the maximum time permissible.

Lastly, it is what we call the reward system. The use of rewards within the classroom is a form of extrinsic motivation for students. It encourages them to participate cooperatively in academic and social learning experiences. Especially under these changing futures of distance learning, students tend not to participate because of not being familiar with new technologies which come with new futures. Through a reward system, we are able to increase motivation, which will assist students to develop interest and increase their participation in everyday classrooms, organised orientations and educational workshops.

Keywords: Connection, Open Distance Learning, Communication, Online, Students, Accesses

Conclusion

The futures of quality open, flexible, and distance learning models and technologies are poised to reshape the landscape of education profoundly. Therefore, student support it's at the centre of the learning experience. personalized learning experiences, early alert system, reward system. Are just a few of the factors we should zoom into closely because it is the backbone of student success that will define the future of education. As these support initiatives evolve, they will empower learners across the globe with accessible, engaging, and relevant educational opportunities, preparing them for success in an increasingly interconnected and dynamic world.

Sustainability and Digital Transformation: Key Insights from University-Industry Co-Creation Workshops

Carles Bruguera[1], Natalí Basilico[2], Carmen Pagés[3], Mitchell Peters[4]

[1] Universitat Oberta de Catalunya (UOC), Spain, cbruguerat@uoc.edu
[2] Universitat Oberta de Catalunya (UOC), Spain, nbasilico@uoc.edu
[3] Universitat Oberta de Catalunya (UOC), Spain, cpagesserra@uoc.edu
[4] Universitat Oberta de Catalunya (UOC), Spain, mjosephp@uoc.edu

Correspondence: Carles Bruguera: cbruguerat@uoc.edu

Abstract:

The simultaneous shifts towards digitalization and sustainability, known as the twin transition, are reshaping the economic and organizational landscape. The World Economic Forum's Future of Jobs 2025 report highlights that AI, automation, and energy innovations are poised to transform 60% of businesses by 2030. To navigate these changes, it is essential to align educational programs with industry needs. This alignment depends on robust collaboration between universities and organisations to identify the competencies and professional profiles required for the evolving labor market. Co-creation workshops present a valuable platform for facilitating this collaboration. This study examines the outcomes of the first of a series of participatory workshops organized by the Open University of Catalonia (UOC), which brought together 30 organizations from Catalonia that are navigating this twin transition. The workshop explored three key areas: (1) key professional profiles that are essential yet hard to recruit, (2) key competencies needed in the rapidly changing job market, and (3) emerging trends shaping the twin transition. The findings reveal that these organizations are struggling with significant talent shortages, particularly in roles that demand expertise in data analytics and sustainability. Participants stressed that sustainability should be integrated into all professional roles, rather than being confined to specialized positions. Additionally, the importance of continuous learning emerged as a central theme, with flexible training formats—such as micro-credentials and modular programs—identified as vital for keeping professionals up-to-date with technological and regulatory developments. Soft skills development in the workplace was also an important part of the conversation. The workshop highlighted the strategic value of direct collaboration between academia and industry. Such initiatives not only identify skill gaps but also actively contribute to curriculum development, ensuring that academic programs are closely aligned with industry demands. By integrating real-world challenges into academic training, co-creation workshops enhance the adaptability and relevance of higher education, ultimately preparing graduates to lead the twin transition and address its complex challenges.

Keywords: Higher Education, Labor market, Twin transition, Lifelong learning

References

Bjorn, G., & Kerrigan, M. R. (2023). Labor market information (LMI) usage in postsecondary institutions: A systematic literature review. *Educational and employment research center.* https://doi.org/10.35542/osf.io/pfa35

Thi Ngoc Ha, N., Van Dyke, N., Spittle, M., Watt, A., & Smallridge, A. (2024). Micro-credentials through the eyes of employers: benefits, challenges and enablers of effectiveness. *Education+ Training*, *66*(7), 948-963.

World Economic Forum. (2023). *The future of jobs report 2023.* World Economic Forum. https://www3.weforum.org/docs/WEF_Future_of_Jobs_2023.pdf

World Economic Forum. (2025). The Future of Jobs Report 2025. World Economic Forum. https://www.weforum.org/reports/the-future-of-jobs-report-2025

Varadarajan, S., Koh, J. H. L., & Daniel, B. K. (2023). A systematic review of the opportunities and challenges of micro-credentials for multiple stakeholders: learners, employers, higher education institutions and government. *International Journal of Educational Technology in Higher Education*, *20*(1), 13.

Zeivots, S., Hopwood, N., Wardak, D., & Cram, A. (2024). Co-design practice in higher education: practice theory insights into collaborative curriculum development. *Higher Education Research & Development*, 1–15. https://doi.org/10.1080/07294360.2024.2410269

Future Ready: Integrating Future Skills and Learner Agency in Dual Higher Education

Aleydis Kleine-Allekotte[1], Ulf-Daniel Ehlers[2]

[1] Business department, DHBW Karlsruhe, Germany, aleydis.kleineallekotte@dhbw-karlsruhe.de
[2] Business department, DHBW Karlsruhe, Germany, ulf-daniel.ehlers@dhbw-karlsruhe.de

Correspondence: Aleydis Kleine-Allekotte: aleydis.kleineallekotte@dhbw-karlsruhe.de

Abstract:

New societal challenges—ranging from climate change to social inequality and the growing impact of digitalization and generative AI—are transforming the way we live, work, and learn (George and George, 2024). These emergent, often unpredictable changes demand a shift in how higher education institutions prepare their students for these unfamiliar situations. It is no longer sufficient to transmit fixed knowledge; instead, higher educational institutions must equip their students with the capabilities to navigate uncertainty, complexity, and change (Hadar, et al., 2020).

This context places *Future Skills* (Ehlers, 2020)—such as self-efficacy, adaptability, creativity, and systems thinking—at the heart of educational transformation. They are essential for learners to thrive in digitally saturated, rapidly shifting environments. The central question this initiative addresses is therefore: **How can learners in dual study programs effectively reflect on, assess, and develop their Future Skills within an integrated educational experience?**

To explore this, we present a research and practice initiative that deeply embeds Future Skills into the curricula of eight selected dual study programs across disciplines. The foundation is the **NextSkills framework** (Ehlers, 2020), which defines the core competencies needed for future readiness. We base our understanding of competencies on the concept of behavioural competence (Weinert, 2001, Erpenbeck and Heyse, 1999), we argue that the development of *Future Skills* must be grounded in **self-directed learning (Morris, 2019)** and oriented toward strengthening **learner agency (Blaschke, Bozkurt, and Cormier, 2021)**. In this context, **challenge-based learning scenarios** provide a suitable pedagogical approach to support students in actively developing the competencies needed for navigating complex, uncertain environments (Gallagher and Savage, 2023). The project focuses on rethinking the dual study model—traditionally marked by weakly linked academic and practical learning—by creating a tightly integrated, competence-oriented structure.

At the core of the initiative is an innovative **didactic concept**: a digitally supported, peer-based reflection process implemented over a full academic year. This involves a combination of:

- a **digital learning journal** app and ePortfolio that scaffold continuous, situational reflection;
- structured **peer learning circles** that foster collaborative meaning-making and feedback;
- and **curriculum-integrated Future Skills modules**, enabling students to actively engage with and personalize their competence development.

To make this learning visible and verifiable, a **micro-credentialing system based on Open Badges** certifies the acquisition of competencies, supporting transparency and transferability across educational and professional contexts.

The concept is piloted through three application scenarios—curriculum-deep integration, modular learning, and self-directed formats—accompanied by iterative refinement through co-creation with students, teachers, and mentors from the field. Rather than focusing solely on digital transformation or AI literacy, this initiative develops a scalable model for embedding Future Skills into higher education, enabling learners to respond creatively and competently to the complex challenges of a society in flux.

Keywords: Future Skills, personalized learning, professional development, digital education

References

Blaschke, L. M., Bozkurt, A., & Cormier, D. (2021). Learner agency and the learner-centred theories for online networked learning and learning ecologies. *Unleashing the power of learner agency. EdTech Books*.

Ehlers, U.-D. (2020). *Future Skills. The Future of Learning and Higher Education.* https://nextskills.org/downloads/Future-Skills-The-Future-of-learning-and-higher-education.pdf

Erpenbeck, J., & Sauer, J. (2001). Das Forschungs-und Entwicklungsprogramm „Lernkultur Kompetenzentwicklung ". *Arbeiten und Lernen. Lernkultur Kompetenzentwicklung und Innovative Arbeitsgestaltung. QUEM-report, 67*, 9-65.

Gallagher, S. E., & Savage, T. (2023). Challenge-based learning in higher education: an exploratory literature review. *Teaching in higher education*, *28*(6), 1135-1157.

George, A. S., & George, A. H. (2024). Towards a Super Smart Society 5.0: Opportunities and Challenges of Integrating Emerging Technologies for Social Innovation. *Partners Universal International Research Journal*, *3*(2), 01-29.

Hadar, L., Ergas, O., Alpert, B., & Ariav, T. (2020). Rethinking teacher education in a vuca world: student teachers' social-emotional competencies during the covid-19 crisis. European Journal of Teacher Education, 43(4), 573-586. https://doi.org/10.1080/02619768.2020.1807513

Morris, T. H. (2019). Self-directed learning: A fundamental competence in a rapidly changing world. *International Review of Education*, *65*(4), 633-653.

The Community in Us: An Online Learning View of Data Science Education

Daniela Castellanos-Reyes[1], Stefan Stenbom[2]

[1] Teacher Education and Learning Sciences Department, North Carolina State University, USA; dcastel2@ncsu.edu
[2] Department of Learning in Engineering Sciences, KTH Royal Institute of Technology, Sweden; stkn@kth.se

Correspondence: Daniela Castellanos-Reyes: dcastel2@ncsu.edu

Abstract:

As the field of data science (DSC) - an interdisciplinary approach to leverage unstructured data for decision-making - expands, many are introduced to it through online education. Before the rapid growth and increased enrollment in formal DSC programs (Coffey, 2024), various educational vendors offered many non-credit online courses for those interested in DSC. However, the curricula from most providers tend to concentrate heavily on developing technical skills, such as data curation, wrangling, and cleaning, while often neglecting the broader application of DS within diverse social contexts. Additionally, they frequently overlook the value of online communities, like Stack Overflow, which learners leverage to solve programming challenges and exchange knowledge. Consequently, it is crucial to explore how online DSC education can evolve beyond merely imparting technical knowledge, fostering computer-mediated communication and collaborative skills, and preparing learners for careers in DSC, where engaging with online communities is essential to thrive.

Online Learning in DSC Education

The Community of Inquiry (CoI) framework is a process model of online teaching and learning. It comprises three interconnected elements: social, cognitive, and teaching presence. Cognitive Presence (CP) is how learners construct and confirm meaning through sustained reflection and discourse (Stenbom & Cleveland-Innes, 2024). Inquiry-based tasks, like programming challenges, guide learners through the triggering event, exploration, integration, and resolution phases used to operationalize CP, helping them build deep understanding and practical data analysis and interpretation skills. Social Presence (SP) refers to the extent to which learners perceive each other as "real" in computer-mediated communication (Stenbom & Cleveland-Innes, 2024). In DSC education, SP fosters environments where students feel comfortable sharing ideas, collaborating on projects, and seeking help from one another. The last element of CoI is teaching presence (TP). This refers to the design, facilitation, and direction of cognitive and social processes for realizing educational outcomes (Stenbom & Cleveland-Innes, 2024). In DSC education, effective TP includes creating a well-structured curriculum that balances theory and application, offering guidance on using DSC tools, and providing timely feedback.

This Proposal

This proposal addresses the question, "What does it mean to have a Community of Inquiry in Data Science?" Building on the assumption that learning is a social event, we will address the paradox that DSC educators and learners face in online learning environments in which opportunities for face-to-face interaction are hindered. We capitalize on the CoI framework to explore how collaborative meaning-making processes occur in online learning DSC by integrating social network analysis and the CoI instrument to propose new data collection instruments to explore online students' communities of inquiry. Specifically, we build on Castellanos-Reyes et al. (2024) work that uses name generators - a social network analysis data collection technique - for CoI research to propose a network questionnaire and network map to assist researchers and educators in collecting both qualitative and quantitative data for mixed-method research designs. The proposed instrument reconciles decades of work on CoI research primarily focused on quantitative approaches (e.g., survey research and quantitative content analysis) to give learners, practitioners, and researchers a community-centered perspective.

Keywords: Online learning, data science education, community of inquiry, social presence, teaching presence, cognitive presence

References

Castellanos-Reyes, D., Richardson, J. C., & Maeda, Y. (2024). The evolution of social presence: A longitudinal exploration of the effect of online students' peer-interactions using social network analysis. The Internet and Higher Education, 61, 100939. https://doi.org/10.1016/j.iheduc.2024.100939

Coffey, L. (2024, January 25). Data science major takes off. *Inside Higher Ed*. https://www.insidehighered.com/news/tech-innovation/teaching-learning/2024/01/25/data-science-major-takes-across-college-campuses

Stenbom, S., & Cleveland-Innes, M. F. (2024). Introduction to the community of inquiry theoretical framework. In *The Design of Digital Learning Environments* (pp. 3-25). Routledge.

Building Pathways: International Collaboration for Flexible Learning

Brian Shee[1], Sarah Brady[2], Michael Hennessy[3]

[1] Graduate and Professional Studies, University of Limerick, Ireland; brian.shee@ul.ie
[2] Graduate and Professional Studies, University of Limerick, Ireland; sarah.brady@ul.ie
[3] Graduate and Professional Studies, University of Limerick, Ireland; michael.hennessy@ul.ie

Correspondence: Michael Hennessy: michael.hennessy@ul.ie

Abstract:

The Irish MicroCreds initiative and Erasmus+ projects are revolutionising lifelong learning by breaking down barriers and offering flexible, accessible micro-credentials. University of Limerick's innovative approach empowers disadvantaged learners, fostering international collaboration and creating pathways to success in a rapidly evolving global landscape.

The MicroCreds project is an Irish Government initiative aimed at mainstreaming micro-credentials and addressing barriers to lifelong learning, such as time constraints and inflexibility in traditional programme delivery (MicroCreds, 2023). Micro-credentials offer flexibility, allowing learners to access education in small units at their own pace, balancing life and work commitments (Irish Universities Association, 2020).

As a founding partner in the MicroCreds project, the University of Limerick has extensive expertise in developing and delivering micro-credentials. With over 150 micro-credentials developed in collaboration with industry and academic partners, the University of Limerick showcases how higher education institutions can integrate relevant and flexible learning pathways (University of Limerick, 2025). Their learner-centred design and robust quality assurance processes ensure these offerings are accessible and relevant to the evolving labour market and address social needs as appropriate.

Building on this success, the University of Limerick has expanded its reach through two Erasmus+ projects aimed at developing new learning routes for disadvantaged groups. The Learn-to-Learn MicroCred project enhances the international micro-credentialing ecosystem by co-creating, piloting, and evaluating high-quality micro-credentials across multiple countries (L2L MicroCred, 2024). This project involves partners from Australia, Norway, Italy, and Ireland, fostering transnational collaboration to identify and address the needs of disadvantaged learners through targeted micro-credentials. By integrating rigorous needs analysis with iterative course design, Learn-to-Learn MicroCred aims to create a responsive and adaptable approach to lifelong learning.

The second project, part of the Emerge initiative, focuses on co-creating and scaling flexible learning pathways through micro-credentials for disadvantaged and marginalised groups. This project brings together educators from Cyprus, Germany, Greece, Ireland, France, Norway, Slovakia, and Spain, engaging with industry representatives, policymakers, and other stakeholders. The goal is to develop, deliver, and test micro-credential offerings for disadvantaged learners across eight countries. The resulting framework will serve as a key resource for developing future international micro-credentials for disadvantaged groups (Emerge, 2024).

Both Erasmus+ projects demonstrate how international partnerships can transform traditional educational approaches. They leverage the University of Limerick's experience and commitment to flexible pathways, focusing on new learning opportunities for disadvantaged groups in multiple countries. By fostering a collaborative environment where diverse expertise converges, these projects address regional and sectoral needs and contribute to a broader vision of lifelong learning that is adaptive, accessible, and universally recognised.

In conclusion, the convergence of the national Irish MicroCreds project and these Erasmus+ initiatives, through the University of Limerick, offers an opportunity to redefine lifelong learning for disadvantaged groups. The integration of digital innovation, collaborative best practices, and flexible micro-credentialing pathways heralds a new era in education, equipping disadvantaged learners with the skills needed for success in a rapidly evolving global landscape.

Keywords: Micro-credentials; Inclusive Learning; Erasmus+; Accessible Learning; Learning Pathways; International Collaboration

References

Emerge (2024) *Empowering the Margins of Europe through Regional and Global Engagement*, available: https://euemerge.eu/, [accessed 18/02/2025]

Irish Universities Association (2020) *MicroCreds Project Overview*, available: https://www.iua.ie/overview-microcreds/, [accessed 13/02/2025]

L2L MicroCred (2024) *Learning to Learn Through Micro-Credentials in a Regional Setting*, available: https://www.l2lmicrocred.net/, [accessed 18/02/2025]

MicroCreds (2023) *Re-Imagining Lifelong Learning in Ireland*, available: https://microcreds.ie/about [accessed 10/02/2025]

University of Limerick (2025) *Micro-credentials: Build Your Learning Pathway*, available: https://www.ul.ie/gps/microcredentials, [accessed 21/01/2025]

Assessments in Online Courses and the Influence of Artificial Intelligence

Florence Martin[1], Stella Kim[2], Doris Bolliger[3]

[1] Department of Teacher Education and Learning Sciences, North Carolina State University, USA; fmartin3@ncsu.edu
[2] Department of Educational Leadership, University of North Carolina Charlotte, USA; skim113@charlotte.edu
[3] Department of Curriculum and Instruction, Texas Tech University, Lubbock, USA; dorisbolliger@gmail.com

Correspondence: Florence Martin: fmartin3@ncsu.edu

Abstract:

Assessments are an important aspect of the teaching and learning process, as they facilitate learning and engagement, and enhance student participation in the course (Owan et al., 2023). Instructors and instructional designers must also be aware of the benefits and challenges in the design and implementation of assessments due to the influence of artificial intelligence (AI) (Swiecki et al., 2022).

This study used a survey methodology to examine instructional designers' perceptions on assessment types, assessment strategies, and the influence of artificial intelligence (AI) in online assessments. Research questions included:
1. What types of assessment types and assessment strategies are considered effective by instructional designers in online courses in higher education?
2. How does the integration of artificial intelligence (AI) influence assessments in online courses?

Instructional designers at several universities were invited to participate in the study, and 103 individuals completed the survey. The survey used a 5-point Likert-type scale for effectiveness with 1 = not effective to 5 = extremely effective, for assessment types and assessment strategies, and open-ended questions.

Assessment Types

Notably, about 10% of participants (n = 10) indicated they had never used proctored exams as an assessment tool for online courses. In terms of mean ratings, case study analysis received the highest value (M = 4.11), followed closely by electronic portfolios (M = 3.99), and design projects (M = 3.99). By contrast, non-proctored exams (M = 2.72), proctored exams (M = 2.97), and asynchronous participation (M = 2.97) were rated as the least effective assessment types.

Additionally, open-ended responses for assessment types were collected. Top responses included authentic assessment, weekly discussion, and social annotations.

Assessment Strategies

Grading rubrics/criteria was rated as the most effective strategy for evaluating student learning (M = 4.13), with most participants selecting "moderately effective", "very effective", or "extremely effective." Other strategies rated highly included multiple attempts/submissions (M = 3.87) and formative assessment (M = 3.83). By contrast, ungraded assignments (M = 2.62) and automated graded assignments (M = 2.72) received the lowest ratings, followed by open-book/note assessments (M = 3.06). Instructor-graded assignments were rated moderately effective (M = 3.74), whereas peer feedback (M = 3.30) and peer evaluation (M = 3.26) were viewed as less effective.

Additionally, open-ended responses on assessment strategies were collected. Top responses included synchronous sessions for assessments, progressive assignments (submitted in stages), and the opportunity to revise and resubmit.

Influence of AI on Perceived Effectiveness of Assessment Types, Strategies and Feedback

Three categories emerged in the open-ended data: the use of AI, alternatives, and challenges. The topmost frequent responses in each of the three categories included the use of AI to create rubrics, Use of machine-graded/automated graded quizzes and feedback, assessments where students have to use higher-order thinking skills, authentic assessments, conducting oral exams, not using AI yet and concerns pertaining to academic integrity.

Results of this study provide IDs, online instructors, administrators, researchers, and students with an understanding of effective student assessments in the age of artificial intelligence.

Keywords: Online Assessments, Artificial Intelligence, Online Instructors, Instructional Designers

References

Owan, V. J., Abang, K. B., Idika, D. O., Etta, E. O., & Bassey, B. A. (2023). Exploring the potential of artificial intelligence tools in educational measurement and assessment. *Eurasia Journal of Mathematics, Science and Technology Education, 19*(8), Article em2307. https://doi.org/10.29333/ejmste/13428

Swiecki, Z., Khosravi, H., Chen, G., Martinez-Maldonado, R., Lodge, J. M., Milligan, S., Selwyn, N., & Gašević, D. (2022). Assessment in the age of artificial intelligence. *Computers and Education: Artificial Intelligence*, *3*, Article 100075. https://doi.org/10.1016/j.caeai.2022.100075

Improving Students' Engagement in Distance Education Through Innovative Assignments

Inés Gil-Jaurena[1], Daniel Domínguez[2], Belén Ballesteros[3], Ana Martínez Ortiz de Zárate[4], Sergio López-Ronda[5], Aitor López-González[6]

[1] Faculty of Education, Universidad Nacional de Educación a Distancia (UNED), Spain; inesgj@edu.uned.es
[2] Faculty of Education, Universidad Nacional de Educación a Distancia (UNED), Spain; ddominguez@edu.uned.es
[3] Faculty of Education, Universidad Nacional de Educación a Distancia (UNED), Spain; bballesteros@edu.uned.es
[4] Faculty of Education, Universidad Nacional de Educación a Distancia (UNED), Spain; amartinezortizdezarate@edu.uned.es
[5] Faculty of Education, Universidad Nacional de Educación a Distancia (UNED), Spain; slopezr@edu.uned.es
[6] Faculty of Education, Universidad Nacional de Educación a Distancia (UNED), Spain; aitorlopezgonzalez@edu.uned.es

Correspondence: Inés Gil-Jaurena: inesgj@edu.uned.es

Abstract:

In 2024-25, we are involved in a teaching innovation project where we want to promote students' active participation through the design and development of renewable assignments in various distance education undergraduate and postgraduate courses that we teach at the National Distance Education University (*Universidad Nacional de Educación a Distancia* - UNED) Faculty of Education in Spain. `Renewable´ assignments –unlike `disposable´ assignments– are 'assignments which both support an individual student's learning and result in new or improved OER that provide a lasting benefit to the broader community of learners' (Wiley & Hilton, 2018), which is aligned with open educational practices (OEP), that include active participation and production of knowledge by students (Paskevicius, 2017). In renewable assignments, students share their work openly, and the artefact developed has value beyond the student's own learning (Wiley, 2013). Students' contributions produce relevant content not only for being assessed by the teacher, but that is available also for other students in the same course, in other courses, or in the wider community, depending on each assignment's characteristics and the type of use the students have allowed.

Our first experience with this type of innovative assignments and assessment methods in 2023-24 –that involved the creation of a collaborative online map about community development projects (Gil-Jaurena et al., 2024)– showed the interest of this task for engaging students as producers and for enriching the course content. In 2024-2025, we have converted our traditional or disposable assignments into renewable ones in various courses. In the presentation, we will share examples of these innovative experiences, and the results obtained. By the end of the semester in June 2025, we will explore the impact of these experiences in terms of students' engagement and academic achievement. For the analysis, we will consider students' perceptions collected via surveys, students' performance in the online course, and academic rates (assessment rates and average scores).

In relation to generative AI, we consider that this type of assignments –that facilitate collaborative learning in distance education environments, students' engagement and public sharing–can promote a more ethical use of AI as a support tool, and not as a replacement tool. As we demand our students to be active and critical agents in their learning process and show their productions publicly, we consider that this can prevent the misuse of generative AI tools. In the project, we will reflect on these aspects based on the results obtained.

Keywords: renewable assignments; engagement; collaborative learning; open educational practice; distance education

References

Gil-Jaurena, I.; López-González, A.& Domínguez, D. (2024). Open collaborative map in distance education: an experience with renewable assignments. *EDEN 2024 Research Workshop Proceedings: Emerging Technologies, Challenges and Opportunities in Education and Research*, Timisoara, Romania, 16-18 October 2024 (pp. 1-2). https://eden-europe.eu/wp-content/uploads/2024/11/2024-RW-proceedings_short-papers.pdf

Paskevicius, M. (2017). Conceptualizing Open Educational Practices through the Lens of Constructive Alignment. *Open Praxis, 9*(2), 125–140. http://doi.org/10.5944/openpraxis.9.2.519

Wiley, D. (2013). *What is open pedagogy?* https://opencontent.org/blog/archives/2975

Wiley, D., & Hilton III, J.L. (2018). Defining OER-enabled pedagogy. *The International Review of Research in Open and Distributed Learning, 19*(4). https://doi.org/10.19173/irrodl.v19i4.3601

Engaging with Generative AI in Assessment: Perceptions, Practices and Professional Development Needs at a South African University

Sukaina Walji[1], François Cilliers[2], Soraya Lester[1], Cheng-Wen Huang[1], Sanet Steyn[3]

[1] Centre for Innovation in Learning and Teaching, University of Cape Town, South Africa; Sukaina.Walji@uct.ac.za
[2] Centre for Higher Education Development, University of Cape Town, South Africa; Francois.Cilliers@uct.ac.za
[3] Centre for Educational Assessments, University of Cape Town, South Africa; Sanet.Steyn@uct.ac.za

Correspondence: Sukaina Walji: Sukaina.Walji@uct.ac.za

Abstract:

The rapid advancement of Generative Artificial Intelligence (GenAI) is disrupting traditional assessment practices in higher education, compelling teaching staff to rethink assessment strategies, integrity policies, and learning outcomes (Awadallah Alkouk & Khlaif, 2024; Coleman & Van Belle, 2025). While discussions about GenAI's impact are widespread, there remains uncertainty about how university educators are actually responding to these changes in practice. Understanding these responses is crucial for informing staff development initiatives that support effective and ethically sound engagement with AI in assessment.

This study addresses this gap by presenting findings from a survey conducted at the University of Cape Town (UCT), capturing teaching staff's engagement with, perceptions of, and practices related to GenAI in assessment. The survey examined changes in assessment design, the use of AI for evaluating student work, perceived impacts on academic integrity, and staff confidence in employing GenAI tools effectively. As members of a central academic development unit, we aimed to use these insights to shape targeted professional development initiatives that respond to emerging challenges and opportunities in AI-enabled assessment.

Our questionnaire gathered responses about changes in assessment design in response to GenAI, usage of AI for assessing student work, perceived impacts on assessment integrity, and staff confidence in employing GenAI tools effectively. Preliminary analysis reveals varying practices and attitudes across faculties. While some academics have proactively adapted assessment instructions explicitly addressing GenAI use, others maintain traditional methods without modifications. Notably, most staff express significant concerns about GenAI undermining learning outcomes and assessment integrity. A minority currently incorporate GenAI tools into assessment processes, primarily for question design and marking assistance.

Confidence levels among staff about using AI vary considerably, indicating a gap in training and in departmental and institutional support. Respondents highlighted GenAI's potential for enhancing feedback mechanisms and formative assessment practices positively, but also voiced apprehensions about inflated student performance and diminished critical thinking skills. Some expressed concerns with ethical considerations of AI in education, particularly in relation to bias, accessibility, and the broader implications for equity and inclusion. At the same time, there is notable interest among academics in developing skills related to automated marking, AI-driven feedback and AI-supported academic integrity practices.

This study has promoted reflection on the need to provide dynamic and evolving professional development offerings that track the pace of developments around GenAI technologies. The findings underscore an urgency for clearer and responsive institutional guidance and policies, targeted professional development and aligned communications at multiple levels. Opportunities are also needed to enable teaching staff to responsibly integrate GenAI within their disciplinary contexts. There is a need for balanced approaches promoting innovative assessment practices that could leverage GenAI's benefits while safeguarding academic integrity and supporting student learning outcomes. The findings contribute to ongoing discussions around strategies to shape engagement, integration and ethical use of GenAI in assessment designs.

Keywords: Assessment; Academics; Generative AI; Professional Development; AI literacy; Innovation

References

Awadallah Alkouk, W., & Khlaif, Z. N. (2024). AI-resistant assessments in higher education: practical insights from faculty training workshops. *Frontiers in Education, 9*. https://doi.org/10.3389/feduc.2024.1499495

Coleman, M., & Van Belle, J. P. (2025). Perceptions of educators on the use of text-generative AI in South African higher education. In N. Hasteer, S. McLoone, P. Sharma, & R. Nallamalli (Eds.), *Adaptive Intelligence. InCITe 2024. Lecture Notes in Electrical Engineering* (Vol. 1280). Springer, Singapore. https://doi.org/10.1007/978-981-97-9045-6_4

Quality Link: The Standards and Quality Criteria for Learning Opportunities, Leading to Micro-Credentials

Estela Daukšienė[1], Elena Trepulė[2], Jochen Ehrenreich[3], Colin Tück[4], Arantza Mongelos Garcia[5], Tiago Simões[6]

[1] EDEN Digital Learning Europe, Estonia; estela.dauksiene@vdu.lt
[2] EDEN Digital Learning Europe, Estonia; elena.trepule@vdu.lt
[3]Baden-Wuerttemberg Cooperative State University (DHBW), Germany; jochen.ehrenreich@heilbronn.dhbw.de
[4]Knoledge Innovation Centre, Slovenia; colin@knowledgeinnovation.eu
[5]Mondragon University, Spain; amongelos@mondragon.edu
[6]European University Foundation, Hungary; tiago.simoes@uni-foundation.eu

Correspondence: Estela Daukšienė: estela.dauksiene@vdu.lt

Abstract:

QualityLink is an Erasmus+ project which focuses on aggregating quality indicators on learning opportunities leading to micro-credentials. The QualityLink project expert group set out the list of possible quality domains and indicators for the courses leading to micro-credentials, and the partner institutions addressed the students or lifelong and other stakeholders (teachers, course designers, university program leaders and other university staff, employers, etc) for their feedback to validate the indicators and their importance. The short abstract indicates the micro-credential quality domains and provides a glimpse into the survey results. The complete survey and project results are to be presented at the conference.

Keywords: micro-credentials, learning opportunities, quality, indicators

The project experts defined micro-credentials following the EU Council Recommendations (2021) as a "record of the learning outcomes that a learner has acquired following a small volume of learning. These learning outcomes will have been assessed against transparent and clearly defined criteria. Learning experiences leading to micro-credentials are designed to provide the learner with specific knowledge, skills and competencies that respond to societal, personal, cultural or labour market needs."
The QualityLink project expert group (Trepule et al., 2024) recommended a list of possible quality domains and indicators for the courses leading to micro-credentials, indicating five quality domains with the following indicators:

1. Content Relevance, Labor Market Demand, and Accuracy:
   - Accurate and up-to-date information
   - Demand for skills in micro-credentials
   - Specific requests for skills / micro-credentials
   - Stackability
   - Additional QA / Labels
   - Quality Assurance (ESG)

2. Teaching Methods and Pedagogy
   - Quality Assurance (based on the European Standards and Guidelines)
   - Platform QA / Eligibility Policies of Major Platforms
   - Active methodologies
   - Tutoring
   - Student/staff ratio
   - Assessment methods used
   - Virtual learning environment available
3. Accessibility and Inclusivity
   - Make-up/diversity of the student body
   - Recognition of prior learning
   - Learner support services
   - Eligibility for grants /loans
4. Learner-Centred Approach, Satisfaction and Success
   - Student ratings
   - Graduation rate
   - Student ratings of educators
   - Student/graduate performance
   - Grade distribution
   - Course description
5. Institutional Reputation
   - Expertise of Lecturers
   - Ranking of the Institution
   - Network membership
   - Recognition history (direct and/or skills).

More relevance and more in-depth explanations of the quality domains and indicators can be found in the QualityLink report (Trepule et al., 2024), available on the project website. The results of the domain validations and indicators and the importance rating will be presented at the conference. The preliminary results show that students and other stakeholders prioritise Content relevance and alignment with industry demands and put less priority on Accessibility and inclusivity. The results also show that students prefer more information about the course to be available and more passive teaching methods in the course, but they count on the opinions of other students while choosing learning opportunities. The stakeholders stress the relevance of recognition of prior learning and focus more on quality labels than on students.

This project has been funded with support from the European Commission. This publication reflects the views only of the authors, and the Commission cannot be held responsible for any use which may be made of the information contained therein.

References

EU Council. (2022). COUNCIL RECOMMENDATION of 16 June 2022 on a European approach to micro-credentials for lifelong learning and employability (2022/C 243/02; Official Journal of the European Union, pp. 10–22). https://eur-lex.europa.eu/legal-content/EN/TXT/PDF/?uri=CELEX:32022H0627(02)

Trepulė, E., Čepauskiene, R., Braun, C. & Tück, C. (2024) Quality Domains and Indicators: QualityLink report. https://quality-link.eu/quality-domains-and-indicators/

QualityLink project (2024). QualityLink project website: https://quality-link.eu

Micro-credentials for Lifelong Earners/Learners: A National Survey on Up/Reskilling Preferences and Perceptions

Mitchell Peters[1], Natalí Basilico[2], Carles Bruguera[3], Paula Pedro[4]

[1] Universitat Oberta de Catalunya (UOC), Spain, mjosephp@uoc.edu
[2] Universitat Oberta de Catalunya (UOC), Spain, cbruguerat@uoc.edu
[3] Universitat Oberta de Catalunya (UOC), Spain, nbasilico@uoc.edu
[4] Universitat Oberta de Catalunya (UOC), Spain, paupeaz@uoc.edu

Correspondence: Mitchell Peters: mjosephp@uoc.edu

Abstract:

Rapid technological change is reshaping the labor market, driven by digitalization, A.I. automation, and the green transition, creating an urgent need for responsive, flexible, and relevant post-secondary educational opportunities(Bruguera et al., 2024, Cedefop, 2022). The policy context for the development of novel forms of lifelong learning for employability is linked to the European Commissions´ (2025) Union of Skills, which aims to ensure that everyone in Europe is empowered to build in-demand and foundational skills by engaging in quality lifelong upskilling and reskilling. In alignment with the European Union's goal of achieving a 60% adult participation rate in annual training by 2030, lifelong learning initiatives—such as micro-credentials—are being promoted as innovative solutions to meet labor market demands and support workers' professional development through flexible and personalized reskilling and upskilling itineraries (Pouliou, 2025). This study analyzes data from the Continuous Training Needs Survey conducted by the UOC's Labor Market Analysis Unit (Basilico et al., 2025). The survey, which sampled 1,787 individuals aged 25 to 65 in Spain (with a representative margin of error <5%), provides valuable insights into training preferences and awareness, with a focus on micro-credentials. The Survey aimed: (1) to identify the educational objectives of the Spanish working-age population (25-64 years); (2) to determine training preferences and needs, considering the differences among demographic groups; (3) to evaluate the perception and assessment of short training programs (micro-credentials), considering the challenges of an evolving labor market and the changing role of higher education institutions.

Results reveal that participants, particularly working professionals, show a strong preference for training that is short, moderately demanding, online, and asynchronous. However, familiarity with the concept of micro-credentials was low, and most respondents had not participated in such programs. As for micro-credential courses, respondents indicated a preference for intermediate-level content, durations of one to three months, moderate time commitments, afternoon scheduling, and online asynchronous delivery. Participants identified key benefits and advantages of micro-credentials, including opportunities for professional reskilling and upskilling, flexible learning formats compared to longer programs, and access to updated, industry-relevant content. On the other hand, notable concerns included overqualification, limited recognition by employers and educational institutions, and insufficient course depth. In this regard, the main barriers to engaging in micro-credentials were cited as financial costs, difficulty finding programs aligned with personal needs or interests, and limited awareness of available offerings. These findings highlight the need to increase public awareness and accessibility of micro-credentials while improving their design, relevance, and institutional recognition (Brown et al., 2023; Peters et al., 2025). Efforts by higher education institutions to foster lifelong learning for employability are essential in addressing the evolving training needs of the Spanish workforce and supporting their adaptation to a rapidly changing labor market.

Keywords: Micro-credentials, Upskilling, Reskilling, Lifelong learning, Professional Development

References

Basilico, N., Bruguera Trabal, C., Durán Martínez, M., Pedro Aznar, P., & Peters, M. (2025). Enquesta de Necessitats de Formació Contínua (ENFC) de la població espanyola. http://hdl.handle.net/10609/152032

Brown, M., McGreal, R., & Peters, M. (2023). A strategic institutional response to micro-credentials: Key questions for educational leaders. *Journal of Interactive Media in Education, 2023*(1). https://doi.org/10.5334/jime.801

Bruguera, C., Pagés, C., Peters, M., & Fitó, À. (2024). Micro-credentials and soft skills in online education: the employers' perspective. *Distance Education*, 1–21. https://doi.org/10.1080/01587919.2024.2435645

Cedefop. (2022). Microcredentials for labour market education and training: First look at mapping microcredentials in European labour-market-related education, training and learning: take-up, characteristics and functions. *Cedefop research paper, 87*. https://www.cedefop.europa.eu/en/publications/5587

European Commission. (2025). *Union of Skills*. https://commission.europa.eu/topics/eu-competitiveness/union-skills_en

Peters, M., Beirne, E., & Brown, M. (2025). Micro-credentials and its implications for lifelong learning–global insights and critical perspectives. *Distance Education*, *46*(1), 1-7. https://doi.org/10.1080/01587919.2025.2463137

Pouliou, A. (2025). Deepening the focus on microcredentials—labour market sector relevance, quality and inclusion: a critical commentary. *Distance Education*, 1–10. https://doi.org/10.1080/01587919.2025.2453457

The Voice of Youth Gamers: Uses, Gratifications and Considerations

Meital Amzalag[1], Sharon Hardof-Jaffe[2]

[1] Holon Institute of Technology, Israel; meitalam@hit.ac.il
[2] Levinsky-Wingate Academic College, Israel; sharon.hardof@l-w.ac.il

Correspondence: Meital Amzalag: meitalam@hit.ac.il

Abstract:

Video games today are highly complex, requiring advanced visuals and real-time interactions, typically demanding powerful computers or gaming consoles (Blumberg et al., 2024; Kultima, 2009). They offer benefits such as emotional regulation, empathy, and enhanced learning, supporting cognitive development and digital literacy (Blumberg et al., 2019; Flynn et al., 2021). However, they also pose challenges, including reduced sleep, weight gain, and increased aggression linked to violent gameplay (Blumberg et al., 2019; Chatterjee, 2021). For gamers, gaming is a core part of life, fostering performance improvement, learning, and identity formation. It fulfills needs such as entertainment, knowledge acquisition, curiosity, and social recognition (Authors, 2024). This study amplifies gamers' voices on their experiences and gaming's broader implications. Using a qualitative approach, it analyzes pre- and post-gaming session interviews with 22 young gamers (ages 13–17).

Preliminary Findings

Uses

Interviews reveal that video game usage is diverse, with six key characteristics. First, gaming devices are powerful, consisting of dedicated consoles or high-performance computers with advanced graphics and computational capabilities. Second, gameplay is complex and spans various genres, including war, strategy, and fantasy games. Third, gaming sessions are extensive, often lasting several hours per day and continuing late into the night. Fourth, some games incorporate physical elements, such as hand movement speed, controller vibration responsiveness, and full-body motion in console and virtual reality games. Fifth, gaming often involves multitasking, such as listening to music while playing.

Gratifications

The interviews identified three categories of needs that video games fulfill. **Social** – Video games help players connect with friends and meet new people. **Emotional** – Games evoke emotions like joy, excitement, frustration, and achievement. They provide enjoyment, relaxation, escapism, and immersion in a flow state. Some participants noted their role in emotional regulation and a sense of control. **Informal Learning** – Video games boost motivation and develop skills like strategic thinking, concentration, and learning from mistakes. Players gain knowledge, especially in language learning, history, geography, and technological literacy. The learning process is experiential, with reinforcement, feedback, and navigating success and failure, fostering continuous improvement.

Consideration

The study highlights the extensive decision-making processes involved in gaming. Players exercise judgment regarding the duration of gameplay, the selection of games based on complexity and quality, and the strategic choices that maximize their chances of success. Additionally, they demonstrate awareness of online risks, carefully selecting gaming partners, controlling their exposure, and monitoring their gameplay habits.

Gamer Identity Development

The findings indicate that being a **gamer** is an evolving identity. Participants describe distinct characteristics that differentiate them from general computer users and non-gaming peers. They actively self-identify as gamers and are recognized as such by others. A strong sense of belonging to the gaming community emerges, alongside a distinction from non-gaming adolescents.

Implications

These findings highlight the broad impact of video games on youth, influencing social connections, emotional well-being, cognitive growth, and identity formation. Understanding their potential as a tool for learning and self-expression can help educators, parents, and policymakers promote responsible gaming and harness it for educational and developmental benefits.

Keywords: Gaming; Video games; Youth; Uses and Gratifications Theory; Informal learning

References

Blumberg, F. C., Deater-Deckard, K., Calvert, S. L., Flynn, R. M., Green, C. S., Arnold, D & ,.Brooks, P. J. (2019). Digital games as a context for children's cognitive development: Research recommendations and policy considerations. *Social Policy Report, 32*(1), 1-33 .

Blumberg, F. C., Flynn, R. M., Homer, B. D., Bailey, J. O., Eng, C. M., Green, C. S., ... & Gentile, D. A. (2024). Current state of play: Children's learning in the context of digital games. *Journal of Children and Media, 18*(2), 293-299. https://doi.org/10.1080/17482798.2024.2335725

Chatterjee, S. (2021). Dark side of online social games (OSG) using Facebook platform: effect of age, gender, and identity as moderators. *Information Technology & People, 34*(7), 1800-1818. https://doi.org/10.1108/ITP-05-2020-0267

Flynn, R. M., Kleinknecht, E., Ricker, A. A., & Blumberg, F. C. (2021). A narrative review of methods used to examine digital gaming impacts on learning and cognition during middle childhood. *International Journal of Child-Computer Interaction*, 30, 100325. https://doi.org/10.1016/j.ijcci.2021.100325

Kultima, A. (2009, September). Casual game design values. In *Proceedings of the 13th international MindTrek conference: Everyday life in the ubiquitous era* (pp. 58-65).

Empowering Mid-Level Technicians: A Competence Framework for Future Skills in Europe's Twin Transition

Florian Linscheid[1]

[1] Department of Education and Future Skills, Baden-Württemberg Cooperative State University, Germany; Florian.linscheid@dhbw-karlsruhe.de

Correspondence: Florian Linscheid: florian.linscheid@dhbw-karlsruhe.de

Abstract

To meet its climate and digital transformation goals, the European Union must empower mid-level technical professionals (EQF 5–6) with transversal Future Skills. These professionals are central to operationalising sustainability, innovation, and digitalisation across European industries. This paper presents the results of the HUCO Labs project (EU Grant 101186024), which developed a competence framework tailored to this need. The framework is based on a mixed-methods study including a survey of 150 European stakeholders and eleven in-depth interviews with representatives from industry, vocational education, and applied research. The findings highlight four competence domains that should shape future vocational curricula: Innovation, Green Transformation, Digital Transformation, and Management.

Main Text

Europe's green and digital transitions require a qualified and adaptable workforce. While high-level policy frameworks such as DigComp, GreenComp, and EntreComp outline strategic directions, they often overlook mid-level technicians who act as implementation agents in applied settings. The HUCO Labs project addresses this gap by developing a competence framework specifically for EQF 5–6 professionals in sectors such as manufacturing, automotive, IT, and biomedical engineering.

The study followed a multistage methodology combining desk research, a Europe-wide survey (n = 150), and twelve qualitative interviews conducted in Germany, France, Italy, Poland, and the UK. Despite sectoral variation, participants agreed on the increasing importance of transversal competences: problem-solving, adaptability, data literacy, systems thinking, and interdisciplinary collaboration. These were seen as essential complements to technical skills like digital simulation, cybersecurity, and sustainable process design.

Figure 1 illustrates these findings through a relevance matrix that maps individual Innovation competences by their average importance and correlation with the overall competence domain. Core competences such as Creativity & Problem-Solving (r = .40, M = 4.57) and Innovation Management (r = .46, M = 4.14) are positioned in the upper-right quadrant, while competences like Digital Simulation and Ethical Research appear as hidden potentials with high strategic value despite lower ratings.

We ground our understanding of competence in the concept of behavioural competence (Weinert, 2001; Erpenbeck & Heyse, 1999), and argue that Future Skills must be fostered through self-directed learning (Morris, 2019) and strengthened learner agency (Blaschke et al., 2021). Challenge-based learning was identified as a promising pedagogical approach to support the development of such skills (Gallagher & Savage, 2023).

The final framework is structured around four strategic competence domains:

- Innovation,
- Green Transformation,
- Digital Transformation,

- Management.

This structure enables a modular approach to curriculum development that aligns with both policy goals and real-world workplace requirements.

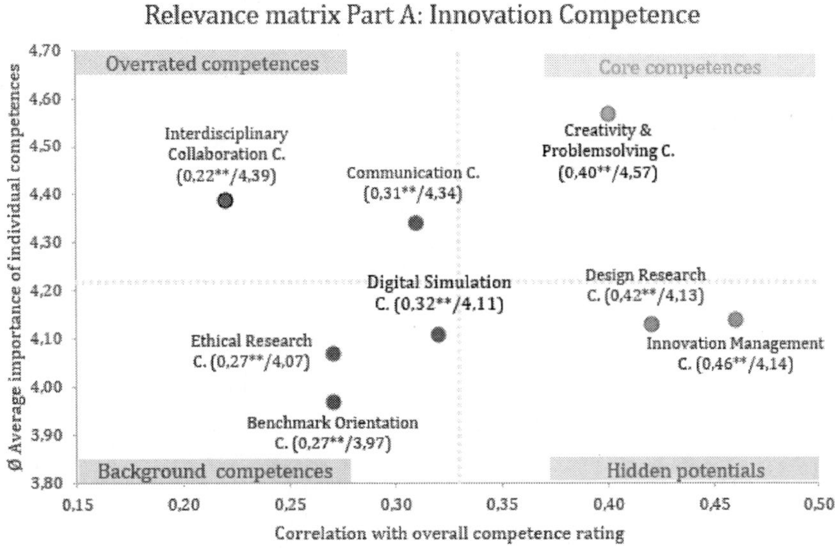

Figure 1 - Relevance matrix Innovation Competence Part A (n=150)

Conclusion

This contribution offers a validated and operational competence map to strengthen technician-led innovation and ensure workforce resilience in the face of Europe's twin transition. It supports educators, policymakers, and industry in rethinking technical education at EQF 5–6.

Keywords: Future Skills, Technical Education, Innovation, Green Transition, Digital Transformation, Competence Framework

References

Bacigalupo, M., Kampylis, P., Punie, Y., & Van den Brande, G. (2016). *EntreComp: The entrepreneurship competence framework*. Publications Office of the European Union. https://doi.org/10.2791/593884

Carretero, S., Vuorikari, R., & Punie, Y. (2017). *DigComp 2.1: The digital competence framework for citizens.* Publications Office of the European Union. https://doi.org/10.2760/38842

Cedefop. (2022). *Vocational education and training in Europe: Recent developments and challenges.* Publications Office of the European Union. https://www.cedefop.europa.eu/

Cuccovillo Foundation. (2021). *RECAPHE: Recognising and promoting research competences in applied higher education*. https://recaphe-project.eu

Ehlers, U. D. (2020). *Future Skills: The future of learning and higher education*. Springer VS.

European Commission. (2019). *The European Green Deal.* https://eur-lex.europa.eu/legal-content/EN/TXT/?uri=CELEX:52019DC0640

European Commission. (2020). *European Skills Agenda for sustainable competitiveness, social fairness and resilience*. https://ec.europa.eu/social/main.jsp?catId=1223

European Commission. (2022). *European sustainability competence framework – GreenComp*. Publications Office of the European Union. https://data.europa.eu/doi/10.2760/13286

Redecker, C. (2021). *AI and education: Guidance for policy-makers*. UNESCO. https://unesdoc.unesco.org/ark:/48223/pf0000376709

Fostering Critical Thinking in Psychology Students through the Use of AI

Nijel Ratonel[1]

[1] Product Innovation, Torrens University, Australia; nijel.ratonel@torrens.edu.au

Correspondence: Nijel Ratonel: nijel.ratonel@torrens.edu.au

Abstract:

The integration of Torrino, a bespoke chatbot, into the Bachelor of Psychological Science presents an innovative approach to using AI in education to develop and enhance students' critical thinking. Trained on current, relevant and peer-reviewed organisational psychology literature, Torrino simulates the role of a human resources manager. As students reflect on their interactions with the AI and its responses, they learn the application of theories to workplace wellbeing and engagement. In this transformative project, the assessment strategy shifts from traditional, passive methods, such as online tests, to an authentic strategy that positions the learner in an active role of retrieving their prior knowledge to construct meaning and new insight.

The first assessment of the Organisational Psychology subject involves a generative artificial intelligence (Gen AI) consultation in which students interact with an AI human resources (HR) manager powered by an in-house large language model (LLM) called Torrino. Students are required to write question prompts aimed at enhancing workplace mental health and wellbeing, and critically reflect on their interaction with the AI HR manager. This innovative project considers the validity lens for summative assessments, envisioning future workplaces where AI is ubiquitous and ensuring learning outcomes are sufficiently demonstrated (Lodge et al., 2023; Dawson et al., 2024; Ellis & Lodge, 2024). Furthermore, the strategy to integrate AI into a summative assessment ensures that the target students will experience authentic, relevant and sustainable learning. This initiative aligns with the imperative to keep the Psychology curriculum abreast of the broadening and ever-changing digital landscape. Additionally, the Torrino chatbot project introduces the responsible and ethical use of Gen AI in a first-year subject, modelling a strong foundation for professional settings where Gen AI literacy and skills are highly valued (World Economic Forum, 2025).

By challenging students to tap into their higher-order thinking skills, such as analysis and evaluative judgment, they develop critical thinking (Gerlich, 2025) by reflecting on how the AI HR manager's responses connect or challenge what they already know about workplace wellbeing and engagement. Through Torrino's immediate and contextualised responses, students enhance their knowledge of organisational issues, including their impact on worker mental health and quality of work life.

The Torrino chatbot project's approach to assessment redesign in the age of AI adopts a scaffolded learning experience. In the Organisational Psychology subject, students are instructed to engage in formative learning activities such as AI prompt writing and reflective thinking and writing using Driscoll's Model of Reflection (as cited in Rolfe & Freshwater, 2010). These activities prepare students for a purposeful consultation with the AI HR manager for their first assessment. By critically and ethically engaging with the Torrino chatbot, students develop metacognitive skills, allowing them to discern when AI can support their learning and regulate their reliance on it.

The project successfully navigated the copyright challenges of scraping reading resources to create datasets for training Torrino. The lessons learnt from the scraping phase of the project and strategies used to address the concerns of authors and publishers can serve as a model for like-minded professionals and institutions planning to adopt AI in their teaching and learning practices and mitigate the risks of misuse of their AI models.

Keywords: AI in education, assessment redesign, psychological science, critical thinking, metacognition

References

Dawson, P., Bearman, M., Dollinger, M., & Boud, D. (2024). Validity matters more than cheating. *Assessment & Evaluation in Higher Education*, 49:7, 1005-1016, https://doi.org/10.1080/02602938.2024.2386662

Ellis, C. & Lodge, J. (2024). *Stop looking for evidence of cheating with AI and start looking for evidence of learning*. LinkedIn. https://www.linkedin.com/pulse/stop-looking-evidence-cheating-ai-start-learning-cath-ellis-h0zzc/

Gerlich, M. (2025). AI tools in society: Impacts on cognitive offloading and the future of critical Thinking. *Societies, 15*(1), 6. https://doi.org/10.3390/soc15010006

Lodge, J. M., S. Howard, M. Bearman, and P. Dawson. (2023). *Assessment reform for the age of artificial intelligence*. Canberra: Tertiary Education Quality and Standards Agency (TEQSA). https://www.teqsa.gov.au/sites/default/files/2023-09/assessment-reform-age-artificial-intelligence-discussion-paper.pdf

Rolfe, G. & Freshwater, D. (2010). *Critical reflection in practice: Generating knowledge for care*. Bloomsbury. https://ebookcentral.proquest.com/lib/think/reader.action?docID=6406408&ppg=59

World Economic Forum. (2025). *Future of jobs report 2025: Insight report January 2025*. https://www.weforum.org/publications/the-future-of-jobs-report-2025/

Bring it Out of the Appendix: Capturing Student Critical Thinking Development in Conversations with GenAI

Alison Casey[1], Joseph Boulis[2]

[1]The University of Sydney Business School, The University of Sydney, Australia; alison.casey@sydney.edu.au
[2]The University of Sydney Business School, The University of Sydney, Australia; joseph.boulis@sydney.edu.au

Correspondence: Alison Casey: alison.casey@sydney.edu.au

Abstract:

Student use of and subsequent reflection upon generative AI (GenAI) has become an increasingly mainstream assessment model to cultivate students' evaluative judgement and critical thinking (Bearman et al., 2024; Perkins et al., 2024). This work demonstrates that student conversations with GenAI should be examined alongside their reflections upon it, rather than relegating these to the appendix as is currently common practice. This combination has the potential to provide a more complete picture of critical thinking capabilities than the reflection piece on its own.

Students in an undergraduate business course were asked to converse with a GenAI agent in order to create a report and write a reflection on the process of developing the report. The assessment piece was the report plus the reflection; students were required to submit conversation histories as an appendix. The authors, wishing to understand the nature of student use of the GenAI agent in this assessment, downloaded the full set of conversations (deidentified, under ethics application 2024/HE000760; N=1478 discrete exchanges with the agent). The authors initially conducted a manual semantic scan of the dataset to identify any patterns in how students utilized the agent, coding each exchange. It was determined that there were five distinct ways students employed the agent: *ideation, seeking information, using a framework, writing report sections, and refining their writing*. Student reflections, unsurprisingly, mapped to elements of Ennis' critical thinking abilities (Ennis et al., 2015), predominantly 'bases for inference' and 'inference'. Our analysis of the conversations with the GenAI agent revealed complementary critical thinking abilities. Most prevalent were 'basic clarification' and 'advanced clarification', and these correlated with the ways students engaged with the agent. For instance, 'ask clarification questions' appeared in both *ideation* and *seeking information*, 'define terms and judge definitions' emerged in *seeking information* and *using a framework*, while 'think suppositionally' was evident in *using a framework* and *refining writing*. We propose that combining GenAI agent conversations with reflections on its use can provide a more comprehensive picture of a student's critical thinking capabilities than reflections alone.

These observations raised the ethical imperative to share the potential for the development of critical thinking abilities in this assessment with students themselves in the next iteration of the course (currently running). A full map of the Ennis critical thinking abilities to opportunities in the assessment, as identified above, modelled after Calma & Davies (2025), has been supplied to students, including the five productive ways to converse with the GenAI agent uncovered in the first iteration of the course as articulated above. The language and hierarchy of the Ennis critical thinking abilities have been embedded in all assessment rubrics in the course in order to be able to simultaneously track and model the development of student critical thinking abilities throughout the semester. The assessment data will be evaluated to identify any gaps in the development of critical thinking abilities and to identify which affordances in the assessments, including the use of the GenAI agent, were most valuable in developing these abilities.

Keywords: GenAI, critical thinking, evaluative judgement, reflection, assessment

References

Bearman, M., Tai, J., Dawson, P., Boud, D., & Ajjawi, R. (2024). Developing evaluative judgement for a time of generative artificial intelligence. *Assessment and Evaluation in Higher Education*, *49*(6), 893–905. :10.1080/02602938.2024.2335321

Calma, A., & Davies, M. (2025). Assessing students' critical thinking abilities via a systematic evaluation of essays. *Studies in Higher Education*, 1–16. :10.1080/03075079.2025.2470969

Ennis, R. H., Barnett, R., & Davies, M. (2015). Critical Thinking: A Streamlined Conception. In *The Palgrave Handbook of Critical Thinking in Higher Education* (pp. 31–47). Palgrave Macmillan US. :10.1057/9781137378057_2

Perkins, M., Furze, L., Roe, J., & MacVaugh, J. (2024). The Artificial Intelligence Assessment Scale (AIAS) : A Framework for Ethical Integration of Generative AI in Educational Assessment. *Journal of University Teaching & Learning Practice*, *21*(6), 49–66. :10.53761/q3azde36

Spinning New Tales with ChatGPT: AI-Assisted Fairy Tale Rewriting and Its Impact on Creativity

Ka Yan LAM[1]

[1] Department of Applied Foreign Languages, National Taiwan University of Science and Technology, Taiwan; anniselam@mail.ntust.edu.tw

Correspondence: Ka Yan Lam: anniselam@mail.ntust.edu.tw

Abstract:

Artificial intelligence (AI) has revolutionized personalized learning through adaptive platforms, chatbots, and data-driven tools. ChatGPT, in particular, has gained widespread popularity, assisting students in brainstorming, writing, and summarizing, improving efficiency in academic tasks (Niloy et al., 2023). AI-powered tools also support creative writing in generating ideas, structuring plots, and refining content across genres (Coenen et al., 2021; Fiialka et al., 2024). However, most research on ChatGPT's impact focuses on essays and scientific writing (Ingley & Pack, 2023; Liu et al., 2023; Niloy et al., 2023), with limited studies exploring creative writing (Kartal, 2024).

To address this gap, this study in progress investigates ChatGPT's influence on creativity in English creative writing by introducing fairy-tale rewriting as an innovative pedagogical approach to engage students in reinterpretations of fairy-tale narratives. The choice of this genre is justified by two reasons. First, students' prior knowledge of fairy tales provides a familiar foundation for creative expression, allowing them to build confidence and develop original narratives by modifying familiar themes, motifs, and structures. Second, fairy-tale rewriting fosters critical literacy by encouraging students to engage with texts from multiple perspectives and reflect on social issues (Freire, 1970; Lewison et al., 2002; Luke & Freebody, 1999). Combining AI-assisted writing with this approach enables students to explore AI's influence on creativity while promoting responsible AI use in learning.

Participants in this study are 23 sophomores from a reading and writing class at a university in Taiwan. A mixed-method research design combines both quantitative and qualitative data to assess ChatGPT's impact on creativity. Students rewrite fairy tales with and without the assistance of ChatGPT, and their works are assessed using an integrated set of rubrics derived from previous studies (Cheung et al., 2001; Mozaffari, 2013; Niloy et al., 2023), with statistical comparisons to measure creativity levels. Additional data are gathered from surveys, reflective writings, interviews, and ChatGPT conversation records. The reflective writings and interviews are analyzed inductively to identify participants' perceptions of AI-assisted fairy-tale rewriting and its impact on creativity. Preliminary findings will highlight discussion points, including (1) differences in creativity levels between AI-assisted and non-AI-assisted fairy-tale rewriting, (2) students' perceptions of using ChatGPT for fairy-tale rewriting and its impacts on their creativity, and (3) their ethical concerns for AI's potential homogenizing effects on originality.

This study contributes to the growing body of research on AI in education, offering recommendations for integrating AI and innovative pedagogy into language classrooms to foster creativity and critical engagement. It also underscores the importance of cultivating ethical awareness among university students, who are increasingly reliant on various generative AI tools for their studies. By advancing knowledge and practical strategies for AI-assisted creative writing, this study seeks to maximize AI's potential while addressing its challenges in literary education.

Keywords: ChatGPT, creative writing, fairy-tale rewriting, creativity, critical literacy

References

Cheung, W. M., Tse, S. K., & Tsang, W. H. H. (2001). Development and validation of the Chinese creative writing scale for primary school students in Hong Kong. *The Journal of Creative Behavior*, *35*(4), 249-260:10.1002/j.2162-6057.2001.tb01049.x

Coenen, A., Davis, L., Ippolito, D., Reif, E., & Yuan, A. (2021). Wordcraft: A human-AI collaborative editor for story writing. *arXiv: 2107.07430v1*:10.48550/arXiv.2107.07430

Fiialka, S., Kornieva, Z., & Honcharuk, T. (2024). The use of ChatGPT in creative writing assistance. *XLinguae*, *17*(1): 10.18355/XL.2024.17.01.01

Freire, P. (2000). *Pedagogy of the oppressed* (M. B. Ramos, Trans.). Continuum.

Ingley, S. J., & Pack, A. (2023). Leveraging AI tools to develop the writer rather than the writing. *Trends in Ecology & Evolution*, *38*(9), 785-787:10.1016/j.tree.2023.05.007

Kartal, G. (2024). The influence of ChatGPT on thinking skills and creativity of EFL student teachers: A narrative inquiry. *Journal of Education for Teaching*, *50*(4), 627-642:10.1080/02607476.2024.2326502

Lewison, M., Flint, A. S., & Sluys, K. V. (2002). Taking on critical literacy: The journey of newcomers and novices. *Language Arts*, *79*(5), 382-392:10.58680/la2002255

Liu, C., Hou, J., Tu, Y. F., Wang, Y., & Hwang, G. J. (2023). Incorporating a reflective thinking promoting mechanism into artificial intelligence-supported English writing environments. *Interactive Learning Environments*, *31*(9), 5614-5632:10.1080/10494820.2021.2012812

Luke, A., & Freebody, P. R. (1999). Further notes on the four resources model. *Practically Primary*, *4*(2), 5-8.

Mozaffari, H. (2013). An analytical rubric for assessing creativity in creative writing. *Theory and Practice in Language Studies*, *3*(12):10.4304/tpls.3.12.2214-2219

Niloy, A. C., Akter, S., Sultana, N., Sultana, J., & Rahman, S. I. U. (2024). Is ChatGPT a menace for creative writing ability? An experiment. *Journal of Computer Assisted Learning*, *40*(2), 919-930:10.1111/jcal.12929

How Does AI-Driven Conversation Training Shape Human Communication?

Hannah Nermerich[1], Denise Rupprecht[2], Katharina Frosch[3], Olga Levina[4], Friederike Lindauer[5], Carmen Winkel[6]

[1,2,3,4] Department of Business and Management, Brandenburg University of Applied Sciences, Germany
[5] Project ELI Incubator, Brandenburg University of Applied Sciences
[1] nermeric@th-brandenburg.de
[2] rupprech@th-brandenburg.de
[3] katharina.frosch@th-brandenburg.de
[4] levina@th-brandenburg.de
[5] lindauer@th-brandenburg.de
[6] carmen.winkel@th-brandenburg.de

Correspondence: Hannah Nermerich; nermeric@th-brandenburg.de

Abstract:

By enabling realistic, simulated conversations, chatbot-assisted learning presents an opportunity to expand upon and refine traditional communication training. This study examines how chatbot-assisted conversation training influences face-to-face communication and whether engaging in such chatbot-mediated training leads to changes in human communication patterns. As prior research suggests (e.g., Zhang et al., 2024; Huang, Hew, & Fryer, 2022; Wang, Cheung, & Chai, 2024), chatbots used as conversational partners have shown particular relevance in language learning contexts, which closely aligns with the training approach examined in this study.

Although we may profit from positive effects of human-to-chatbot communication training, it is also imperative to consider potential adverse outcomes, such as loosing empathy, oversimplifying complex emotional cues, normalizing transactional rather than relational communication (Huang, Hew, & Fryer, 2022). When implementing AI-driven training in educational contexts, such ethical considerations must be accorded the highest priority.

This study examines the impact of AI-driven conversation training on human-to-human communication through a field experiment. It explores whether engaging in human-to-chatbot interactions influences human-to-human communication. To address these research questions, a deductive content analysis of N=90 selected conversation transcripts was conducted, focusing on key dimensions of effective leadership communication. The analysis was structured around predefined communication strategies, following established theoretical frameworks for active listening (Decuypere & Pircher Verdorfer, 2022), motivational language (Men et al., 2021; Mayfield & Mayfield, 2017) and goal setting (Latham & Locke, 2007; London et al., 2004).

The study employs a cross-over design with two experimental groups, where participants engage in both chatbot-based conversations and human-to-human (H2H) interactions with a role-play partner. To control for sequencing effects, the order of these interactions is varied. This structured approach enables a comparative analysis of how AI-driven training influences interpersonal communication. Transcripts from human-to-chatbot

(H2Chatbot) and H2H interactions are analyzed using qualitative content analysis with frequency counts to assess the implementation of key communication strategies and evaluate the impact of chatbot-based training on face-to-face communication

While final results are still pending, preliminary findings suggest that individuals trained with AI may exhibit more structured but less emotionally nuanced communication when transitioning to human dialogue. This has significant implications for educational settings, where AI may be increasingly used for communication training. If chatbot-assisted training fosters clarity and efficiency but reduces empathy and adaptive listening, its educational application must be critically evaluated. The study's findings will contribute to discussions on the ethical use of chatbot-assisted communication training, helping educators develop balanced approaches that leverage AI's benefits while mitigating potential drawbacks.

Keywords: AI-driven Conversation, human-to-human-communication, chatbot-assisted communication training, Ethical Aspects, Field Experiment

References

Decuypere, A., & Pircher Verdorfer, A. (2022). *Leader Attentive Communication: A new Communication Concept, Validation and Scale Development*. Journal of Leadership & Organizational Studies, 29, pp. 424-442. https://doi.org/10.1177/15480518221100922.

Huang, W., Hew, K. F., & Fryer, L. K. (2022). *Chatbots for language learning—Are they really useful? A systematic review of chatbot-supported language learning*. Journal of Computer Assisted Learning, 38(1), pp. 237–257. https://doi.org/10.1111/jcal.12610

Latham, G. P., & Locke, E. A. (2007). *New Developments in Goal Setting Theory.* Organizational Behavior and Human Decision Processes, 102(1), pp. 1-27.

London, M., Mone, E. M., & Scott, J. C. (2004). *Performance Management and Assessment: Methods for Improved Rater Accuracy and Employee Goal Setting.* Human Resource Management, 43(4), pp. 319-336.

Mariacher, N., Schlögl, S., & Monz, A. (2019). *Investigating perceptions of social intelligence in simulated human-chatbot interactions.* In: Progresses in Artificial Intelligence and Neural Systems, p. 513-529. DOI:10.1007/978-981-15-5093-5_44

Mayfield, M., & Mayfield, J. (2017). *Leader Talk and the Creative Spark: A Research Note on How Leader Motivating Language Use Influences Follower Creative Environment Perceptions.* International Journal of Business Communication, 54(2), pp. 210-225.

Mayfield, M., Mayfield, J. R., & Kopf, J. (2018). *The Effects of Motivating Language on Subordinate Performance and Satisfaction.* Human Resource Management, 57, pp. 241-257.

Men, R., Qin, Y.S., & Jin, J. (2021). *Fostering Employee Trust via Effective Supervisory Communication during the COVID-19 Pandemic: Through the Lens of Motivating Language Theory.* International Journal of Business Communication, 59(2), pp. 193-218.

Wang, F., Cheung, A. C. K., & Chai, C. S. (2024). *Language learning development in human-AI interaction: A thematic review of the research landscape. System*, 125, p. 103424. Available at: https://doi.org/10.1016/j.system.2024.103424

Zhang, R., Zou, D. and Cheng, G. (2023). *A review of chatbot-assisted learning: pedagogical approaches, implementations, factors leading to effectiveness, theories, and future directions.* Interactive Learning Environments, 32(8), pp. 4529–4557.

AI Ethics in Education: A Framework for Responsible Integration and Alignment with EU Values

Alexia Antzaka[1], María Orcasitas-Vicandi[2], Gorka Roman Etxebarrieta[3], Asier León Nuñez[4], Natalia Louleli[5]

[1] Department of Educational Psychology and Psychobiology, Universidad Internacional de la Rioja (UNIR), Spain; alexia.antzaka@unir.net
[2]Department of English and German Philology, Translation and Interpretation, University of the Basque Country, Spain; maria.orcasitas@ehu.eus
[3]Department of Language and Literature Didactics, University of the Basque Country, Spain; gorka.roman@ehu.eus
[4]Deusto University, Spain; asier.leon@opendeusto.es
[5] Department of Language and Literature Didactics, University of the Basque Country, Spain; Department of Educational Psychology and Psychobiology, Universidad Internacional de la Rioja (UNIR), Spain; natalia.louleli@ehu.eus

Correspondence: Alexia Antzaka: alexia.antzaka@unir.net

Abstract:

The increasing integration of artificial intelligence (AI) in education necessitates frameworks to evaluate its ethical implications and ensure responsible adoption. The AI Pioneers project, an ERASMUS+ Forward Looking initiative (2023–2025), aims to support the responsible integration of AI in Adult Education and Vocational Education and Training (VET). As part of this effort, the project introduces the "Evaluation schema for AI in education on data, privacy, ethics, and EU values", a structured inquiry framework designed to help institutions reflect on the ethical dimensions of AI adoption. Rather than a prescriptive tool, the schema provides guiding questions and interpretative support to facilitate informed decision-making.

The schema was developed through a review of existing guidelines and research on ethical AI in education (e.g., Chan, 2023; European Commission, 2022; Nguyen et al., 2023; Şenocak et al., 2024). Following this initial phase, it was refined based on feedback from the partner consortium. The schema consists of five interrelated components. The first, **Assessing current AI use, AI maturity, and related AI ethical concerns**, provides questions to help institutions understand their level of AI integration and readiness. This section is informed by AI maturity (JISC, 2022), which evaluates how institutions utilize AI and the organizational support for these technologies. By assessing AI maturity, educational centers can identify gaps and areas needing development. The second component, **AI Governance and Monitoring**, addresses compliance with legal and ethical standards, including data protection, transparency, accountability, diversity, and fairness. This section is particularly relevant for senior management, IT staff, and AI providers collaborating with educational centers. While some aspects, such as adherence to legislation, are straightforward, others, like ensuring non-discrimination and fairness, require a nuanced approach.

The third component, **Operational Considerations**, focuses on the ethical implications of AI for teachers, learners, and IT staff. It emphasizes AI literacy, training, and ongoing support to ensure human agency and oversight. Promoting AI literacy helps foster democratic participation in educational AI policies and practices, upholding equity and accountability. The fourth component, **Pedagogical Considerations**, centers on the role of AI in teaching, learning, and assessment. It examines ethical dilemmas such as AI's impact on assessment fairness, potential biases in AI-generated content, and copyright issues. This section explores how AI can empower educators and prepare students for an AI-driven workforce, with particular attention to Adult Education and Vocational Education and Training (Attwell et al., 2021; UNESCO, 2019). The final component, **Other Considerations**, tackles broader ethical concerns, including sustainability, ethical design, and commercialization. These aspects are often overlooked but are critical to ensuring the long-term responsible deployment of AI in education (Şenocak et al., 2024).

By offering structured guidance and reflection points, this schema supports educational institutions in making informed decisions about AI adoption. It provides a flexible framework that can be adapted to different educational settings, helping stakeholders navigate the ethical challenges of AI while maximizing its benefits for learners and educators.

Keywords: Artificial Intelligence in Education, Ethical AI, Evaluation Framework, Adult Education, Vocational Education and Training (VET)

References

Atwell, G., Bekiaridis, G., Deitmer, L., Perini, M., Roppertz, S., Stieglitz, D., & Tutlys, V. (2021). *Artificial intelligence & vocational education and training. How to shape the future.* Taccle AI. Retrieved from: https://taccleai.eu/wp-content/uploads/2021/12/TaccleAI_Recommendations_UK_compressed.pdf

Chan, C. K. Y. (2023). A comprehensive AI policy education framework for university teaching and learning. *International Journal of Educational Technology in Higher Education, 20*(1), 38. https://link.springer.com/article/10.1186/s41239-023-00408-3

European Commission, Directorate-General for Education, Youth, Sport, and Culture. (2022). *Ethical guidelines on the use of artificial intelligence (AI) and data in teaching and learning for educators.* Publications Office of the European Union. https://data.europa.eu/doi/10.2766/153756

JISC (2022). *AI in tertiary Education. A summary of the current state of play.* JISC Repository. Retrieved from https://repository.jisc.ac.uk/8783/1/ai-in-tertiary-education-report-june-2022.pdf

Nguyen, A., Ngo, H. N., Hong, Y., Dang, B., & Nguyen, B. P. T. (2023). Ethical principles for artificial intelligence in education. *Education and Information Technologies, 28*(4), 4221-4241. https://doi.org/10.1007/s10639-022-11316-w

Şenocak, D., Bozkurt, A., & Koçdar, S. (2024). Exploring the Ethical Principles for the Implementation of Artificial Intelligence in Education: Towards a Future Agenda. In *Transforming Education With Generative AI: Prompt Engineering and Synthetic Content Creation* (pp. 200-213). IGI Global.

UNESCO (2019). Artificial Intelligence in Education: Challenges and Opportunities for Sustainable Development. Retrieved from: https://unesdoc.unesco.org/ark:/48223/pf0000366994

Integrating AI into General Education University-Level Courses in the U.S.

Eva Badowska[1]

[1] Dean of the College of Liberal Arts and Sciences, Hofstra University, United States; eva.badowska@hofstra.edu

Correspondence: Eva Badowska: eva.badowska@hofstra.edu

Abstract:

As generative AI reshapes the world of knowledge work, universities in the U.S. are starting to integrate preparation for working with AI into what is often called General Education (Gen Ed) in the American college curriculum. While students are rapidly adopting AI tools (Coffey, 2023), faculty remain divided on how to incorporate them into foundational courses (Salhab, 2024). This paper explores strategies for integrating AI into Gen Ed courses, balancing the need for AI literacy with the broader goals of typical Gen Ed programs, which often include critical thinking, ethical reasoning, and interdisciplinary inquiry.

AI's impact on cognitive effort and student confidence (Lee, 2025; Gerlich, 2025) raises concerns not just about academic honesty but about overreliance. Yet emerging frameworks suggest that AI can enhance learning when paired with active engagement and metacognitive strategies (Bowen & Watson, 2024). Institutions must move beyond reactive policies and adopt structured interdisciplinary approaches that equip students to assess AI content critically (Sidorkin, 2025). Working with AI requires integration across humanities, social sciences, and STEM disciplines and may take different forms, from specialized AI literacy courses to AI integration into specific foundational courses (e.g., composition courses) to „AI across the curriculum" that includes integration in the majors.

Drawing from recent research and institutional case studies, the paper proposes a model for AI integration in Gen Ed curricula that aligns, first and foremost, with Gen Ed's learning outcomes around critical thinking. It considers AI's potential to support inquiry-driven learning (Mollick, 2024), while addressing faculty concerns about academic integrity and „cognitive offloading" (Gerlich, 2025). This paper concludes with recommendations for institutional policies that foster AI fluency without undermining the intellectual rigor that Gen Ed seeks to cultivate. By framing AI as a tool for inquiry rather than a shortcut to answers, universities can prepare students to engage with AI critically, ethically, and creatively in academic, professional, and personal contexts.

Keywords: General Education (Gen Ed), artificial intelligence (AI), critical thinking, inquiry-driven learning, cognitive offloading

References

Biswas, J., Fussell, D., Stone, P., Patterson, K., Procko, K., Sabatini, L., & Xu, Z. (2025). The essentials of AI for life and society: An AI literacy course for the university community. *ArXiv.org*. https://arxiv.org/abs/2501.07392

Bousquette, I. (2024, August 26). Inside universities' love-hate relationship with ChatGPT. *The Wall Street Journal.* *https://www.wsj.com/articles/inside-universities-love-hate-relationship-with-chatgpt-92808293?utm_source=chatgpt.com*

Jose Antonio Bowen, & C. Edward Watson. (2024). *Teaching with AI: A practical guide to a new era of human learning*. Johns Hopkins University Press.

Coffey, L. (2023, October 31). Students outrunning faculty in AI use. *Inside Higher Ed.* https://www.insidehighered.com/news/tech-innovation/artificial-intelligence/2023/10/31/most-students-outrunning-faculty-ai-use

Gerlich, M. (2025). AI tools in society: impacts on cognitive offloading and the future of critical thinking. *SSRN Electronic Journal*. https://papers.ssrn.com/sol3/papers.cfm?abstract_id=5082524

Hanstedt, P. (2024). *General education essentials: A guide for college faculty.* Second edition. Taylor & Francis.

Lee, Hao-Ping, Sarkar, A., Tankelevitch, L., Drosos, I., Rintel, S., Banks, R., & Wilson, N. (2025). The impact of generative AI on critical thinking: Self-reported reductions in cognitive effort. *CHI '25: Proceedings of the 2025 CHI Conferenceon Human Factors in Computing Systems*. Article no. 1121, pp. 1-22. https://doi.org/10.1145/3706598.3713778

Mollick, E. (2024). *Co-intelligence: Living and working with AI*. Penguin.

Salhab, R. (2024). AI literacy across curriculum design: Investigating college instructors' perspectives. *Online Learning*, 28(2). https://olj.onlinelearningconsortium.org/index.php/olj/article/view/4426

Sidorkin, A.M. (2025). AI integration blueprint: Transforming higher education for the age of intelligence. *AI-EDU arXiv.* https://journals.calstate.edu/ai-edu/article/view/5126

Sills, Adam. (2025). *How I learned to stop worrying and love ChatGPT: A manifesto*. Unpublished manuscript.

Student Guide to Artificial Intelligence (2024, August 22). https://studentguidetoai.org/

University of Delaware AI for Teaching and Learning Working Group. (2024). *Considerations for integrating AI within teaching and learning.* https://www.udel.edu/content/dam/udelImages/artificial-intelligence/Considerations_for_Integrating_AI_Within_Teaching_and_Learning_FINAL.pdf

Who Are the Actors? Directing AI Innovation in a University Teaching and Learning Ecosystem

Stephen Marquard[1], Sukaina Walji[2]

[1] Centre for Innovation in Learning and Teaching, University of Cape Town, South Africa; stephen.marquard@uct.ac.za
[2] Centre for Innovation in Learning and Teaching, University of Cape Town, South Africa; sukaina.walji@uct.ac.za

Correspondence: Stephen Marquard: stephen.marquard@uct.ac.za

Abstract:

The widespread availability of new AI capabilities, including GenAI, has led to a dramatic change of pace in the introduction of new educational technologies in universities. A decade ago, the affordances and functional behaviour of edtech solutions could be well described. Today, AI-driven capabilities are offered with high promise but high uncertainty, and evaluating the possible benefits or potential harms of these solutions across different learning contexts with confidence may be out of reach for many institutions.

Bearman et al (2023) argue that AI tools should be accepted as unknowable and propose a set of pedagogical strategies for working with these tools with students which embrace the unknowability. In a socio-technical model, AI's are regarded as agentic, although not sentient. These scenarios set out a triad of educator, student and AI.

Institutional decision-makers face the challenge of shaping AI adoption to support the distinct processes of teaching and learning in responsible and sustainable ways. AI capabilities appear at every turn, in existing institutional platforms, pitches from edtech vendors, and direct-to-consumer services ("bring your own AI"). These bring additional external actors into the pedagogical space: the creators of machine learning (ML) and large language models (LLMs), and intermediaries who build solutions using these models. Institutional role-players who select, configure and represent AI products and solutions to educators and students in different ways are a further type of actor.

What happens if these actors all have a different script? What is the scope and consequence of divergent understanding and expression by different actors, human and technological, about pedagogies and learning strategies given that "the search space of optimal pedagogical strategies" (Jurenka et al, 2024) is vastly underdeveloped, and there may be no clear agreement on what is "optimal"?

We explore a conceptual model for institutional decision-making on AI adoption which explicitly recognizes the broad set of actors introduced by AI capabilities, with the learning affordances of the play emerging from the dynamic improvisation between actors, which unfolds over time. The model is presented in relation to the authors' experience in managing an AI Teaching Innovation Grants process at the University of Cape Town, as a means of developing a responsive and coherent evaluation approach to a wide variety of applications of AI in teaching and learning contexts.

Keywords: AI; EdTech; Affordances; Teaching; Learning; Actors

References

Bearman, M., & Ajjawi, R. (2023). Learning to work with the black box: Pedagogy for a world with artificial intelligence. *British Journal of Educational Technology*, 54, 1160–1173. https://doi.org/10.1111/bjet.13337

Jurenka, I., Kunesch, M., McKee, K. R., Gillick, D., Zhu, S., Wiltberger, S., ... & Ibrahim, L. (2024). Towards responsible development of generative AI for education: An evaluation-driven approach. arXiv preprint arXiv:2407.12687. https://goo.gle/LearnLM

Responsible and Transparent Use of GenAI in Online Assessment: A Case Study at the Universidade Aberta, Portugal

João Paz[1], António Moreira Teixeira[2]

[1] Laboratório de Educação a Distância e eLearning, Universidade Aberta, Portugal: joao.paz@uab.pt
[2] Laboratório de Educação a Distância e eLearning, Universidade Aberta, Portugal: Antonio.Teixeira@uab.pt

Correspondence: João Paz: joao.paz@uab.pt

Abstract:

The introduction of education tools based on Generative Artificial Intelligence (GenAI) is proving to be highly disruptive. The impact is even greater than the traditional examples of the introduction of calculators and the use of the Internet. This has created the need for all actors in the educational field, from institutions to teachers and students, to adjust. A complex process which is still in progress. One of the educational dimensions which has been more affected by this phenomenon is learning assessment and evaluation. That is one of the areas identified in systematic literature reviews that produced a typology of research areas in AI in Education: Profiling and Prediction, Intelligent Tutoring Systems, Assessment and Evaluation, and Adaptive Systems and Personalisation (Bond et al., 2024; Zawacki-Richter et al., 2019).

One of the main decisions teachers have to make these days regarding learning assessment is whether to allow or to completely ban the use of GenAI-powered tools in assessment assignments. Although several arguments may be mobilised in support of each position, there is one strong argument in favour of restricting the use of such tools (if not in all, at least in part) in assessment assignments. This is the need to ensure the validity of the assessment process. "A validity perspective makes the claim: a student's assessment submission is valid if it represents their actual capability" (Dawson et al., 2024, p. 1010).

Nevertheless, the practicality of the Gen AI use identification is an issue which remains to be solved, particularly in online Education. Unlike plagiarism, which can be detected, there are no tools at the moment capable of detecting GenAI use with enough reliability. The use of these tools is hindered by too many false positives (Hardie et al., 2024). So, one of the more appropriate strategies may be to make the student's use of GenAI transparent, within a framework of an adequate institutional policy for the use of GenAI.

In this paper, we describe a case study currently being carried out at the Universidade Aberta, in Portugal, a European public distance learning and research university. This experiment is part of an innovative practice in a Degree in Education provided by the Department of Education and Distance Learning, in which the transparent use of Gen AI is being promoted. The Higher Education institution has an AI institutional policy in place for promoting such a high level of transparency.

The Research Questions are as follows:

To what extent are student using GenAI in their assessment assignments?

What are the main GenAI tools being used?

What are the typical use cases of GenAI in their assessment assignments?

The participants in the case study are characterized as well as the Curricular Units involved (one from the first semester of the first year of the course, other from the first semester of the last year of the course, from a Degree in Education; and one from a first semester from first year of a teacher´s professionalization course). The results were subject to an exploratory analysis of the Self Reports which the students were asked to send as part of a GenAI Use Report accompanying the assignments in which they were allowed to use these tools.

The results showed significant differences between students enrolled in the first year and the ones enrolled in the last year, as well as different patterns of use. This is particularly the case for the trainees enrolled in the teachers' professionalization course, which ranges from writing support, answer structuring and correction of References to understanding the questions asked and even tutoring advice on how to answer. Several inferences could also be made about the AI Prompt literacy from the participants and the typology of good and bad practices of the GenAI use. These results will enable us to get a better understanding of the students' use of GenAI, with further research needed to enhance the comprehension of the phenomenon and guide us in improving future course development.

Keywords: Generative Artificial Intelligence, Assessment, Online Education, Ethical and responsible academic practice

References

Bond, M., Khosravi, H., De Laat, M., Bergdahl, N., Negrea, V., Oxley, E., Pham, P., Chong, S. W., & Siemens, G. (2024). A meta systematic review of artificial intelligence in higher education: a call for increased ethics, collaboration, and rigour. *International Journal of Educational Technology in Higher Education*, 21(1), 4. https://doi.org/10.1186/s41239-023-00436-z

Dawson, P., Bearman, M., Dollinger, M., & Boud, D. (2024). Validity matters more than cheating. *Assessment & Evaluation in Higher Education*, 49(7), 1005–1016. https://doi.org/10.1080/02602938.2024.2386662

Hardie, L., Lowe, J., Pride, M., Waugh, K., Hauck, M., & Ryan, F. (2024). *Developing robust assessment in the light of Generative AI developments*. https://oro.open.ac.uk/99447/

Zawacki-Richter, O., Marín, V. I., Bond, M., & Gouverneur, F. (2019). Systematic review of research on artificial intelligence applications in higher education – where are the educators? *International Journal of Educational Technology in Higher Education*, 16(1), 39. https://doi.org/10.1186/s41239-019-0171-0

Transforming the Student Experience Through Learner Empowerment and Digital Education Innovation at the Atlantic Technological University in Ireland

Carina Ginty[1], Jessica Duffy[2]

[1] Atlantic Technological University (ATU), Ireland; carina.ginty@atu.ie
[2] Atlantic Technological University (ATU), Ireland: Jessica.duffy@atu.ie

Correspondence: Carina Ginty: carina.ginty@atu.ie

Abstract:

Ireland's technological sector, combining five new technological universities and two institutes of technology, formed a partnership to develop and deliver on the National Technological University Transformation for Recovery and Resilience (N-TUTORR) programme from 2022-2025. This programme, was EU funded (40 million euro) and overseen by the Higher Education Authority (HEA) Ireland, it utilised the national scale and scope of the technological university sector to deliver a best-practice suite of initiatives and opportunities for the learner, for staff development and supported by necessary enabling technologies.

N-TUTORR is a national programme of work and it is was designed to enable and leverage digital transformations to achieve sustainable and long-lasting change in the higher education student experience. The project was structured as 4 streams delivering 12+ work packages across 6 themes. The Student Empowerment Stream transformed the student experience through learner empowerment. Key work packages included: the development of a TU sector 'Digital Backpack' (MyDigitalBackpack.ie) co-created with 100 national student champions; the creation of a digital and sustainable futures student competency framework named AREA including digital and AI competency assessment; establishing a student champion team of 100; creating a students as partners in innovation and change fellowship programme including 175 national projects with 35 situated in ATU. Initiatives under this work stream covered academic integrity, universal design for learning, equality diversity and inclusion, digital transformation in teaching and learning, employability, and education for sustainable developement.

This paper shares outputs and learnings from the national student empowerment program and the impact on students and staff across 9 ATU campuses in the West and Northwest of Ireland.

Keywords: Digital Learning, Student Empowerment, Digital Skills, Sustainable Development Goals, Student Partnership, Digital Innovation.

Summary

Ireland's technological sector, combining five new technological universities and two institutes of technology, has formed a partnership to develop and deliver on the National Technological University Transformation for Recovery and Resilience (NTUTORR) programme in 2023 and 2024. This programme, which is EU-funded (40 million euro) and overseen by the Higher Education Authority (HEA) Ireland, utilises the national scale and scope of the technological university sector to deliver a best-practice suite of initiatives and opportunities for the learner, for staff development and supported by necessary enabling technologies.

N-TUTORR is a national programme of work designed to enable and leverage digital transformations to achieve sustainable and long-lasting change in the higher education student experience. The project is structured as 4 streams delivering 10+ work packages across 6 themes. The Student Empowerment Stream worked on transforming student experience through learner empowerment. A standout work package, 'Building an academy for education for sustainability, leadership and employability' included the development of a TU sector 'Student Digital Backpack' (MyDigitalBackpack.ie), the creation of a digital and sustainable futures student champions and a fellowship programme supporting student partnership.

Student-staff partnerships can be difficult to define, and there are numerous attempts to describe them in the literature. However, a commonly used definition is a collaborative, reciprocal process through which all participants have the opportunity to contribute equally, although not necessarily in the same ways, to curricular or pedagogical conceptualisation, decision making, implementation, investigation, or analysis (Cook-Sather et al., 2014, p.6-7 cited in Carroll, Ginty & Maguire 2023).

The Student Digital Backpack (mydigitalbackpack.ie), is a Virtual Learning Environment (VLE) platform for students across the Technological University (TU) sector (ATU, MTU, SETU, TUS, TU Dublin, DKIT and IADT) to complete short non-accredited courses and gain digital badges. The collaboratively developed and adapted courses provide students with additional skills to complement their existing programmes of study. They include Digital Discovery; Sustainable Development Goals; Civic Engagement; Academic Integrity; and Gender Based Violence on Campus.

The Digital and Sustainable Futures Student Champion Programme offered 100 students across 5 universities and 2 institutes of technology the opportunity to learn and develop skills in one of the key N-TUTORR priority areas (Academic Integrity, Digital Transformation, Equality, Diversity & Inclusion, Education for Sustainability, Universal Design for Learning) in addition to developing leadership, collaboration and communication skills. The conference presentation will discuss:

- the open education principles and practices (Bali, 2022; Cronin, 2020) that have underpinned the development journey of the Digital Backpack to date and learnings from the pilot experience across the sector.
- the role of the student champions and the impact they made in ATU and beyond
- the student champion digital engagement initiatives that are transforming the learning and teaching experience at a local and national level.
- the AREA Student Competency Framework, including a digital and AI competency online self-assessment tool leading to a digital open badge.

The Partners in Innovation and Change Fellowship Programme included 175 projects (35 in ATU) from across the technological university sector in Ireland, awarded funding grants (min. 5,000 euro per project) in 2023-24 to transform learning on programmes of study or through student services available on campus or off campus. Each fellowship project supported student empowerment and involved a collaboration between learners and staff, and focused on enhancing the experience of students at technological universities across all of N-TUTORR's core themes. A catalogue of the 175 project proposals is available at https://issuu.com/atlantictechnologicaluniversity/docs/postcards_flipbook1. Student empowerment happens in HE when students are given the power to make decisions and drive change and innovation in their university.

When Students are empowered to make decisions it will enhance the learning, teaching or assessment experience at the university. N-TUTORR funding provided the enabler for this opportunity and a vehicle to create a culture of student Empowerment across the Irish technological higher education sector. This conference presentation will present on the impact and outputs from the digital transformation fellowship award projects from ATU (see impact book here) and discuss how we might build on these outputs to further support the university's digital transformation journey.

Finally, this paper presentation will demonstrate how the student empowerment program at ATU aligned with the Sustainable Development Goals and encouraged students to further explore and learn key skills focused on global priorities and challenges.

References

Bali, M. (2022). Outside-In: Entangled Openness as Subversion Influencing Emergent Change. OTESSA Journal, 1(1). DOI: https://doi.org/10.18357/otessaj.2022.1.1.25

Carroll, S., Antropova, O., Ginty, C., & Maguire, M,. (2024). Student Empowerment in the Technological Universities and Institutes of Technology in Ireland: A collection of impact case studies from the N-TUTORR students as partners in innovation and change fellowship programme 2022-2024 . N-TUTORR. ISBN: 978-1-7395019-5-2. Access at https://issuu.com/atlantictechnologicaluniversity/docs/20241111_fellowship_impact_book_with_digital_cover

Carroll. S., Ginty, C., Maguire, M. (2023): Transforming Learning Together: The Power of Student-staff Partnerships in Higher Education

Cronin, C. (2020). Open education: Walking a critical path. In D. Conrad & P. Prinsloo (Eds.), Open(ing) education: Theory and practice. Brill. doi: 10.1163/9789004422988_002

Ginty, C., (2023), Choosing Sustainable Futures: The N-TUTORR Project and Student Empowerment in the Irish Technological University Sector in Ireland. Panel member and chaired by Prof. Gilly Salmon on Truly Transforming Higher Education. Beyond Tradition, Beyond Our Wildest Dreams. OEB Berlin 2023, https://oeb.global/conference.

SOCIOGAMERS: Integrating Virtual Reality for Teaching Sociology

Simona Barsotti[1], Valentina Goglio[2], Giorgio Borla[3], Renzo Carriero[4], Silvia Gerbi[5], Valentina Moiso[6]

[1] Department of Cultures, Politics and Society, University of Turin, Italy; simona.barsotti@unito.it
[2] Department of Cultures, Politics and Society, University of Turin, Italy; valentina.goglio@unito.it
[3] Department of Philosophy and Educational Science, University of Turin, Italy; giorgio.borla@unito.it
[4] Department of Cultures, Politics and Society, University of Turin, Italy; renzo.carriero@unito.it
[5] Department of Philosophy and Education Science, University of Turin, Italy; silvia.gerbi@edu.unito.it
[6] Department of Cultures, Politics and Society, University of Turin, Italy; valentina.moiso@unito.it

Correspondence: Valentina Goglio: valentina.goglio@unito.it

Abstract:

In the field of innovative technologies for education, interest in Virtual Reality (VR) has grown significantly over the past decade. Recent studies have investigated the potential of this tool, highlighting both direct and indirect benefits (through affective-cognitive factors) on learning outcomes (Ding & Li, 2022; Makransky & Petersen, 2021). Indeed, the immersive and interactive nature of this technology fosters active student engagement and the mobilization of attentional resources, making learning more motivated and effective (Di Natale et al., 2020). The characteristics of VR share common ground with gamification and Game-Based Learning, allowing for integrated use (Lampropoulos & Kinshuk, 2024). However, the adoption of these tools is primarily concentrated in scientific and technological disciplines, with only marginal implementation in the humanities and social sciences (Ding & Li, 2022; Hamilton et al., 2022).

The "Sociogamers" project aligns with this emerging field of research, aiming to integrate VR into social sciences curricula at the University of Turin to enhance and strengthen the learning process in three different study programs. Adopting an interdisciplinary and circular approach, the study follows a multi-phase development process structured according to the Design Thinking methodology. The learning needs assessment of a sociology course (Network Society) has identified critical areas for intervention, forming the basis for the development of educational resources. These resources, referred to as "sociogames," are currently under development and will be created using a bottom-up approach by students from the Education Sciences program (Sociology of Education and Game-Based Learning), utilizing the CoSpaces platform. Implementation is scheduled for the 2025/2026 academic year, targeting first-year students of the Network Society course, who will assess its usability and effectiveness.

A key strength of the project lies in its distinct interdisciplinarity, reflected in its circular and networked design process. Students not only engage with VR resources but also actively participate in their design and evaluation, following a bottom-up and user-generated model. The content can be adapted to different cognitive styles, allowing for a personalized learning experience that aligns with the core principles of Universal Design for Learning and offering additional resources to students with higher support needs (Ślósarz et al., 2022).

In line with existing literature, the project anticipates improvements in the acquisition, retention, and transfer of sociological knowledge for Network Society students, as well as enhanced design skills for Education Sciences students. The introduction of engaging and interactive activities also addresses additional identified needs, such as developing transferable skills for the labor market (Jaramillo-Mediavilla et al., 2024; Boyle et al., 2016) and the promotion of steady student progression in their academic careers (Elsherbiny & Al Maamari, 2021). The developed resources will be further refined and adapted for use in other contexts: released with Creative Commons licenses, these will be made available to partner institution of a European project consortium (www.hespriproject.eu/).

Keywords: Virtual Reality, Game-Based Learning, Personalized learning, Sociology, Education quality, Interdisciplinarity.

References

Boyle, E. A., Hainey, T., Connolly, T. M., Gray, G., Earp, J., Ott, M., Lim, T., Ninaus, M., Ribeiro, C., & Pereira, J. (2016). An update to the systematic literature review of empirical evidence of the impacts and outcomes of computer games and serious games. *Computers & Education*, 94, 178–192. https://doi.org/10.1016/j.compedu.2015.11.003

Di Natale, A. F., Repetto, C., Riva, G., & Villani, D. (2020). Immersive virtual reality in K-12 and higher education: A 10-year systematic review of empirical research. *British Journal of Educational Technology*, 51(6), 2006–2033. https://doi.org/10.1111/bjet.13030

Ding, X., & Li, Z. (2022). A review of the application of virtual reality technology in higher education based on Web of Science literature data as an example. *Frontiers in Education*, 7, 1048816. https://doi.org/10.3389/feduc.2022.1048816

Elsherbiny, M. M. K., & H. Al Maamari, R. H. (2020). Game-based learning through mobile phone apps: effectively enhancing learning for social work students. *Social Work Education*, 40(3), 315–332. https://doi.org/10.1080/02615479.2020.1737665

Hamilton, D., McKechnie, J., Edgerton, E., & Wilson, C. (2021). Immersive virtual reality as a pedagogical tool in education: A systematic literature review of quantitative learning outcomes and experimental design. *Journal of Computers in Education*, 8, 1–32. https://doi.org/10.1007/s40692-020-00169-2

Jaramillo-Mediavilla, L., Basantes-Andrade, A., Cabezas-González, M., & Casillas-Martín, S. (2024). Impact of gamification on motivation and academic performance: A systematic review. *Education Sciences*, 14(6), 639. https://doi.org/10.3390/educsci14060639

Lampropoulos, G., & Kinshuk. (2024). Virtual reality and gamification in education: A systematic review. *Education Tech Research and Development*, 72, 1691–1785. https://doi.org/10.1007/s11423-024-10351-3

Makransky, G., & Petersen, G. B. (2021). The Cognitive Affective Model of Immersive Learning (CAMIL): A theoretical research-based model of learning in immersive virtual reality. *Educational Psychology Review*, 33, 937–958. https://doi.org/10.1007/s10648-020-09586-2

Ślósarz, L., Jurczyk-Romanowska, E., Rosińczuk, J., & Kazimierska-Zając, M. (2022). Virtual Reality as a Teaching Resource Which Reinforces Emotions in the Teaching Process. *Sage Open*, 12(3). https://doi.org/10.1177/21582440221118083

Investigating AI Policy in Higher Education Through an Ecopedagogical Framework

Stephanie Wilson[1], Dewa Wardak[2]

[1]The University of Sydney Business School, The University of Sydney, Australia; stephanie.wilson@sydney.edu.au
[2]The University of Sydney Business School, The University of Sydney, Australia; dewa.wardak@sydney.edu.au

Correspondence: Stephanie Wilson: stephanie.wilson@sydney.edu.au

Abstract:

In this presentation, we will share the process and preliminary findings of a project that reviews literature and policy in relation to education with, for and about Artificial Intelligence (AI) in the Australian higher education context. We use content analysis (Drisko & Maschi, 2016) to investigate whether AI policy in education is informed by the principles of ecopedagogy which include environmental awareness, sustainability and social justice.

Ecopedagogies is an area of educational research and practice that supports critical examinations of the politics of socio-environmental connections through local, global and planetary lenses (Ford & Jandrić, 2022; Jandrić, MacKenzie & Knox, 2023). In using ecopedagogies as a framework, we reflect on its value in helping us critically explore the challenges and opportunities of AI in higher education. In particular, we consider how it can be used to shape approaches to AI integration for a more just and sustainable world.

In terms of the environment, ecopedagogies assist us in understanding how digitisation in the age of AI distances (or de-distances) us from nature (Misiaszek, 2023), how AI uses nature as a resource for the generation of digital data (Stewart, 2023), and how AI both addresses and contributes to environmental crises through the consumption and 'prosumption' of nature (Price, 2023b). While technologies in the age of AI are often espoused as providing solutions, including in education, they can generate more problems than they solve in relation to sustainability through the creation of social inequalities and the depletion of planetary resources (Price, 2023a). In addition to helping us reveal the hidden environmental costs of AI use in education, ecopedagogies may help us understand AI's contribution to forms of biocapitalism in education and how this can be mitigated through biopolitics (Pierce, 2013; Bourassa, 2024).

By understanding AI not as separate from society but as deeply integrated with social, environmental and political issues (Jandrić, MacKenzie & Knox, 2023), we can begin to rethink how AI can be used in higher education 'for good' (Pechenkina (2023) and shape ways of integrating AI that support the environment and societal wellbeing now and into the future.

The presentation provides an opportunity to connect the preliminary findings of this study in the Australian context with the global community, and for participants to consider the application of an ecopedagogies framework to support research and discussion in relation to education with, for and about AI.

Keywords: Ecopedagogies, artificial intelligence, sustainability, environmental awareness, social justice

References

Bourassa, G. (2024). Postdigital biopolitics. In P. Jandrić (Ed.), *Encyclopedia of Postdigital Science and Education*. Springer, Cham. :10.1007/978-3-031-35469-4_70-1

Drisko, J. W., & Maschi, T. (2016). *Content analysis*. Oxford university press.

Ford, D., & Jandrić, P. (Eds.) (2022). *Postdigital ecopedagogies: Genealogies, contradictions, and possible futures*. Postdigital Science and Education Book Series. Springer Cham. :10.1007/978-3-030-97262-2

Jandrić, P., MacKenzie, A., & Knox, J. (Eds). (2023). *Postdigital research: Genealogies, challenges, and future perspectives.* Springer Cham. :10.1007/978-3-031-31299-1

Pechenkina, E. (2023). Artificial intelligence for good? Challenges and possibilities of AI in higher education from a data justice perspective. In L. Czernowitz & C. Cronin (Eds.), *Higher education for good: Teaching and learning futures*. Open Book Publishers. :10.11647/OPB.0363

Pierce, C. (2013). *Education in the age of biocapitalism: Optimizing educational life for a flat world*. Palgrave Macmillan. :10.1057/9781137027832

Price, C. (2023a). Postdigital environmental crisis. In P. Jandrić (Ed.), *Encyclopedia of Postdigital Science and Education*. Springer, Cham. :10.1007/978-3-031-35469-4_6-2

Price, C. (2023b). Postdigital nature 2.0. In P. Jandrić (Ed.), *Encyclopedia of Postdigital Science and Education*. Springer, Cham. :10.1007/978-3-031-35469-4_6-1

Stewart, G. T. (2023). Postdigital nature(s). In P. Jandrić (Ed.), *Encyclopedia of Postdigital Science and Education*. Springer, Cham. :10.1007/978-3-031-35469-4_17-2

From Classroom to Community: Student Civic Engagement for Future Skills Learning

Monica Gago Garcia[1], Laura Eigbrecht[2], Jörn Allmang[3], Agurtzane Martinez Gorrochategui[4], Ane Urizar Zugazagoitia[5], Ulf-Daniel Ehlers[6]

[1] Mondragon University, Spain; mgago@mondragon.edu
[2] Baden-Wuerttemberg Cooperative State University Karlsruhe, Germany; laura.eigbrecht@dhbw-karlsruhe.de
[3] Baden-Wuerttemberg Cooperative State University Karlsruhe, Germany; joern.allmang@dhbw-karlsruhe.de
[4] Mondragon University, Spain; amartinez@mondragon.edu
[5] Mondragon University, Spain; aurizar@mondragon.edu
[6] Baden-Wuerttemberg Cooperative State University Karlsruhe, Germany; ulf-daniel.ehlers@dhbw-karlsruhe.de

Correspondence: Laura Eigbrecht: laura.eigbrecht@dhbw-karlsruhe.de

Abstract:

Civic participation is a multidisciplinary concept that refers to the active involvement of individuals in community initiatives. It encompasses voluntary actions aimed at collective well-being (Cnaan and Park, 2016; Guthrie, 1995 [1994]) and social transformation. Such activities also generate benefits for the individuals involved in them. Civic engagement encompasses various forms of civic involvement, such as electoral participation, membership in organisations, volunteering and collective action (Adler and Goggin, 2005; Warren, Sulaiman & Jaafar, 2014), but beyond mere participation, this concept reflects a concern for others and leads to action for the common good.

At the university level, research has analysed the role of higher education institutions in promoting civic engagement. In addition to the academic and professional training traditionally associated with the concept of student engagement, universities should prepare students for active citizenship in democratic societies (Fellner et al., 2022) and should foster student civic engagement. We agree with Adler and Goggin (2005) that the latter focuses on collaborations between students and organisations within and outside the (higher) educational context with the aim of supporting others and serving the community. It is essential that universities foster critical thinking, cooperation and empathy, forming individuals capable of acting with equity and social justice and facilitating the development of civic responsibility and democratic values - human rights, respect and social inclusion. Student participation and civic engagement are linked to the development of competences that strengthen a participatory culture (Almond & Verba, 1963; Burns, Schlozman, & Verba, 2001; Verba & Nie, 1972, cited in Melkumyan, Pavlyutkin & Prutskova, 2015) through collaborative activities between universities and community entities.

In this context, universities should design pedagogical activities that cultivate civic competences essential for active participation and civic engagement. Examples of such activities include service-learning and volunteering, which link academic education with practical experiences of social impact. These and other activities offer space for experiential learning and the development of competences that include but also transcend civic competences: the authors argue that these are learning settings for important Future Skills that allow individuals to successfully act in emerging contexts (Ehlers, 2020). However, in order to enhance awareness and visibility for these Future Skills, it is necessary to establish spaces and tools for reflection. For this reason, an international initiative has started to develop a competence framework and a reflection guideline for Future Skills learning in student participation and civic engagement. The research is based on a systematic literature review on the topic, a thorough analysis of existing frameworks and complemented by several student and experts focus groups. The methodology as well as the first findings and the competence framework will be presented.

Keywords: Future Skills, civic engagement, Service Learning, student participation, student engagement

References

Adler, R. P., & Goggin, J. (2005). What do we mean by "civic engagement"? *Journal of Transformative Education, 3*(3), pp: 236–253.

Cnaan, R. A., Park, S. (2016). The Multifaceted Nature of Civic Participation: A Literature Review. *Brill Research Perspectives. Vol, 1,* pp: 1-73. https://doi.org/10.1163/24054933-12340001

Ehlers, U.-D. (2020). *Future Skills. The Future of Learning and Higher Education.* https://nextskills.org/downloads/Future-Skills-The-Future-of-learning-and-higher-education.pdf

Fellner, K. D. (2019). Iskotew & crow: Reigniting narratives of Indigenous survivance & trauma wisdom in the classroom. In S. Carr-Stewart & J. Ottmann (Eds.), *Knowing the Past, Facing the Future: Indigenous education in Canada* (pp. 143-170). University of British Columbia Press.

Guthrie, R. (1995 [1994]). Civic, civil or servile? *The Philanthropist, 4*(12), pp: 45–57.

Melkumyan, E., Pavlyutkin, I., & Prutskova, E. (2015). Civic effects of higher education in Russia: Religiosity, social capital and the 'pure teaching effect' of educational programmes. *Tertiary Education and Management, 21*(3), pp: 215-228. https://doi.org/10.1080/13583883.2015.1044021

Warren A. M.; Sulaiman, A. & Jaafar, N.I (2014). Social media effects on fostering online civic engagement and building citizen trust and trust in institutions. *Government Informazion Quarterly, 31* (2), pp: 291-301. http://dx.doi.org/10.1016/j.giq.2013.11.007

Distance Education, Social Class and Graduate Employability; Thinking with and Against Bourdieu in the Age of AI

Lorraine Delaney[1]

[1]Institute of Education, Dublin City University, Ireland. lorraine.delaney@dcu.ie

Correspondence: Lorraine Delaney lorraine.delaney@dcu.ie

Abstract:

This paper draws on Bourdieu's concepts of habitus, field and capital to explore the university access and employability experiences of distance graduates. Thinking with and against Bourdieu in the age of AI, data is drawn from institutional records (n=268), online surveys (126 respondents) and 17 semi-structured interviews.

Bourdieu's conceptualisation of habitus (1973) relates to class-specific dispositions. Bourdieu presents the field of higher education as a structured space (1993), with institutions ranked in relation to the capital they can bestow. Capital is any resource which has symbolic value and can act as currency (Bourdieu 1986).

Graduates in this study were primarily (64%) from a lower socio-economic background. Many (40%) had been participating in HE since leaving school, often in short, non-university courses which allowed them to enter the labour market quickly and become financially independent. Bourdieu (1973) helps us understand this action as part of a totality of structures (economic, social and cultural). Graduates' completion of a degree is delayed or protracted for reasons relating to social class. This impacts their ability to leverage financial capital in the labour market.

Bourdieu (1979 p. 104/5) contends that in terms of scholastic age, and in relation to educational capital, 'lost years are a step towards relegation or elimination'. The graduates in this study do successfully transition into graduate-level employment, but this happens slowly. They need time to position themselves to avail of opportunities, or they require further post-graduate study. While it can be difficult to make up for early experiences of educational disadvantage, the graduates in this study are more likely to have been positively 'distinguished' rather than 'eliminated' by their completion of a university degree through distance education. Resulting from their studies, they regularly attain graduate-level employment and upward social mobility.

The graduates present the challenges they face as ones of individual agency. However, social structures are equally conspicuous in their accounts. Although capable of university study, they are funnelled into lower-status courses (Smyth 2018). Targeting school leavers with distance education opportunities would result in earlier degree completion with consequential benefits in the labour market. While Bourdieu promotes full-time university access for the working class, this study revealed that the system of full-time degree completion does not suit everyone; some want or need financial independence and require flexible study options.

And what might Bourdieu have to say about AI? Bourdieu thought deeply about a two-tiered society. As with full-time university access, AI is extraordinarily profitable for those who control it. AI extracts from the earth in terms of fossil energy (Crawford 2022), and extracts from humans in terms of knowledge and labour. Bourdieu would understand this as the logic of capitalism. The true cost and benefit of AI have yet to be determined.

Keywords: Bourdieu; graduates; distance education, employability, social class.

References

Bourdieu, P. (1973). Cultural Reproduction and Social Reproduction. *IN*: Brown, R. (ed.) *Knowledge, Education and Cultural Change*. London: Tavistock

Bourdieu, P. (1986). The forms of capital.*IN:* Robinson, J.G. (ed.), *Handbook of theory and research for the sociology of education.* New York: Greenwood Press.

Bourdieu, P. (1990). *The logic of practice*. Stanford University Press.

Bourdieu, P. (1993). *Sociology in question*. London: Sage.

Crawford, K. (2021). *Atlas of AI: Power, Politics, and the Planetary Costs of Artificial Intelligence*. Yale University Press.

Smyth, E. (2018), "Widening Access to Higher Education: Balancing Supply and Demand in Ireland", Riddell, S., Minty, S., Weedon, E. and Whittaker, S. (Ed.) *Higher Education Funding and Access in International Perspective* (*Great Debates in Higher Education*), Emerald Publishing Limited, Bingley, pp. 121-142. https://doi.org/10.1108/978-1-78754-651-620181007

The Impact of Online Study on Students' Mental Health and Well-being

Dasa Grajfoner[1], Ziva Veingerl Cic[2]

[1] DOBA Business School, Slovenia, Dasa.Grajfoner@doba.si
[2] DOBA Business School, Slovenia, ziva.veingerl-cic@doba.si

Correspondence: Dasa Grajfoner: Dasa.Grajfoner@doba.si

Abstract:

The rapid shift towards online education has brought about significant transformations in the learning experience of students. While online study offers advantages such as flexibility, accessibility, and personalized learning, it also presents challenges that can impact students' mental health and overall well-being. This study examines the effects of online education on students' mental health, with a particular focus on work-life-study balance, psychological resilience and coping strategies. Conducted at DOBA Business School, the biggest online Higher Education Institution in Slovenia, the research employed a mixed-methods approach, combining quantitative survey data with qualitative insights from structured interviews. A total of 507 students participated in the study, providing data on their academic experiences, stress levels, and mental health indicators.

The results indicate that online study poses unique challenges, particularly for students juggling academic, professional, and personal responsibilities (Pološki Vokić et al., 2021). Approximately 72% of working students reported high stress levels, with Croatian students experiencing greater difficulty balancing their commitments compared to Slovenian students. The study also highlights the role of psychological resilience and emotional intelligence in mitigating stress. Students with higher emotional intelligence exhibited better mental health outcomes, suggesting that self-regulation and adaptive coping mechanisms are critical for success in online learning environments. Moreover, students in leadership roles demonstrated greater resilience, indicating that active engagement and structured responsibilities can serve as protective factors against stress.

Further analysis of student mental health and well-being revealed that a lack of face-to-face interaction and increased self-discipline demands contribute to anxiety and feelings of isolation (Akpınar, 2021). The study emphasizes the importance of institutional support, including mental health counseling, structured peer support programs, and interactive virtual communities. The study proposes several interventions to enhance student well-being, including digital well-being resources, resilience training, and flexible study schedules tailored to students' needs.

The findings align with existing literature on online education and mental health, reinforcing the need for comprehensive strategies to support students in virtual learning environments (Abbaszadeh et al., 2023). As online education continues to evolve, higher education institutions must adopt a holistic approach that integrates mental health services, social engagement initiatives, and personalized academic support. Future research should explore the long-term effects of online study on students' mental health and the potential role of emerging technologies, such as virtual reality and artificial intelligence, in enhancing the online learning experience.

This study contributes to the growing discourse on online education and mental health by providing empirical evidence on the challenges and opportunities associated with online learning. The recommendations derived from this research can inform policy decisions and institutional practices aimed at fostering a more supportive and mentally healthy online learning environment. By addressing the mental health challenges faced by online students, educational institutions can enhance student engagement, academic success, and overall well-being.

Keywords: online study, mental health, psychological well-being, work-life-study balance, resilience.

References

Abbaszadeh, S., Keshavarz, M., & Yavari, A. (2023). Resilience and academic success: The impact of online education challenges on university students. *Journal of Higher Education Research*, 48, 134–151.

Akpınar, B. (2021). The psychological impact of online education during the COVID-19 pandemic: A case of anxiety and depression among university students. *Journal of Educational Research*, 35, 105–117.

Pološki Vokić, N., Sontor, T., & Tomljenović, M. (2021). Work-study-life balance among students: Challenges and coping strategies. *Journal of Student Life Research*, 10(3), 201–216.

Digital Technologies and Museum Learning for Developing Multilingual Competence

Maria Tolaini[1]

[1] Languages and Cultures Department, University of Genova, Italy; maria.tolaini@edu.unige.it

Correspondence: Maria Tolaini: maria.tolaini@edu.unige.it

Abstract:

Multilingual competence is recognized as a fundamental skill for active societal participation (European Council, 2018). Ensuring equitable access to language learning opportunities, irrespective of socio-economic status or disabilities, is a priority for inclusive education policies (European Council Conclusions, 2021). This need is particularly pronounced for upper secondary students, as proficiency in multiple languages significantly enhances their academic and professional prospects. However, a 2024 European Commission report indicates that only 34% of Italians feel sufficiently skilled to engage in an English conversation (European Commission, 2024). The European Union proposes several practical strategies to enhance multilingual competence, including integrating classroom learning with informal learning sites, such as museums (Cedefop, 2015). Another key aspect highlighted by the EU is the integration of digital technologies into instructional design (European Council, 2019). The existing literature extensively documents the advantages of digital technologies, and the European Commission itself has published action plans and reference frameworks to support these innovations (European Commission, 2020; Vuorikari, 2022). Based on these guidelines, the present research explores the contributions of educational digital technologies and informal learning environments, such as museums, to develop multilingual competence, assessing their effectiveness and inclusiveness for upper secondary school students. Based on systematic literature reviews and case study analysis, and incorporating the principles of Universal Design for Learning (Gordon, 2024), the research was designed to include museum-based language learning experiences supported by digital educational technologies and assess their effectiveness in terms of learning outcomes and levels of inclusion with pilot and experimental testing. The pilot phase lasted five weeks and involved 41 students from a high school in Genoa, Italy, divided into a control group and three experimental groups, which attended different experimental language-based experimental activities both in the museum and at school. The results of this participation were assessed by pre-test and post-test essays and a questionnaire. The results of the pilot experience informed the implementation of the experimental phase, which lasted 26 weeks and involved 131 students from two schools in Genoa. Compared to the pilot phase, this phase increased the number of museum activities, refined the workshop activities and also used pre-, post-, and follow-up lexical-grammar tests. However, the main difference between the pilot and the experimental phase was the increased and diversified use of digital educational technologies such as Virtual Reality, Augmented Reality, a real-time collaborative web platform and a blended learning platform. This contribution focuses on describing these technologies, highlighting their inclusive characteristics, explaining their selection based on Universal Design for Learning principles, and detailing how they were integrated and utilized within the learning pathways. It also examines the benefits and challenges they presented.

Keywords: digital educational technology; museum learning; multilingual competence; inclusive learning

References

Cedefop (2015). *European guidelines for validating non-formal and informal learning. Cedefop ref-erence series, no. 104*. Publications Office.

European Commission (2020). *Digital Education Action Plan (2021-2027). Resetting education and training for the digital age*. Publications Office of the European Union.

European Commission (2024). *Europeans and their language*. Publications Office of the European Union.

European Council (2018). *Council Recommendation of 22 May 2018 on key competences for life-long learning (Text with EEA relevance) 2018/C 189/01*. Publications Office of the Europe-an Union.

European Council (2019). *Council Recommendation of 22 May 2019 on a comprehensive approach to the teaching and learning of languages 2019/C 189/03*. Publications Office of the Europe-an Union.

European Council (2021). *Council conclusions on equity and inclusion in education and training in order to promote educational success for all 2021/C 221/02*. Publications Office of the Euro-pean Union.

Gordon, D. (2024). *Universal Design for Learning: Principles, Framework, and Practice*. CAST Pubblications

Vuorikari, R., Kluzer, S., & Punie, Y. (2022). *DigComp 2.2: The Digital Competence Framework for Citizens EUR 31006 EN*. Publications Office of the European Union.

Extended Reality (XR) in Higher Education: Building an Immersive, Personalised Learning Experience

Geraldine McDermott[1]

[1]Centre for Pedagogical Innovation and Development, Technological University of the Shannon, Ireland; geraldine.mcdermott@tus.ie

Correspondence: Geraldine McDermott: geraldine.mcdermott@tus.ie

Abstract:

Extended Reality (XR) provides students with opportunities for spatial visualisation, experiential learning, and the development of transversal skills, such as problem-solving, critical thinking, and communication skills. Noted by Alvar (2024) as one of the key trends to watch for 2025, the technological affordances of Extended Reality respond to the call from the European Commission's Digital Education Action Plan (2020), which "sets out a common vision of high-quality, inclusive, and accessible digital education in Europe," noting that "digital education content is more engaging, interactive, and embedded in diverse formats and platforms."

This presentation reports on an ambitious initiative to embed XR education within an Irish Technological University. It charts the journey from a small-scale XR research project through engagement with faculty and students to the establishment of a community of practice of XR researchers and educators. It also documents the requisite engagement with the wider university services to establish the infrastructure necessary for the scalability of such an initiative.

Innovativeness and responsiveness are key features of this pedagogical approach, and students from different faculties (Science, Business, Engineering) across the distributed campus are now supported to use Virtual Reality, harnessing the potential of AI to provide personalised learning opportunities. VR applications provide access to otherwise inaccessible locations and enable enhanced comprehension within an immersive, multimodal, inclusive environment. As these technologies become more affordable and more robust, they offer greater potential for our educational context.

The competencies developed within an immersive learning environment are particularly relevant to the digital world our graduates will work in. This presentation will share the experiences of educators as they respond to the need for adaptive and immersive educational environments.

Keywords: Virtual Reality, immersive technologies, higher education

References

European Commission (2020). Digital Education Action Plan (2021-2027). Available at: https://education.ec.europa.eu/focus-topics/digital-education/action-plan.

Alvarez, G. (2024). Gartner Top 10 Strategic Technology Trends for 2025. Available at: https://www.gartner.com/en/articles/top-technology-trends-2025.

Towards Inclusive Education through Educational Robotics: Supporting Diverse Learning Needs

Muhammad H. Al Omoush[1], Monica Ward[2]

[1,2] Faculty of Engineering and Computing, Dublin City University, Dublin, Ireland
[1] muhammad.menazelalomoush2@mail.dcu.ie
[2] monica.ward@dcu.ie

Correspondence: Muhammad H. Al Omoush: muhammad.menazelalomoush2@mail.dcu.ie

Abstract:

Inclusive education aims to accommodate diverse learning needs, ensuring that all students have equal access to quality education regardless of their cognitive or physical challenges (DEC & NAEYC, 2009; Love & Horn, 2021; Pelatti et al., 2016). One of the most promising advancements in this field is the integration of educational robotics (ER), which provides interactive, adaptive, and engaging learning experiences (Zhong & Xia, 2020). Interactive ER features can boost engagement and offer personalised feedback, helping students develop skills beyond a teacher's traditional role (Fung et al., 2025).

This paper is based on the ongoing development of a low-cost educational robot designed as an inclusive learning tool to enhance engagement, accessibility, and mathematical comprehension for primary school students with signs of dyslexia or dyscalculia. The authors highlight the ER's potential to support students with learning difficulties such as dyslexia and dyscalculia and emphasise how ER could potentially foster personalised learning pathways that align with students' strengths and challenges. ER facilitates multimodal instruction, enabling students to interact with content through visual, auditory, and kinaesthetic means (Ritschel et al., 2017). For example, speech-to-text (STT) and text-to-speech (TTS) functions can enhance reading comprehension and phonological processing for students with dyslexia (Bäck et al., 2024; Edyburn, 2021; Ok & Rao, 2019). These features are already built into some robots or can be added as needed. Students with dyscalculia can engage with tactile and visual mathematical representations, improving number sense and problem-solving skills.

Beyond personalised learning, ER contributes to collaborative and inclusive classroom environments. Robotics-based learning activities not only encourage peer interactions, teamwork, and experiential learning but also foster a supportive and cooperative learning culture. ER provides teachers with real-time feedback on student progress, enabling educators to personalise instruction and interventions effectively. Also, ER could offer a safe space for students to practise without fear of mistakes, potentially fostering exploration, learning, and inclusivity. Capacity-building initiatives for teachers play an essential role in maximising the potential of ER, equipping educators with the necessary skills to integrate ER into diverse learning environments effectively (Toh et al., 2016).

Integrating ER into inclusive education presents a range of benefits, but it also poses challenges related to cost, infrastructure, and teacher acceptance and training. However, the accessibility and affordability of learning with ER are supported by open-source options such as the Robot Operating System (ROS)[1] and low-cost development boards like Arduino[2] and Raspberry Pi[3], while all benefit from strong community support. Virtual robotics platforms and simulators further reduce barriers by enabling learners to experiment, program, and test robots in digital environments without physical hardware. That is particularly valuable in regions with limited access to specialised resources and classrooms with high student-teacher ratios. This paper will share the development process of a low-cost educational robot, present initial findings on students' reception of the robotics integration into mathematics, and outline plans for testing and evaluating this integration. Future research should explore longitudinal studies on the impact of ER on student outcomes, as well as strategies to scale robotics-based learning interventions across different socio-economic settings.

1: https://www.ros.org
2: https://www.arduino.cc
3: https://www.raspberrypi.com

Keywords: Educational robotics, Inclusive education, Dyslexia, Dyscalculia, Multimodal instruction

Acknowledgement

This work was conducted with the financial support of the Research Ireland Centre for Research Training in Digitally-Enhanced Reality (d-real) under Grant No. 18/CRT/6224. For the purpose of Open Access, the author has applied a CC BY public copyright licence to any Author Accepted Manuscript version arising from this submission.

References

Bäck, A., Lindeblad, G., Elmqvist, E., & Svensson, C. (2024). Dyslexic students' experiences in using assistive technology to support written language skills: a five-year follow-up. Disability and Rehabilitation: Assistive Technology, 19(4), 1217–1227.

Early childhood inclusion: A joint position statement of the Division for Early Childhood (DEC) and the National Association for the Education of Young Children. (2009). NAEYC.

Edyburn, D. L. (2021). Universal usability and universal design for learning. Intervention in School and Clinic, 56(5), 310–315. https://doi.org/10.1177/1053451220963082

Fung, K. Y., Fung, K. C., Lui, T. L. R., Sin, K. F., Lee, L. H., Qu, H., & Song, S. (2025). Exploring the impact of robot interaction on learning engagement: a comparative study of two multi-modal robots. Smart Learning Environments, 12(1).

Love, H. R., & Horn, E. (2021). Definition, context, quality: Current issues in research examining high-quality inclusive education. Topics in Early Childhood Special Education, 40(4), 204–216.

Ok, M. W., & Rao, K. (2019). Digital tools for the inclusive classroom: Google Chrome as assistive and instructional technology. Journal of Special Education Technology: A Publication of Utah State University, the Association for Special Education Technology, and the Technology and Media Division of the Council for Exceptional Children, 34(3), 204–211. https://doi.org/10.1177/0162643419841546

Pelatti, C. Y., Dynia, J. M., Logan, J. A., Justice, L. M., & Kaderavek, J. (2016). Examining quality in two preschool settings: Publicly funded early childhood education and inclusive early childhood education classrooms. Child & Youth Care Forum, 45, 829–849.

Ritschel, H., Baur, T., & Andre, E. (2017). Adapting a Robot's linguistic style based on socially-aware reinforcement learning. 2017 26th IEEE International Symposium on Robot and Human Interactive Communication (RO-MAN).

Toh, L. P. E., Causo, A., Tzuo, P. W., Chen, I. M., & Yeo, S. H. (2016). A Review on the Use of Robots in Education and Young Children. Educational Technology & Society, 19(2), 148–163.

Zhong, B., & Xia, L. (2020). A systematic review on exploring the potential of educational robotics in mathematics education. International Journal of Science and Mathematics Education, 18(1), 79–101. https://doi.org/10.1007/s10763-018-09939-y

Exploring University Students' Concerns About AI in Higher Education

Dewa Wardak[1]

[1]The University of Sydney Business School, Australia; dewa.wardak@sydney.edu.au

Correspondence: Dewa Wardak: dewa.wardak@sydney.edu.au

Abstract:

The Ipsos (2023) global survey of 31 countries found Australians had the lowest trust and positive feelings about AI, though reasons for these concerns were not explored. Chung et al. (2024) surveyed over 8,000 students across Australian universities, revealing widespread AI use but also concerns about cheating, rule violations, and inadequate guidance. My ongoing study focuses on international students at a large Australian university, exploring their specific concerns about using AI in group projects. In this presentation, I will share preliminary results aligned with the conference theme of student and societal well-being. Using Clarke and Braun's (2017) thematic analysis approach, three key themes emerged from the written responses: AI-induced distrust in peer collaboration, AI diminishing creativity, and concerns about students becoming dependent on AI.

AI-induced distrust: Preliminary data from 50 responses shows students worry about peers using AI in group assessments, making detection difficult. For example, one respondent stated, "group members use entirely AI-generated content, and we need to take time to see the parts to find out and need extra time to change the parts". While research on AI-induced distrust among students is limited, Luo (2024) highlights a lack of two-way transparency in AI-mediated assessments, where students face surveillance but teachers remain unclear about grading, fostering a low-trust environment.

AI diminishing creativity: Respondents voiced concerns that AI generates generic, low-quality outputs and that relying on it could stifle creativity. One student, for instance, stated, "I feel like it ruins creativity and people don't think enough, and it also gives poor quality". Habib et al. (2024) examined the impact of generative AI on students' creative thinking and concluded that while AI can be beneficial for some tasks, it can have negative effects on students' creative confidence.

Becoming dependent on AI: Responses in this category revealed students' concerns about becoming overly dependent on AI. One response stated "AI is making me soft, and slowly I am being dependent on it in a way that in the future I will not be nearly as productive as I was, and I won't be able to do menial tasks without it". While some studies point to the risks of over-relying on AI (Owais, 2025; Liu, 2025), empirical evidence is limited. Nonetheless, excessive dependence on AI can lead to a loss of autonomy and accountability in both everyday life and critical decision-making (Szmyd & Mitera, 2024).

I frame these findings through the lens of Ryan and Deci's (2000) Self-Determination Theory (SDT), emphasising the critical roles of autonomy, competence, and relatedness in education. I argue that AI in education must be carefully managed to support, rather than undermine, these fundamental psychological needs. Recent applications of SDT in various contexts have explored its relevance to AI, such as examining AI literacy among university students (Wang et al., 2025), mediating the link between AI literacy and innovative behaviour (Ji et al., 2025), and investigating how AI-enhanced collaborative learning can improve knowledge and reduce cognitive load (Li et al., 2025).

Keywords: AI concerns; Self-Determination Theory; Trust; Creativity; Dependency

References

Chung, J., Henderson, M., Pepperell, N., Slade, C., Liang, Y. (2024). Student perspectives on AI in Higher Education: Student Survey. Student Perspectives on AI in Higher Education Project. https://doi.org/10.26180/27915930

Clarke, V., & Braun, V. (2017). Thematic analysis. *The Journal of Positive Psychology, 12*(3), 297–298.

Habib, S., Vogel, T., Anli, X., & Thorne, E. (2024). How does generative artificial intelligence impact student creativity? *Journal of Creativity, 34*(1), 100072. https://doi.org/10.1016/j.yjoc.2023.100072

Ipsos. (2023, July). *Global views on A.I. 2023: How people across the world feel about artificial intelligence and expect it will impact their life.* Ipsos. https://www.ipsos.com/sites/default/files/ct/news/documents/2023-07/Ipsos%20Global%20AI%202023%20Report-WEB_0.pdf

Ji, Y., Zhong, M., Lyu, S., & others. (2025). How does AI literacy affect individual innovative behavior: The mediating role of psychological need satisfaction, creative self-efficacy, and self-regulated learning. *Education and Information Technologies.* https://doi.org/10.1007/s10639-025-13437-4

Li, T., Zhan, Z., Ji, Y., & Li, T. (2025). Exploring human and AI collaboration in inclusive STEM teacher training: A synergistic approach based on self-determination theory. *The Internet and Higher Education, 65*, 101003. https://doi.org/10.1016/j.iheduc.2025.101003

Liu, Q. (2025). *Design and evaluation of AI-aided writing: Managing user burden and improving content quality. SIGHCI 2024 Proceedings*, 20. https://aisel.aisnet.org/sighci2024/20

Luo (Jess), J. (2024). How does GenAI affect trust in teacher-student relationships? Insights from students' assessment experiences. *Teaching in Higher Education*, 1–16. https://doi.org/10.1080/13562517.2024.2341005

Owais, A. K. (2025). AI in English teaching with ChatGPT: Does it really work?. In *Using AI tools in text analysis, simplification, classification, and synthesis* (pp. 199-228). IGI Global Scientific Publishing.

Ryan, R. M., & Deci, E. L. (2000). Self-determination theory and the facilitation of intrinsic motivation, social development, and well-being. *American Psychologist, 55*(1), 68–78.

Szmyd, K., & Mitera, E. (2024). The impact of artificial intelligence on the development of critical thinking skills in students. *European Research Studies Journal, 27*(2), 1022-1039.

Wang, K., Cui, W., & Yuan, X. (2025). Artificial intelligence in higher education: The impact of need satisfaction on artificial intelligence literacy mediated by self-regulated learning strategies. *Behavioral Sciences, 15*(2), 165. https://doi.org/10.3390/bs15020165

Educational Futures as Imagined by the EDEH Futuring Squad: Four Scenarios for 2040

Deborah Arnold[1], Gül Akcaova[2]

[1] NTT DATA, France; deborahjane.arnold@gmail.com
[2] SURF, The Netherlands; Gul.akcaova@surf.nl

Correspondence: Deborah Arnold: deborahjane.arnold@gmail.com

Abstract:

The digital education landscape is rapidly evolving, driven by technological advancements and changing societal needs. This paper presents the work of the European Digital Education Hub (EDEH) Futuring Squad, which convened between September and December 2024 to explore various dimensions of (future) trends in digital education, including innovations in learning technologies, pedagogical strategies, and the broader implications for learners, educators, institutions and society. Trends addressed included artificial intelligence (AI) to personalise learning experiences, immersive technologies such as virtual and augmented reality for creating engaging learning environments, and data analytics for monitoring and enhancing educational outcomes. The discussions also included societal and ethical considerations relating to equitable access, digital literacy and the challenges of climate change.

Drawing on prior work in the field of educational futuring (Bayne & Ross, 2024; European University Association, 2021a, 2021b; Larsen, 2020), the squad took the year 2040 as being not too close to, and not too far ahead of, the present. The squad adopted the four scenario archetypes (Dator & Dator, 2019) of continued growth, constraint/discipline, collapse/decline, and transformation. Each scenario described the social, political, economic and educational landscape in 2040, identified key factors, and was illustrated by "day in the life" descriptions to anchor the scenarios in imagined futures.

The growth scenario considered that education in 2040 is driven by advanced technologies such as AI-powered personal assistants, augmented and virtual reality and data-driven personalisation, in a culture of lifelong learning, and international collaboration. However, this was not a naively optimistic scenario, with risks identified as being societal polarisation, the digital divide and exclusion, data, cybersecurity and ethical AI usage concerns, as well as mental health and cognitive overload.

The constraint scenario imagined a more reasonable and accountable framework for education. Key factors here are a more regulated educational framework, growing scepticism towards technological advancements, a more sophisticated approach to digital literacy inclusion and a more responsible use of digital resources. Challenges were identified as equity in digital learning quality, student engagement and motivation in virtual environments, assessment and accreditation of digital learning, data privacy and security, and scalability of digital learning models.

The collapse/decline scenario asked the provocative question of whether 2040 sees the end of human knowledge and digital education, on the premise that a lack of appropriate legislation and an overoptimistic faith in techno-solutionism have resulted in the evolution of technology becoming uncontrollable. Legislative loopholes undermine privacy, public trust and innovation, science drowns in AI-driven fraud, there is a two-tier education system with inequality designed in, data spaces are at risk from cyber-attacks, AI and human-generated content are indistinguishable, the expert community has all but disappeared, and climate disruption is at breaking point.

Finally, the transformation scenario identified societal trends feeding transformation, focusing on empathy, critical thinking, emotional intelligence and practical stills; a deep connection with environmental issues embedded in education, civic engagement, well-being, lifelong learning, supported by a host of technologies from new generation learning environments to immersive technologies and neural interfaces.

References

Dator, J., & Dator, J., (2019). Alternative futures at the Manoa School. *Jim Dator: A Noticer in Time: Selected work, 1967-2018*, 37-54.

European University Association, (2021a). *Universities without walls: A vision for 2030*, Higher Education Report, European University Association.

European University Association. (2021b). *Pathways to the future. A follow-up to Universities without walls–A vision for 2030.* Higher Education Report, European University Association.

Larsen, N. (2020). *Using the Future: Embracing Uncertainty, Improving Decision-Making, and Democratising Tomorrow*. Copenhagen Institute for Futures Studies

Note

The final report from the EDEN Futuring Squad is expected to be published in the first half of 2025. The link to the full report will be shared during the presentation. Should the report not be published by the time of the EDEN Annual Conference, the link will be made available via the EDEH and other social media channels.

Investigating the Use of Social Robotics to Support Student Learning and Well-Being in Higher Education

Karol Fitzgerald[1], Geraldine McDermott[2], Geraldine Maughan[3]

[1] Department of Software Engineering, Technological University of the Shannon, Ireland; karol.fitzgerald@tus.ie
[2] Centre for Pedagogical Innovation and Development, Technological University of the Shannon, Ireland; geraldine.mcdermott@tus.ie
[3] Department of Applied Social Sciences, Technological University of the Shannon, Ireland; geraldine.maughan@tus.ie

Correspondence: karol.fitzgerald@tus.ie

Abstract:

Third-level education often poses unique challenges for students with additional needs, in particular disabilities, neurodivergence, or stress and anxiety. Addressing their needs requires innovative solutions that promote personalised learning, inclusivity and mental well-being. Recent research in the domain of social robotics suggests that there is potential to support students in their learning and well-being, within a tertiary education context, through engagement with a social robot.

A review by Youssef et al (2023) presents a variety of applications for social robotics in education, noting the potential of social robots for learning assistance and language learning; while Johal et al. (2022) identified personalized learning as a key area for future research, noting that the affective nature of the robot was considered important for learner interaction. Popular robots such as Pepper© and Nao© are frequently chosen for research in social robotics, because of their expressive body movements and personality traits (see Velentza et al. (2021) and Belpaeme and Tanaka (2021) for examples). However, robots such as these are quite expensive, so social robots such as Zenbo© and Buddy © are more accessible and often used to explore how social robotics could support students through task-based scenarios and affective interactions.

This presentation will provide an overview of a research project involving senior faculty from the disciplines of Engineering, Education and Social Sciences, who introduced a social robot to students on campus, inviting them to interact with the robot to complete specific tasks. The presentation will also share feedback from students, gathered via an anonymous questionnaire to capture key insights into students' perceptions of and reactions to social robots as a tool to support learning and student well-being.

Keywords: social robotics, student wellbeing, higher education

References

Belpaeme, T., & Tanaka, F. (2021). Social robots as educators. In *OECD digital education outlook 2021 pushing the Frontiers with artificial intelligence, blockchain and robots: pushing the Frontiers with artificial intelligence, blockchain and robots* (p. 143). Paris: OECD Publishing.

Johal, W., Belpaeme, T., & Chetouani, M. (2022). Robots for learning. *Frontiers in Robotics and AI*, *9*, 1050658.

Velentza, A. M., Fachantidis, N., & Pliasa, S. (2021). Which one? choosing favorite robot after different styles of storytelling and robots' conversation. *Frontiers in Robotics and AI*, *8*, 700005.

Youssef, K., Said, S., Alkork, S., & Beyrouthy, T. (2023). Social robotics in education: A survey on recent studies and applications. *International Journal of Emerging Technologies in Learning (Online)*, *18*(3), 67.

Enhancing Learning Through Virtual Reality in Tourism and Event Management

Noëlle O'Connor[1], Geraldine McDermott[2], Assumpta Byrne[3], Sandra Griselain[4]

[1] Centre for Pedagogical Innovation and Development, Technological University of the Shannon, Ireland; noelle.oconnor@tus.ie
[2] Centre for Pedagogical Innovation and Development, Technological University of the Shannon, Ireland; geraldine.mcdermott@tus.ie
[3] Library, Technological University of the Shannon, Ireland; assumpta.byrne@tus.ie
[4] Department of Hospitality, Tourism and Leisure, Technological University of the Shannon, Ireland; andragriselain@tus.ie

Correspondence: Noëlle O'Connor: noelle.oconnor@tus.ie

Abstract:

As higher education continues to embrace digital transformation, Virtual Reality (VR) technology is emerging as a powerful tool to enhance experiential learning. This research examines the integration of VR in tourism and event management education at the Technological University of the Shannon (TUS) in Ireland, using two case studies that explore VR's impact on student engagement, industry readiness, and practical learning experiences.

The first case study, "Virtual Reality in Visitor Attractions: A Dark Tourism Journey", introduced the Business Studies (Hons.) with Travel and Tourism Management students to VR applications in special interest tourism. Using the Secret Annexe VR app, students explored the Anne Frank House (Amsterdam), analysing visitor motivations, ethical considerations, and the role of VR in heritage tourism.

The second case study, "Virtual Reality in Events: Tomorrowland", engaged the Business Studies (Hons.) with Event Management students in an immersive 360° experience of the Tomorrowland Music Festival (Belgium). The activity allowed students to explore event site design, décor, and entertainment management, offering real-world insights into large-scale event planning without the need for physical travel.

This research revealed several key findings regarding the integration of VR technology in tourism and event management education. VR enhanced student engagement and retention, bridging the gap between theory and practice through immersive and experiential learning. Students also developed digital competency and industry readiness, gaining confidence in using VR technology, a tool that is increasingly relevant in both the tourism and event industries. The research highlighted how VR provides alternative ways to experience tourism sites and events, making learning more interactive and accessible. Additionally, lecturers emphasised the scalability and future integration of VR in tourism and event education, recognising its potential for expanding learning opportunities and deepening student engagement.

This research contributes to the EDEN 2025 Annual Conference's theme, "Shaping the Future of Digital Education," showcasing VR's role in immersive, technology-enhanced learning. Findings offer practical insights for higher education institutions aiming to integrate innovative digital tools into tourism and event management curricula.

Keywords: Enhancing Learning, Virtual Reality, Tourism and Event Management, Ireland

The EduMat+ Project: Teaching Children to Code to Enhance Their Learning Experiences

Stefan Colibaba[1], Irina Gheorghiu[2], Ioan Juncu[3], Alexandra Hanu[4], Carmen Antonita[5]

[1] EuroEd Foundation Iasi, Romania; stefancolibaba@euroed.ro
[2] Albert Ludwigs University Freiburg, Germany; irina_gheorghiu16@yahoo.com
[3,4,5]EuroEd School Iasi, Romania; ioan.juncu@euroed.ro; alexandra.hanu@euroed.ro; carmenantonita@yahoo.com

Correspondence: Stefan Colibaba: stefancolibaba@euroed.ro

Abstract:

This paper highlights the novel rationale and methodology of the EduMat+ project funded by the European Commission under the Erasmus+ programme. The project is implemented through a partnership of universities, primary schools, and NGOs specializing in education and IT across five countries: Italy, Bulgaria, Spain, Portugal, and Romania. The EduMat+ project aims to bridge the digital literacy gap between generations and enhance the effective use of technology as a teaching tool by integrating coding and STEAM (science, technology, engineering, arts, and mathematics) into primary school curricula.

The paper examines the project's innovative teaching strategy, which uses coding to create infographic interactive mats and outlines the children's journey to learn and use coding. Instead of traditional narratives, the project employs infographics to develop engaging, hands-on learning experiences for children. These visual tools facilitate play-based learning, encouraging children to explore real-world issues that require urgent action, while also empowering them to contribute meaningfully to key topics such as environmental sustainability, social inclusion, or climate change. For example, in Module 7, the children were introduced to the concept of inequalities, focusing on disparities in income, education, healthcare, and opportunities across different social groups. Subsequent sessions looked deeper into the root causes of these inequalities and explored potential solutions. Using infographic mats, teachers visually represented disparities in various communities, guiding children to identify real-world examples. The children then analyzed specific causes of inequality, learned about strategies for addressing them, and ultimately designed a solution plan. Finally, they used coding platforms to create their own interactive map to illustrate their proposed interventions, reinforcing both digital literacy and critical thinking skills. Their findings were shared with their peers and parents.

To achieve these objectives, participating teachers engaged in an online course and a workshop focused on creating and using interactive mats with the educational platform Scratch. In parallel, the children attended a Scratch workshop that introduced them to the fundamentals of coding. Scratch encouraged children to not only interact with digital technologies but also create and express themselves through these new tools (Resnik, 2012). This platform empowered them to bring their imaginative ideas to life by designing unique characters, backdrops, and interactive features. Furthermore, Scratch facilitated collaboration and sharing, allowing children to showcase their projects, receive feedback, and enhance their learning experiences together.

The project seeks to increase children's awareness of the importance of information technology in education, encourage the use of new digital technologies to support primary school teachers, and promote active and inclusive child participation. The paper highlights the benefits and challenges of the coding strategy as experienced by the children themselves. The findings of the EduMat+ project (Project Number: 2023-1-IT02-KA220-SCH-000157934) support the use of coding as an innovative and engaging way to educate children. The strategy:

- enables children to create and express themselves through the new technologies;

- teaches children how to work together, identify and resolve issues when they arise, and maintain persistence and perseverance when things aren't functioning as expected;
- merges the physical and digital worlds with a view to fostering a more holistic learning experience.

Keywords: primary school teachers, children, coding, infographic mats, Scratch

References

Bicen, H., & Beheshti, M. (2017). *The psychological impact of infographics in education*. BRAIN (Broad Research in Artificial Intelligence and Neuroscience), 8(4), 99–108. https://doi.org/10.17160/brain.2017.4.1.33

Cortoni, I., Caccamo, A., & Mus, C. (2023). Mapping, coding, learning: When infographic meets digital education – A pilot programme in design school, pp. 549–562.

EduMat project. (n.d.). EduMat project. https://www.edumatproject.eu/index.php

Jeong, D. W., Moon, H., Jeong, S., & Moon, C. (2024). *Digital capital accumulation in schools, teachers, and* students and academic achievement: Cross-country evidence from the PISA 2018. International Journal of Educational Development, 107, Article 103024. https://doi.org/10.1016/j.ijedudev.2024.103024

Kaplancali, U. T., & Demirkol, Z. (2017). *Teaching coding to children: A methodology for kids 5+*. International Journal of Elementary Education, 6(4), 32–37. https://doi.org/10.11648/j.ijeedu.20170604.11

Matrix, S., & Hodson, J. (2014). *Teaching with infographics: Practicing new digital competencies and visual literacies.* Journal of Pedagogic Development, 4, pp. 1–10.

Pitzalis, M., & Porcu, M. (2024). *Digital capital and cultural capital in education: Unravelling intersections and* distinctions *that shape social differentiation*. British Educational Research Journal, 50, pp. 2753–2776. https://doi.org/10.1002/berj.4050

Resnik, M. (2012). Let's teach kids to code [Video]. TED. https://www.ted.com/talks/mitch_resnick_let_s_teach_kids_to_code

Resnik, M., & Rusk, N. (2020). Coding at a crossroads. Communications of the ACM. https://cacm.acm.org/research/coding-at-a-crossroads/

Scratch. (n.d.). Scratch. https://scratch.mit.edu/

Strawhacker, A., & Umaschi Bers, M. (2019). *What they learn when they learn coding: Investigating cognitive domains and computer programming knowledge in young children*. Educational Technology Research and Development, 67, pp. 541–575.

Wahyuningsih, S., et al. (2020). *STEAM learning in early childhood education: A literature review*. International Journal of Pedagogy and Teacher Education, 4(1), pp. 33–44.

Online Learner Success Dimensions and Factors for Online Education: A Systematic Review

Florence Martin[1], Jered Borup[2]

[1] Department of Teacher Education and Learning Sciences, North Carolina State University, USA; fmartin3@ncsu.edu
[2] Division of Learning Technologies, George Mason University, USA; jborup@gmu.edu

Correspondence: Florence Martin: fmartin3@ncsu.edu

Abstract:

Several factors play a role in the success of online learning. We use a multidimensional perspective to identify online learner success factors through the following research questions.
1. What are the dimensions contributing to the success of online learners as identified in existing research?
2. What are the factors contributing to the success of online learners as identified in the existing research?
This review used the DISCAR systematic review process (West and Martin et al., 2024), which involved (a) designing the review, (b) setting inclusion and exclusion criteria, (c) selecting data sources, search strategies, and screening criteria, (d) extracting data from primary studies to address research questions, and (e) analyzing and synthesizing data to report findings.

Dimensions of Online Learning
Building on Martin et al.'s (2020) framework of online learning research themes, which included learner, course and instructor, and organization, in this current framework, we have added program and community as the dimensions of online learning.
Learner. The Learner dimension focuses on the various aspects of the learner who engages in learning through an online setting (Du et al., 2022; Park et al., 2021).
Course and Instructor. The Course and Instructor dimension focuses on the course that is offered online and the instructor who facilitates the course (Mbuva et al., 2023).
Program and Organization. The Program and Organization dimension focuses on the administrative and support structures that are provided by the program and/or organization that extend beyond and across courses (Leary et al., 2020; Linden et al., 2022).
Community. The Community dimension focuses on the personal and professional environments in which students live, work, and learn that can be determining factors in both their decision to enroll and success in online courses (Gravelle et al., 2024; González et al., 2022).

Online Learning Success Factors
This systematic review presents the findings of online learner success dimensions and factors from 260 studies. Focusing on four dimensions a total of 35 success factors were identified. There were 12 learner-related factors, 10 course and instructor-related factors, six program and organisation-related factors, and seven community-related factors

Learner Success Factors included Learner Readiness, Personal and Environmental Factors, Cognitive Factors, Self-Regulation, Time Management, Engagement Level, Motivational Factors, Learner Self-Efficacy, Emotional Factors, Social factors and Technology factors.

Course and Instructor Success Factors included Course Design and Organization, Course Material, Instructional Approaches, Course Activities and Assessment, Accessibility Factors, Cultural Considerations, Instructor Characteristics, Instructor Presence and Communication, Course Technology and Course Support.

Program and Organization Success Factors included Student Orientation, Faculty Professional Development, Student Academic Advising, Student Support Services, Institutional Sense of Community and Belonging and Tutoring.

Community Success Factors included Inter-role Harmony, Autonomy and Control, Emotional Support and Encouragement, Financial Support, Positive and Stable Home Environment, Assistance with Family Responsibilities and Childcare, and Help with Coursework

This online learner success framework assists students, instructors, instructional designers, and administrators in offering multidimensional support for learners to be successful in online courses. The framework with online learner success factors and dimensions also supports researchers to study them.

Keywords: Online Learning, Online Education, Learner Success, Online Instructor, Community, Program, Organization

References

Du, X., Zhang, M., Shelton, B. E., & Hung, J. L. (2022). Learning anytime, anywhere: a spatio-temporal analysis for online learning. Interactive Learning Environments, 30(1), 34-48.

González, C. A. H., & Blackford, B. J. (2022). Engagement as antecedent of academic achievement and the moderating impact of work-family-school inter-role conflict for online graduate students. The International Journal of Management Education, 20(3), 100676.

Gravelle, C. D., Brodsky, J. E., Lodhi, A. K., Zapparrata, N. M., Che, E. S., Ober, T. M., & Brooks, P. J. (2024). Remote online learning outcomes in introductory psychology during the COVID-19 pandemic. Scholarship of Teaching and Learning in Psychology, 10(4), 442–470.

Leary, H., Dopp, C., Turley, C., Cheney, M., Simmons, Z.,; Graham, C. R., & Hatch, R. (2020). Professional development for online teaching: A literature review. Online Learning, 24(4), 254-275.

Linden, K., Teakel, S., & Van der Ploeg, N. (2022). Improving student success with online embedded tutor support in first-year subjects.'A practice report'. Student Success, 13(2), 42-50

Park, J., Yu, R., Rodriguez, F., Baker, R., Smyth, P., & Warschauer, M. (2018). Understanding Student Procrastination via Mixture Models. International Educational Data Mining Society

Martin, F., Sun, T., & Westine, C. D. (2020). A systematic review of research on online teaching and learning from 2009 to 2018. Computers & education, 159, 104009.

Mbuva, J. M. (2023). Understanding the Effects of the Best Practices of Formative Feedback and Intentional Follow-Ups on Online Students' Success. Journal of Higher Education Theory & Practice, 23(18)

West, R. & Martin, F. (2024). What type of paper are you writing? A taxonomy of review and theory scholarship distinguished by their summary and advocacy arguments. Educational Technology Research and Development, 72, 2443-2476

Promoting AI Literacy: A Comprehensive Model for AI Competencies in Higher Education Institutions

Nils Aschhoff[1], Claudia Berg[2], Manuel Geisler[3], Miriam Hägerbäumer[4], Vera Kristina Lenz-Kesekamp[5], Miriam Stehling[6]

[1] Europäische Fernhochschule Hamburg (Euro-FH), Germany, Nils.Aschhoff@euro-fh.de
[2] Europäische Fernhochschule Hamburg (Euro-FH), Germany, Claudia.Berg@euro-fh.de
[3] Europäische Fernhochschule Hamburg (Euro-FH), Germany, Manuel.Geislerf@euro-fh.de
[4] Europäische Fernhochschule Hamburg (Euro-FH), Germany, Miriam.Haegerbaeumer@euro-fh.de
[5] Europäische Fernhochschule Hamburg (Euro-FH), Germany, Vera.Kristina.Lenz-Kesekamp@euro-fh.de
[6] Europäische Fernhochschule Hamburg (Euro-FH), Germany, Miriam.Stehling@euro-fh.de

Correspondence: Miriam Hägerbäumer, Miriam.Haegerbaeumer@euro-fh.de

Abstract:

Due to the growing influence of (generative) AI across various sectors, higher education institutions face the critical task of equipping students with the necessary AI competencies (Ehlers et al., 2023; Laupichler et al., 2022). Therefore, these institutions must integrate a critical examination of the opportunities and challenges of generative AI into their curricula (Bobula, 2024). This paper outlines a project of a German distance-learning university whose goal is to develop a comprehensive AI competency model that will integrate AI-related content into various degree programs.

Acknowledging the multifaceted impact of AI on education (Crompton & Burke, 2023), the project takes into account various perspectives to address AI's implications for teaching, learning, and assessment. As part of the project, an interdisciplinary team is working on creating and refining a cross-program AI competency model. This model is based on an extensive literature review of existing models, empirical findings, and expert evaluations. The identified AI competencies underwent thorough discussion, refinement, and reformulation, with four guiding principles in mind. First, the model should reflect the specific competency needs relevant to future professional fields. Additionally, it should be a general model, applicable across disciplines and functional at both the bachelor's and master's levels. Differentiation between various competency levels (basic AI competencies, competencies for professional AI use, and competencies for AI experts) should be possible. Finally, the model must remain both relevant and manageable, containing only specific AI competencies without generic meta-competencies, ensuring a carefully considered degree of differentiation (Allen & Kendeou, 2024; Annapureddy et al., 2025; Chee et al., 2024).

The competency model is part of an interactive platform designed to inform educators about AI literacy, assist in systematically selecting relevant AI competencies, and link these to appropriate teaching materials. The platform offers educators structured access to AI teaching materials and tools, supporting the integration of AI into curricula (Beninger et al., 2025). By facilitating the sharing of resources, best practices, and innovative approaches, the platform aims to foster exchange among educators and enhance understanding of AI literacy. Preliminary results from pilot applications of the model have received positive feedback. The ongoing elaboration is focused on refining the model's implementation, with the interactive platform's launch anticipated in the coming months.

This project aligns with broader efforts to harness AI's potential for innovation in education while critically addressing ethical considerations, disinformation, and biases (Bond et al., 2024). It contributes to the discussion on shaping digital and AI-driven educational policies that support the development of critical assessment of generative AI among students (Airaj, 2024; Memarian & Doleck, 2023). The paper provides insights into systematically integrating AI competencies in higher education. It outlines the approach of developing the AI competency model and illustrates how this model is practically integrated into the development of programs and modules. In addition to the ongoing evaluation of the AI competency model, the paper also discusses its transferability to other educational institutions.

Keywords: AI Literacy, Competency Model, AI Competencies, Generative AI

References

Airaj, M. (2024). Ethical artificial intelligence for teaching-learning in higher education. *Education and Information Technologies, 29*(13), 17145–17167. https://doi.org/10.1007/s10639-024-12545-x

Allen, L. K. & Kendeou, P. (2024). ED-AI Lit: An interdisciplinary framework for AI Literacy in education. *Policy Insights from the Behavioral and Brain Sciences, 11*(1), 3–10. https://doi.org/10.1177/23727322231220339

Annapureddy, R., Fornaroli, A., & Gatica-Perez, D. (2025). Generative AI Literacy: Twelve defining competencies. *Digital Government: Research and Practice*, *6*(1), 1-21. https://doi.org/10.1145/3685680

Beninger, S., Reppel, A., Stanton, J., & Watson, F. (2025). Facilitating Generative AI Literacy in the face of evolving technology: Interventions in marketing classrooms. *Journal of Marketing Education*, *0*(0), 1-14. https://doi.org/10.1177/02734753251316569

Bond, M., Khosravi, H., De Laat, M., Bergdahl, N., Negrea, V., Oxley, E., Pham, P., Chong, S. W. & Siemens, G. (2024). A meta systematic review of artificial intelligence in higher education: A call for increased ethics, collaboration, and rigour. *International Journal of Educational Technology in Higher Education, 21*, Article 4. https://doi.org/10.1186/s41239-023-00436-z

Bobula, M. (2024). Generative artificial intelligence (AI) in higher education: A comprehensive review of challenges, opportunities, and implications. *Journal of Learning Development in Higher Education, 30*. https://doi.org/10.47408/jldhe.vi30.1137

Chee, H., Ahn, S., & Lee, J. (2024). A competency framework for AI Literacy: Variations by different learner groups and an implied learning pathway. *British Journal of Educational Technology,* 1-37. https://doi.org/10.1111/bjet.13556

Crompton, H. & Burke, D. (2023). Artificial intelligence in higher education: The state of the field. *International Journal of Educational Technology in Higher Education, 20*, Article 22. https://doi.org/10.1186/s41239-023-00392-8

Ehlers, U.-D., Lindner, M., Sommer, S. & Rauch, E. (2023). AICOMP - Future skills in a world increasingly shaped by AI. *Ubiquity Proceedings.* https://doi.org/10.5334/uproc.91

Laupichler, M. C., Aster, A., Schirch, J. & Raupach, T. (2022). Artificial intelligence literacy in higher education: A scoping literature review. *Computers and Education, 3,* Article 100101. https://doi.org/10.1016/j.caeai.2022.100101

Memarian, B. & Doleck, T. (2023). Fairness, Accountability, Transparency, and Ethics (FATE) in Artificial Intelligence (AI) and higher education: A systematic review. *Computers and Education: Artificial Intelligence, 5*, Article 100152. https://doi.org/10.1016/j.caeai.2023.100152

Co-designing Educational Futures in the Age of AI

Stephanie Wilson[1], Carmen Vallis[2], Dewa Wardak[3], Alison Casey[4]

[1] The University of Sydney Business School, The University of Sydney, Australia; stephanie.wilson@sydney.edu.au
[2] The University of Sydney Business School, The University of Sydney, Australia; carmen.vallis@sydney.edu.au
[3] The University of Sydney Business School, The University of Sydney, Australia; dewa.wardak@sydney.edu.au
[4] The University of Sydney Business School, The University of Sydney, Australia; alison.casey@sydney.edu.au

Correspondence: Stephanie Wilson: stephanie.wilson@sydney.edu.au

Abstract:

Recently, research on Generative AI (GenAI) in higher education has surged, but it remains focused on technology rather than pedagogy and ethics (Zawacki-Richter et al., 2024). Participatory approaches are much needed to engage educators and create positive and preferred educational futures.

At the University of Sydney Business School, we use a co-design approach that draws on our experience of facilitating over 150 projects in a six-year strategic education initiative (Wilson et al., 2021; Vallis et al., 2022, Wardak et al., 2024; Zeivots et al., 2024). In this presentation, we share three examples of how co-design has been used to collectively engage teachers, students, educational developers and learning designers in the exploration and development of GenAI in higher education. Our examples demonstrate a novel, strategic approach to integrating AI with pedagogy, rather than merely as a tool to be embedded.

In the first example, interdisciplinary collaboration between business and educational academics was invited in workshops on assessment design that integrates GenAI. For example, co-design between educational developers and experts in international business led to assessments that integrated AI literacy, critical thinking, and professional writing skills, rather than the technology itself. Finance educators and educational developers also co-designed structured writing workshops with students on how to use AI tools to refine reports, improving logic, structure, and research depth (Hendrischke et al., 2025).

In the second example, co-design workshops were run with teachers, third-space professionals and students to explore GenAI through metaphors (Vallis et al., 2024a). In this case, the co-design approach introduced activities for exploring GenAI in imaginative ways. Rather than teaching participants how to prompt or direct them to specific ways of using the technology, metaphors were used to facilitate creative and critical inquiry. In this way, the approach supported critical reflection and collaboration as distinct from instrumental approaches to educational technologies (Gupta, 2024). Participants indicated that the workshop fostered a sense of community and shared learning amongst the diverse group.

The third example describes a project that used co-design to explore the potential of using GenAI for educational video presentations in a module on business ethics (Vallis et al., 2024b). Teachers, educational developers, learning designers and media producers developed AI-generated avatars, along with interactive materials to immerse students in the ethics of business intelligence. The project led to the development of an educational design pattern for adaptation by others (Vallis, 2024).

Our examples emphasise the need for pedagogical responses that are collaborative, active, creative and critical to support the implementation of GenAI as a strategy in higher education. Co-design, as a participatory approach to designing educational experiences using GenAI, supports the co-existence of multiple positions for communal knowledge (Jandric et al. 2023). Our choice of design approach matters, as designing for education is intertwined with politics, personal relationships, legacies of exclusion and oppression, and impacts on the planet (Macgilchrist, 2023).

In this session, participants will discuss the potential of co-design for implementing GenAI in their own contexts and for shaping preferred educational futures. Together we look ahead, and ask: *How might higher education evolve if AI were always co-designed with educators and students at the center?*

Keywords: co-design, participatory approaches, artificial intelligence, higher education, educational futures

---

References

Gupta, A., Atef, Y., Mills, A., & Bali, M. (2024). Assistant parrot or colonizing loudspeaker? ChatGPT metaphors for developing critical AI literacies. Open Praxis, 16(1). : 10.55982/openpraxis.16.1.631

Hendrischke, H., Nagar, S., Sun, J., Petersen, S., & Vallis, C. (2025, February 25). How academics in the business school are using generative AI with report writing. *Teaching@Sydney*. https://educational-innovation.sydney.edu.au/teaching@sydney/how-academics-in-the-business-school-are-using-generative-ai-with-report-writing/

Jandrić, P., Luke, T.W., Sturm, S. *et al.* (2023). Collective writing: The continuous struggle for meaning-making. *Postdigit alScience and Education, 5*, 851–893. :10.1007/s42438-022-00320-5

Kleinsmann, M., & Valkenburg, R. (2008). Barriers and enablers for creating shared understanding in co-design projects. *Design Studies, 29*(4), 369–386. :10.1016/j.destud.2008.03. 003

Macgilchrist, F., Allert, H., Pargman, T. C., & Jarke, J. (2023). Designing postdigital futures. Which designs? Whose futures? *Postdigital Science and Education.* :10.1007/s42438-022-00389-y

Vallis, C., Wilson, S., & Casey, A. (2024a). Generative AI: Beyond the binaries with metaphors. ASCILITE Conference 2024, Melbourne, Australia: ASCILITE. :10.14742/apubs.2024.1408

Vallis, C., Wilson, S., Gozman, D., & Buchanan, J. (2024b). Student perceptions of AI-generated avatars in teaching business ethics: We might not be impressed. *Postdigital Science and Education, 6*(2), 537-555. 10.1007/s42438-023-00407-7

Vallis, C., Wilson, S., Tyrrell, J., & Narayan, V. (2022). Co-design as professional learning: Pulling each other in different directions, pulling together. In D. Forbes, R. Walker (Eds.). Developing Online Teaching in Higher Education: Global Perspectives on Continuing Professional Learning and Development, (pp. 133-146). Cham, Switzerland: Springer.

Vallis, C. (2024). Generative AI for educational video presentations. CLaS Design Patterns, accessed March 16, 2024, https://clasdesignpatterns.com/generative-ai-for-educational-video-presentations/

Wardak, D., Wilson, S., & Zeivotz, S. (2024). Co-design as a networked approach to designing educational futures. *Postdigital Science and Education, 6*(1), 194-210. :10.1007/s42438-023-00425-5

Wilson, S., Huber, E., & Bryant, P. (2021). Using co-Design processes to support strategic pedagogical change in business education. In T.U. Thomsen, A. Lindgreen, A. Kjaergaard, E. Rosier, A. Tuncdogan (Eds.), Handbook of Teaching and Learning at Business Schools: A Practice-Based Approach, (pp. 20-35). Cheltenham: Edward Elgar Publishing.

Zawacki-Richter, O., Bai, J. Y. H., Lee, K., Slagter van Tryon, P. J., & Prinsloo, P. (2024). New advances in artificial intelligence applications in higher education? *International Journal of Educational Technology in Higher Education*, *21*(1), 32. :10.1186/s41239-024-00464-3

Zeivots, S., Hopwood, N., Wardak, D., & Cram, A. (2024). Co-design practice in higher education: Practice theory insights into collaborative curriculum development. *Higher Education Research and Development,* Published Online: 4 October 2024. :10.1080/07294360.2024.2410269

Learning Skills Through the Design of Serious Games in Virtual Reality: The 'Sociogamers' Project

Manuela Repetto[1], Simona Tirocchi[2]

[1] University of Turin, Italy; manuela.repetto@unito.it
[2] University of Turin, Italy; simona.tirocchi@unito.it

Correspondence: Manuela Repetto: manuela.repetto@unito.it

Abstract:

Education in recent years has increasingly interfaced with the world of digital technologies (Selwyn, 2016; 2021), which are contributing to transforming the spaces, times, and styles of teaching and learning. Within the influence exerted by new digital technologies, gamification, game-based learning, and Virtual Reality (VR) also play a role. The development and experimentation of serious games in education already boast extensive literature (Gros, 2007; Bellotti et al., 2011), including references to Virtual Reality aspects (Di Natale et al., 2020; Lampropoulos & Kinshuk, 2024).

The "Sociogamers" project, developed starting in 2024, aims to integrate VR into social sciences curricula at the University of Turin to enhance the learning process across three different study programs. Adopting an interdisciplinary, bottom-up, peer-to-peer, and user-generated approach, the study follows a multi-phase development process structured according to the Design Thinking methodology.

The learning needs assessment of a sociology course ("Network Society") has identified critical themes for intervention, on which immersive educational games are being developed. The ten sociological topics selected for game design cover both sociological theory and social research methodology: *Social Capital, Descriptive Social Norms, Sociological Perspective vs. Individual Perspective, Good Sociological Questions, Status Bias, Group Segregation, Qualitative Interview, Gender Inequality in the Labor Market, Social Control, Self-Fulfilling Prophecy.* Building on this foundation and using a design model based on the identification of learning objectives and on the creation of authentic scenarios and game situations that promote experiential learning (Alrehaili & Osman, 2022; Asad et al., 2021), groups of students from the Sociology of Education and Game-Based Learning courses are developing (March 2025) 40 serious games, referred to as "sociogames". These games, developed through the CoSpaces Edu Pro platform, will subsequently be validated and used by students in the "Network Society" course.

In this context, the development of serious games on sociological themes represents for students an opportunity not only for improving exam performance and acquiring disciplinary and learning design skills, but also for enhancing transversal and soft skills (Buendía García et al., 2013).

Through a qualitative study, conducted using semi-structured questionnaires administered to students participating in the experiment (both the designers and the "developers" of the game), this paper aims to explore (and potentially confirm) the hypothesis that the design and development of serious games can enhance abilities such as communication, collaboration, critical thinking, and problem-solving. The hypothesis suggests that the co-creation process of the game stimulates teamwork, conflict management, and adaptability, while the necessity of modelling social dynamics within gameplay fosters critical reflection and empathy. These aspects are crucial not only in higher education but also in the job market, particularly within the context of a global, post-pandemic society (Jandrić, 2020; Arredondo-Trapero et al. 2024).

In this sense, the integration of serious game design into educational curricula can represent an effective methodology for developing soft skills, which are commonly defined as non-technical skills that enable individuals to interact effectively and cooperatively with others (Kopolovich, 2020; Marin-Zapata, Román-Calderón, Robledo-Ardila, & Jaramillo-Serna, 2022).

Keywords: Digital education, Virtual Reality, Game-Based Learning, Soft skills, UGC, Sociology.

References

Alrehaili, E. A., & Al Osman, H. (2022). A virtual reality role-playing serious game for experiential learning. *Interactive Learning Environments*, *30*(5), 922-935.

Arredondo-Trapero, F. G., Guerra-Leal, E. M., Kim, J., & Vázquez-Parra, J. C. (2024). Competitiveness, quality education and universities: the shift to the post-pandemic world. *Journal of Applied Research in Higher Education*, 16(5), 2140-2154.

Asad, M. M., Naz, A., Churi, P., & Tahanzadeh, M. M. (2021). Virtual reality as pedagogical tool to enhance experiential learning: a systematic literature review. *Education Research International*, *2021*(1), 7061623.

Bellotti, F., Ott, M., Arnab, S., Berta, R., de Freitas, S., Kiili, K., & De Gloria, A. (2011, October). Designing serious games for education: from pedagogical principles to game mechanisms. In *Proceedings of the 5th European Conference on Games Based Learning* (pp. 26-34). Greece: University of Athens.

Buendía García, F., García-Martínez, S., Navarrete-Ibañez, E. M., & Cervelló-Donderis, M. (2013). Designing serious games for getting transferable skills in training settings. *Interaction Design and Architecture (s)*, (19), 47-62.

Gros, B. (2007). Digital games in education: The design of games-based learning environments. *Journal of research on technology in education*, *40*(1), 23-38.

Di Natale, A. F., Repetto, C., Riva, G., & Villani, D. (2020). Immersive virtual reality in K-12 and higher education: A 10-year systematic review of empirical research. *British Journal of Educational Technology*, 51(6), 2006–2033. https://doi.org/10.1111/bjet.13030

Jandrić, P. (2020). Postdigital research in the time of Covid-19. Postdigital Science and Education, 2, 233-238.

Kopolovich, O. (2020). Learning soft skills in the digital age: Challenges and insights from development and teaching'Negotiation Management'MOOC. *Online Journal of Applied Knowledge Management (OJAKM)*, *8*(2), 91-106.

Lampropoulos, G., & Kinshuk. (2024). Virtual reality and gamification in education: A systematic review. *Education Tech Research and Development*, 72, 1691–1785. https://doi.org/10.1007/s11423-024-10351-3

Marin-Zapata, S. I., Román-Calderón, J. P., Robledo-Ardila, C., & Jaramillo-Serna, M. A. (2022). Soft skills, do we know what we are talking about?. *Review of Managerial Science*, *16*(4), 969-1000.

Selwyn, N. (2016), *Is technology good for education?*, John Wiley & Sons.

Selwyn, N. (2021), *Education and technology: Key issues and debates*. Bloomsbury Publishing.

Rewilding Education: Hacking Innovative Pedagogies Across Transnational Contexts to Address Critical Digital Literacies and AI Integration (2022-2025)

Kathrin Otrel-Cass[1], Niels Ruan Lyngdorf[2], Eamon Costello[3], Melanie Gürentz[1], Iris Mendel[1], Olena Beskorsa[1]

[1] University of Graz, Austria; kathrin.otrel-cass@uni-graz.at; melanie.guerentz@uni-graz.at; iris.mendel@uni-graz.at; olena.beskorsa@uni-graz.at
[2] Aalborg University, Denmark; nel@plan.aau.dk
[3] Dublin City University, Ireland; eamon.costello@dcu.ie

Correspondence: Kathrin.otrel-cass@uni-graz.at

Abstract:

We present a synthesis of findings from a series of activities (2022-2025) funded by the European Commission that explored 'Hacking Innovative Pedagogies'. We explored how educational 'hacking'—conceptualised as the creative disruption of conventional pedagogical approaches—promotes critical digital literacies, increases student engagement, and creates more inclusive learning environments. Drawing on transnational collaborations in Nordic, Irish and Austrian educational contexts, we explain our theoretical foundations, methodological approaches, and empirical findings to identify implications for educational practice and future research directions. We have used the notion of "hacking" as a powerful metaphor and a deliberate conceptual move towards subversive, creative approaches to institutional practices (Otrel-Cass et al., 2024). We connect to the conference's focus on AI in education through a hacking lens, to discuss how creative problem solving and the repurposing of existing systems can support new goals. We show how a rewilding approach to conventional pedagogy can support critical literacy and agile thinking. We highlight areas that have been identified by students, teachers and IT expert communities to be 'hackable'—such as outdated assessment systems, content-focused curricula in skills-demanding environments, and educational institutions that replicate rather than challenge social inequalities. We present three emerging areas of future interest: (1) Connections to decolonial pedagogies, to explore the potential convergence between educational "hacking" and decolonial educational frameworks (Stein et al., 2022). (2) Potential applications in addressing educational inequalities to consider applications in different contexts, from serving marginalised communities to educational initiatives for excluded populations. (3) The role of artificial intelligence in enabling or constraining pedagogical innovation and new forms of educational "hacking" through personalisation, simulation, and creative tools that can augment but can never replace human capabilities.

Keywords: Hacking, Rewilding, Creativity

References

Otrel-Cass, K., Costello, E., Lyngdorf, N. E. R., & Mendel, I. (2024). Methods for dreaming about and reimagining digital education. *International Journal of Educational Technology in Higher Education, 21*(1), 31.

Stein, S., Andreotti, V., Ahenakew, C., & Hunt, D. (2022). The complexities and paradoxes of decolonization in education. In *Reimagining globalization and education* (pp. 198-213). Routledge.

Advancing Research in Digital Didactics with AI: DI-daktika project

Giedre Tamoliune[1], Airina Volungevičienė[2], Elena Trepulė[3]

[1] Vytautas Magnus University, Lithuania; giedre.tamoliune@vdu.lt
[2] Vytautas Magnus University, Lithuania; airina.volungeviciene@vdu.lt
[3] Vytautas Magnus University, Lithuania; elena.trepule@vdu.lt

Correspondence: Giedre Tamoliune: giedre.tamoliune@vdu.lt

Abstract:

The European Commission's (2023a) report "Generative AI for School Teachers" highlights AI's potential to transform some aspects of education systems. However, it calls for a critical consideration of what we aim to change and why. Before integrating AI into classroom curriculum, educators must define the specific educational problem(s) it aims to address and decide on the conditions under which the use of AI elements will be considered effective in enhancing teaching, learning, and assessment. This necessitates teachers possess the knowledge, skills and values to make informed decisions regarding using AI elements in classroom curriculum.
The discussions on using and integrating AI into didactical practices and classroom curriculum encompass a broad spectrum of applications. These include, but are not limited to, curriculum content refinement, development of adaptable teaching resources, facilitation of classroom interactions, and implementation of learning assessment strategies (Ligozat, Klette, Almqvist, 2023). Empirical research supports the potential of AI to increase teachers' efficacy by assisting in explanations of complex tasks to students (Deschenes, 2020), providing actionable feedback to teachers (Kurdi et al., 2020), generating diversified and alternative tasks and assessment tools designed for enhancing achievement (Matsuda, Weng, & Wall, 2020), and helping in the learning process planning (Holmes & Tuomi, 2022). Furthermore, AI's educational applications extend to personalized learning support, interactive dialogue systems, intelligent educational games (Su & Yang, 2023; Kurdi et al., 2020), virtual learning assistants, etc.

Despite extensive discussions about AI and the ethical considerations regarding its use, more in-depth research is needed on evidence-based decisions for the didactical changes needed to use elements of AI.

European Commission (2023b) identifies three key elements that need to be considered while planning the use of AI in education: a human-centred design, context-sensitive teaching strategies, and reliable methods for measuring AI's effectiveness in teaching, learning, and assessment. Despite AI's possibilities, it also brings challenges, including the need to improve teachers' digital competence, pedagogical adaptation, system reliability, equity, transparency, and explainability of EdTech solutions, as well as navigating ethical considerations. The European Digital Education Action Plan (European Commission, 2020) acknowledges these challenges, emphasizing that educators' effective deployment of digital technology is crucial for realising high-quality education.

The presentation will introduce the national research project "Questioning Digital Didactics in School Education with the Elements of Artificial Intelligence" (DI-daktika), which aims to identify when digital didactics with elements of AI, informed by LA, enhance teaching, learning, and assessment. This research underscores the critical role of data-informed curriculum design, particularly in teaching, learning, and assessment. As AI becomes more present in education, it is important to equip teachers with AI tools, knowledge, and understanding of the potential of LA to guide their curriculum interventions. Recognising teachers' and learners' existing use of AI, this project aims to promote research-based AI implementation in classroom didactics. Furthermore, the project results will demonstrate the value of data-based decisions regarding AI integration, facilitating sustainable and ethical AI use at the institutional level and leading to enhanced teaching, learning, and assessment.

Keywords: digital didactics, artificial intelligence, learning analytics, classroom curriculum

References

Deschênes, M. (2020). Recommender systems to support learners' Agency in a Learning Context: a systematic review. International Journal of Educational Technology in Higher Education, 17, 50. https://doi.org/10.1186/s41239-020-00219-w

European Commission (2020). Digital Education Action Plan 2021-2027 Resetting education and training for the digital age. https://eur-lex.europa.eu/legal-content/EN/TXT/PDF/?uri=CELEX:52020DC0624

European Commission (2023a). Generative AI for School Teacher. https://wikis.ec.europa.eu/download/attachments/48761872/Generative%20AI%20for%20School%20Teachers_Input%20paper.pdf?version=1&modificationDate=1713272393899&api=v2

European Commission (2023b). 2023 Strategic Foresight Report Sustainability and people's wellbeing at the heart of Europe's Open Strategic Autonomy. https://commission.europa.eu/document/f8f67d33-194c-4c89-a4a6-795980a1dabd_en

Holmes, W. & Tuomi, I. (2022). State of the art and practice in AI in education. European Journal of Education, Research, Development and Policy, 57(4). https://doi.org/10.1111/ejed.12533

Kurdi, Gh., Leo, J., Parsia, B., Sattler, U., Al-Emari, S. (2020). A Systematic Review of Automatic Question Generation for Educational Purposes. International Journal of Artificial Intelligence in Education, 30, 121-204. https://doi.org/10.1007/s40593-019-00186-y

Ligozat, F., Klette, K., Almqvist, J. (eds) Didactics in a Changing World. Transdisciplinary Perspectives in Educational Research, vol 6. Springer, Cham. https://doi.org/10.1007/978-3-031-20810-2_1

Matsuda, N., Weng, W. & Wall, N. (2020). The Effect of Metacognitive Scaffolding for Learning by Teaching a Teachable Agent. International Journal of Artificial Intelligence in Education, 30, 1–37. https://doi.org/10.1007/s40593-019-00190-2

Su, J., & Yang, W. (2023). Unlocking the Power of ChatGPT: A Framework for Applying Generative AI in Education. ECNU Review of Education, 6(3), 355–366. https://doi.org/10.1177/20965311231168423

From Pixels to Pedagogy: Student Teachers Reimagine Learning with Game Based Learning Environment

Aysegul Liman-Kaban[1], Anne O'Dwyer[2], Aisling Leavy[3], Michael McNamara[4], Edward Corry[5], Mairead Ryan[6]

[1] STEM department, Mary Immaculate College, Ireland; Aysegul.limanakaban@mic.ul.ie
[2] STEM department, Mary Immaculate College, Ireland; Anne.ODwyer@mic.ul.ie
[3] STEM department, Mary Immaculate College, Ireland; Aisling.Leavy@mic.ul.ie
[4] STEM department, Mary Immaculate College, Ireland; Michael.McNamara@mic.ul.ie
[5] STEM department, Mary Immaculate College, Ireland; Edward.Corry@mic.ul.ie
[6] STEM department, Mary Immaculate College, Ireland; Mairead.Ryan@mic.ul.ie

Correspondence: Aysegul Liman Kaban: Aysegul.limanakaban@mic.ul.ie

Abstract:

This study investigates how 22 fourth-year teacher candidates in Ireland designed and facilitated a game-based learning initiative using Minecraft Education Edition (MEE) with sixth-grade pupils. Rather than centering solely on engagement, the research critically examines the pedagogical tensions, implementation challenges, and systemic constraints encountered during the process. As part of a structured teacher education program, participants completed a series of targeted MEE training workshops before leading a four-hour classroom session in a local primary school. Qualitative data were gathered through semi-structured focus group interviews—conducted with five groups of 4 participants each—exploring their experiences, perceptions, and emergent complexities. Data were gathered through five semi-structured focus group interviews and analyzed thematically. Findings reveal a complex interplay between teacher candidates' initial digital insecurities and their evolving perceptions of MEE's educational value. While pupils demonstrated high engagement and creativity, candidates encountered persistent challenges in aligning open-ended tasks with curriculum outcomes, particularly in mathematics. Difficulties also emerged in managing collaboration, pacing lessons effectively, and adapting MEE content to different learner profiles. Despite the strong motivational potential of digital games, infrastructural limitations and limited teacher readiness undermined deeper pedagogical integration. The study highlights the need for sustained support, explicit curricular alignment, and critical digital pedagogy frameworks within initial teacher education. Without these, digital innovation risks being reduced to engagement-focused experimentation rather than meaningful educational transformation. These findings resonate with existing literature positioning MEE as a promising yet problematic educational tool. Singh and Sun (2025) frame MEE as a metaverse platform capable of enhancing STEM learning and social presence, while Slattery et al. (2024) highlight its capacity to foster collaboration, creativity, and inclusion. While Minecraft Education Edition offers significant potential to foster creativity, engagement, and student agency, this study underscores that its effective integration into primary education hinges on teacher preparedness, pedagogical coherence, and institutional support structures.

Keywords: Minecraft Education Edition, Game-Based Learning, Initial Teacher Education, Digital Pedagogy, Primary Education

Description of the Initiative

This study was embedded within an initial teacher education (ITE) module aimed at developing fourth-year teacher candidates' critical competencies in digital pedagogy through the practical application of Minecraft Education Edition (MEE). The initiative was conceived as an authentic, school-based intervention designed to explore the pedagogical affordances, constraints, and implementation challenges associated with game-based learning in Irish primary education.

The initiative was structured into three interrelated phases, each informed by principles of experiential learning, reflective practice, and curricular alignment:

Professional Development and Technical Capacity Building

Teacher candidates participated in a sequence of scaffolded workshops delivered by the Microsoft DreamSpace team. These sessions, conducted in both face-to-face and synchronous online formats, aimed to build foundational fluency with MEE. The training introduced participants to key functionalities of the platform (e.g., navigation, collaborative tools, assessment features) and exposed them to curriculum-aligned digital resources, including build challenges and STEM-based learning environments. Additional emphasis was placed on the use of unplugged (offline) preparatory activities and the integration of subject-specific outcomes, particularly in mathematics.

Collaborative Lesson Design and Classroom Implementation

Following the training phase, the 22 ITE candidates were divided into five collaborative planning groups. Each group co-designed and facilitated two MEE-based lessons with a cohort of 27 sixth-grade pupils in a local Irish primary school.

In Session 1, pupils engaged in a "Build Your School Logo" challenge, which encouraged symbolic representation, visual literacy, and creative expression.

In Session 2, pupils participated in a more structured "Build a Bridge" challenge, which required the application of mathematical concepts such as ratio, area, and scale, alongside planning and design skills.

Each lesson incorporated an unplugged activity, where pupils first conceptualized their designs on paper before translating them into digital builds within the MEE environment. Candidates assumed facilitative teaching roles, guiding the learning process, managing collaborative group dynamics, and providing just-in-time support while monitoring curricular engagement and digital task completion.

Reflective Analysis and Data Collection

After implementation, qualitative data were generated through five semi-structured focus group interviews (n=22). These discussions explored candidates' experiences of planning, teaching, and reflecting on MEE integration in a live classroom setting. Transcripts were thematically analyzed to identify key patterns related to pedagogical decision-making, student engagement, infrastructural constraints, and the evolving professional identities of the candidates.

This study demonstrates that while Minecraft Education Edition holds significant promise as a tool for fostering creativity, collaboration, and learner engagement in primary education, its effective pedagogical integration is far from guaranteed. The experiences of 22 fourth-year teacher candidates, working with 27 sixth-grade pupils, revealed a consistent tension between the motivational affordances of game-based learning and the practical challenges of aligning digital tasks with curricular objectives. Candidates grappled with issues of digital fluency, time management, lesson design, and infrastructural limitations, all of which impacted the coherence and impact of their instructional efforts. Importantly, the findings highlight that student engagement—though essential—is insufficient as a sole metric of success; meaningful digital integration demands critical pedagogy, clear learning intentions, and sustained institutional support. As initial teacher education continues to embrace digital tools, there is an urgent need to move beyond instrumental approaches and toward deeper, critically informed frameworks that empower novice teachers to navigate the pedagogical complexities of 21st-century classrooms.

References

Singh, M., & Sun, D. (2025). Evaluating Minecraft as a game-based metaverse platform: exploring gaming experience, social presence, and STEM outcomes. *Interactive Learning Environments*, 1–23. https://doi.org/10.1080/10494820.2025.2459200Books

Slattery, E. J., Butler, D., O'Leary, M., & Marshall, K. (2023). Teachers' experiences of using Minecraft Education in primary school: An Irish perspective. *Irish Educational Studies*, *43*(4), 965–984. https://doi.org/10.1080/03323315.2023.2185276

Empathy through Generative Artificial Intelligence: Implications for the Education of Human-Centered Professionals

Pamsy Hui[1], Sau Fong Leung[2], Kong Yam[3], Catherine Cheung[4], Jacky Ng[5], Amy Ou[6], Melody Chao[7]

[1] Department of Management and Marketing, The Hong Kong Polytechnic University, Hong Kong; pamsy.hui@polyu.edu.hk
[2] School of Nursing, The Hong Kong Polytechnic University, Hong Kong; sau.fong.leung@polyu.edu.hk
[3] Department of Applied Social Sciences, The Hong Kong Polytechnic University, Hong Kong; yam.kong@polyu.edu.hk
[4] School of Hotel and Tourism Management, The Hong Kong Polytechnic University, Hong Kong; catherine.cheung@polyu.edu.hk
[5] Department of Applied Social Sciences, The Hong Kong Polytechnic University, Hong Kong; jackyck.ng@polyu.edu.hk
[6] Department of Management and Marketing, The Hong Kong Polytechnic University, Hong Kong; amy-yi.ou@polyu.edu.hk
[7] Department of Management, Hong Kong University of Science and Technology, Hong Kong; mchao@ust.hk

Correspondence: Pamsy Hui: pamsy.hui@polyu.edu.hk

Abstract:

The tremendous development in Generative Artificial Intelligence (GenAI) in the past few years has attracted much attention and triggered much discussion about how GenAI can be used in human-centric professions (e.g., healthcare and social work). Despite concerns related to biases, empathy and the accuracy of information provided, there is evidence that GenAI can hold tremendous promise in the tackling of complex problems (Blease et al., 2024; Morrow et al., 2023). We investigate how GenAI can be incorporated into the education of responsible human-centred professionals. Specifically, we are interested in the impact of GenAI usage on the efficiency and effectiveness of problem solving among students enrolled in programs in human-centric fields (i.e., mental nursing, social work, and hospitality management). We are also curious how the usage of GenAI influence students' efficacy of the knowledge and skills that they have obtained conventionally in classrooms and through practice (e.g., internship). Students were invited to participate in a survey study. Participants were randomly assigned into one of three conditions: no GenAI, GenAI with specific prompting instructions, and GenAI without instructions. They were then asked to provide a solution to a complex scenario that is specific to their training. Preliminary analyses of a small sample suggested that, consistent with Noy & Zhang (2023), GenAI sped up the problem-solving process, but only if prompting instructions were given. The use of GenAI in general was also found to have increased the satisfaction of, as well as the confidence and optimism, participants felt about the problem-solving process. Interestingly, participants who used GenAI also felt that their professional training was more helpful, used more of that knowledge, and could empathize with the service target better. The differences were particularly evident for students who had some experience in their chosen professions. Analyses examining whether the proposed solutions exhibited qualitative differences were underway. These initial findings show that there is a place for GenAI in the development of empathetic professionals in human-centric fields. However, good prompt engineering and experience in context are critical if one is to make use of GenAI more efficiently and effectively.

Keywords: Generative AI, Empathy, AI in Education, Prompt Engineering

References

Blease, C., Torous, J., McMillan, B., Hägglund, M., & Mandl, K. D. (2024). Generative language models and open notes: Exploring the promise and limitations. *JMIR Medical Education*, 10, e51183. https://doi.org/10.2196/51183

Morrow, E., Zidaru, T., Ross, F., Mason, C., Patel, K. D., Ream, M., & Stockley, R. (2023). Artificial intelligence technologies and compassion in healthcare: A systematic scoping review. *Frontiers in Psychology*, 13, 971044. https://doi.org/10.3389/fpsyg.2022.971044

Noy, S., & Zhang, W. (2023). Experimental evidence on the productivity effects of generative artificial intelligence. *Science*, 381, 187-192. https://doi.org/10.1126/science.adh2586

Responsible and Creative Experimentation with GenAI for Learning and Teaching, Examples from Practice

Chrissi Nerantzi[1], Javiera Atenas[2], Marianthi Karatsiori[3]

[1] School of Education, University of Leeds, United Kingdom; c.nerantzi@leeds.ac.uk
[2] School of Social Sciences and Humanities, University of Suffolk, United Kingdom; j.atenas@uos.ac.uk
[3] Educational and Social Policy Department, University of Macedonia, Greece; mkaratsiori@uom.edu.gr

Correspondence: Chrissi Nerantzi: c.nerantzi@leeds.ac.uk

Abstract:

Students in higher education are using genAI in their learning and assessment more than educators, it seems. The work we would like to present focuses on how we can build AI literacy ethically and responsibly. Existing research indicates that students often harbour misconceptions about AI, such as believing it closely resembles human brain function. Notably, students from non-technical fields tend to exhibit more significant knowledge gaps concerning AI. (Sulmont et al., 2019; Hornberger, Bewersdorff, and Nerdel, 2023), however, AI literacy plays a crucial role in developing students' AI self-efficacy, as at a personal level, learners tend to develop stronger self-efficacy when they experience success through their own efforts (Bewersdorff et al., 2025). In the meantime, educators remain skeptical, and hope that one morning they will wake up and the AI nightmare will be over. Educators are particularly concerned about assessment and rightly so. It is about time to reimagine assessment that is purposeful and meaningful (Picasso et al. 2024; Nerantzi, 2024). Some narratives about students accused of cheating are emerging (Gorichanaz, 2023). How can educators awaken their curiosity and imagination to engage with AI to learn with their students how to use it ethically, critically and creatively? Through responsible and ethical experimentation, use and evaluation in a range of areas of their practice will help them gain insights into its affordances, pitfalls and opportunities for learning (Felix and Webb, 2024). This contribution reports on a series of AI related curricular and extra-curricular projects. These include the co-creation with educators and students in partnership of open educational resources, activities and crowdsourced publications led by the University of Leeds (Brew et al., 2023; Abegglen et al., 2024; Nerantzi et al., 2023) and the international Creativity for learning in higher education (#creativeHE) community (). These aim to showcase and curate novel practices and experimentations but also engage us critically and creatively to develop AI literacy (Atenas et al., 2025) and provide food for thought for others who may be reluctant to engage with genAI. Come along to discuss what we have learnt based on these multiple projects about openness, creativity and collaborative working about learning and teaching with AI and how partnership working with educators and students can uncover valuable ideas for practice.

Keywords: learning with genAI, teaching with genAI, responsible experimentation, genAI projects, open education, partnership working

References

Abegglen, S., Nerantzi, C., Martínez-Arboleda, Karatsiori, M., Atenas, J., & Rowell, C. (Eds.) (2024). Towards AI literacy: 101+ creative and critical practices, perspectives and purposes. #creativeHE. :https://doi.org/10.5281/zenodo.11613520

Atenas J., Havemann L., & Nerantzi C. (2025). Critical and creative pedagogies for artificial intelligence and data literacy: an epistemic data justice approach for academic practice. *Research in Learning Technology, 32*. :https://doi.org/10.25304/rlt.v32.3296

Brew, M., Taylor, S., Lam, R., Havemann, L., & Nerantzi, C. (2023). Towards developing AI literacy: Three student provocations on AI in higher education, Special issue: Generative AI and implications for open online and distance education. *Asian Journal of Distance Education*. :http://www.asianjde.com/ojs/index.php/AsianJDE/article/view/726

Bewersdorff, A., Hornberger, M., Nerdel, C., & Schiff, D. S. (2025). AI advocates and cautious critics: How AI attitudes, AI interest, use of AI, and AI literacy build university students' AI self-efficacy. *Computers and Education: Artificial Intelligence, 8*, 100340. :https://doi.org/10.1016/j.caeai.2024.100340

Felix, J., & Webb, L. (2024). Use of artificial intelligence in education delivery and assessment. UK Parliament Post. 23 February 2024. :https://doi.org/10.58248/PN712

Gorichanaz, T. (2023). Accused: How students respond to allegations of using ChatGPT on assessments, Learning: Research and Practice, *9*(2), 183-196, : https://doi.org/10.1080/23735082.2023.2254787

Hornberger, M., Bewersdorff, A., & Nerdel, C. (2023). What do university students know about Artificial Intelligence? Development and validation of an AI literacy test. *Computers and Education: Artificial Intelligence, 5*, 100165. :https://doi.org/10.1016/j.caeai.2023.100165

Nerantzi, C., Abegglen, S., Karatsiori, M., & Martinez-Arboleda, A. (Eds.) (2023). 101 creative ideas to use AI in Education. #creativeHE. :https://doi.org/10.5281/zenodo.8072949

Nerantzi, C. (2024). Rethinking volume, variety and value of assessment in the era of GenAI, Media & Learning Association. 31 May 2024. :https://media-and-learning.eu/subject/artificial-intelligence/rethinking-volume-variety-and-value-of-assessment-in-the-era-of-genai/

Picasso, F., Atenas, J., Havemann, L., & Serbati, A. (2024). Advancing Critical Data and AI Literacies Through Authentic and Real-World Assessment Design Using a Data Justice Approach. *Open Praxis, 16*(3), 291–310. :https://doi.org/10.55982/openpraxis.16.3.667

Sulmont, E., Patitsas, E., & Cooperstock, J. R. (2019). Can You Teach Me To Machine Learn? *Proceedings of the 50th ACM Technical Symposium on Computer Science Education*, 948–954. :https://doi.org/10.1145/3287324.3287392

Designing Participatory Action Research on Teachers' AI Literacy in Super-Diverse Adult Education

Enrico Vignando[1,2]

[1] DILL, University of Udine, Italy
[2] University of Modena-Reggio Emilia, Italy

Correspondence: Enrico Vignando: enrico.vignando@unimore.it

Abstract:

The research investigates in-service teachers' professional development in AI literacy (Knoth et al., 2024; Laupichler et al., 2022; Sperling et al., 2024), with a closer focus on their interactions with generative artificial intelligence in Provincial Centers for Adult Education (CPIA) in Italy. In CPIAs, adult education and learning, generally influenced by post-digitality (Floreancig et al., 2018, 2020), is also markedly characterized by super-diversity (Pasta & Zoletto, 2023). These two characteristics make CPIAs a rich context for investigating the impact of GenAI on education (Miao & Cukurova, 2024; Sattelmaier & Pawlowski, 2023) and adults' capabilities (Bondi et al., 2021; Markauskaite et al., 2022; Poquet & De Laat, 2021). For this aim, participatory action research is proven to be an effective approach to include different perspectives (Medrado & Verdegem, 2024), encourage teachers' reflection on AI in education, while guaranteeing their active engagement (McTaggart, 1991) and promoting change in their pedagogies (Mezirow, 1991) towards a critical, ethical, and reflective integration of AI in their teaching practices. This contribution illustrates the research design by describing its qualitative methods, theoretical background, teachers' involvement in co-designing and conducting the research, and data collection instruments. Along with detailing the contextual features that have facilitated and hindered the design of participatory action research on professional development of in-service teachers' AI literacy, expected and partial results of the ongoing investigation are presented.

Keywords: participatory action research; super-diversity; adult learning and education; AI literacy; teachers' professional development

References

Bondi, E., Xu, L., Acosta-Navas, D., & Killian, J. A. (2021). Envisioning Communities: A Participatory Approach Towards AI for Social Good. *Proceedings of the 2021 AAAI/ACM Conference on AI, Ethics, and Society*, 425–436. https://doi.org/10.1145/3461702.3462612

Floreancig, P., Fusco, F., Virgilio, F., Zanon, F., & Zoletto, D. (Eds.). (2018). *Tecnologie, lingua, cittadinanza: Percorsi di inclusione dei migranti nei CPIA*. Franco Angeli.

Floreancig, P., Fusco, F., Virgilio, F., Zanon, F., & Zoletto, D. (Eds.). (2020). *Ricerca-azione e trasformazione delle pratiche didattiche: L'esperienza del Piano pluriennale di formazione per le scuole ad alta incidenza di alunni stranieri*. Franco Angeli.

Knoth, N., Decker, M., Laupichler, M. C., Pinski, M., Buchholtz, N., Bata, K., & Schultz, B. (2024). Developing a holistic AI literacy assessment matrix – Bridging generic, domain-specific, and ethical competencies. *Computers and Education Open*, *6*, 100177. https://doi.org/10.1016/j.caeo.2024.100177

Laupichler, M. C., Aster, A., Schirch, J., & Raupach, T. (2022). Artificial intelligence literacy in higher and adult education: A scoping literature review. *Computers and Education: Artificial Intelligence*, *3*, 100101. https://doi.org/10.1016/j.caeai.2022.100101

Markauskaite, L., Marrone, R., Poquet, O., Knight, S., Martinez-Maldonado, R., Howard, S., Tondeur, J., De Laat, M., Buckingham Shum, S., Gašević, D., & Siemens, G. (2022). Rethinking the entwinement between artificial intelligence and human learning: What capabilities do learners need for a world with AI? *Computers and Education: Artificial Intelligence*, *3*, 100056. https://doi.org/10.1016/j.caeai.2022.100056

McTaggart, R. (1991). Principles for Participatory Action Research. *Adult Education Quarterly*, *41*(3), 168–187. https://doi.org/10.1177/0001848191041003003

Medrado, A., & Verdegem, P. (2024). Participatory action research in critical data studies: Interrogating AI from a South–North approach. *Big Data & Society*, *11*(1), 20539517241235869. https://doi.org/10.1177/20539517241235869

Mezirow, J. (1991). *Transformative dimensions of adult learning* (1. ed). Jossey-Bass.

Miao, F., & Cukurova, M. (2024). *AI competency framework for teachers*. UNESCO. https://doi.org/10.54675/ZJTE2084

Pasta, S., & Zoletto, D. (2023). Postdigital Intercultures. Interculture Postdigitali. *Pasta S., Zoletto D. (2023). Postdigital Intercultures. Scholé. Rivista Di Educazione e Studi Culturali, LXI (2), 19-46.*, *2*(LXI), 304.

Poquet, O., & De Laat, M. (2021). Developing capabilities: Lifelong learning in the age of AI. *British Journal of Educational Technology*, *52*(4), 1695–1708. https://doi.org/10.1111/bjet.13123

Sattelmaier, L., & Pawlowski, J. M. (2023). Towards a Generative Artificial Intelligence Competence Framework for Schools. In M. D. Sulistiyo & R. A. Nugraha (Eds.), *Proceedings of the International Conference on Enterprise and Industrial Systems (ICOEINS 2023)* (Vol. 270, pp. 291–307). Atlantis Press International BV. https://doi.org/10.2991/978-94-6463-340-5_26

Sperling, K., Stenberg, C.-J., McGrath, C., Åkerfeldt, A., Heintz, F., & Stenliden, L. (2024). In search of artificial intelligence (AI) literacy in teacher education: A scoping review. *Computers and Education Open*, *6*, 100169. https://doi.org/10.1016/j.caeo.2024.100169

Will AI Hijack our Agency? Four Mindsets for Human-AI Collaboration

Eran Barak-Medina[1]

[1]Holon Institute of Technology, Faculty of Instructional Technologies, Israel

Correspondence: Eran Barak-Medina; eranba@hit.ac.il

Abstract:

There are ways to use AI that could help us thrive, and others that will lead to skill erosion and Agency hijacking. Four distinct human mindsets can be identified in the way people approach AI, each carries benefits and risks:

i. Delegation mindset: Delegating tasks to AI. This approach can lead to time saving and efficiency, but also to dilution of Agency and degradation of skills.

ii. Empowerment mindset: Using AI with the goal of achieving more than a person or AI could do separately. This approach capitalizes on Human-AI collaboration and could increase Agency, but also carries a risk of dependency.

iii. Avoidance mindset: AI is perceived as threatening or not good enough, so its usage is avoided. This approach could lead to becoming irrelevant in a competitive environment.

iv. Suspension mindset: Avoiding the usage of AI deliberately for the purpose of developing skills or for the pure enjoyment of the action. This approach should be seriously considered in training professionals.

The central claim of this proposal is that these four mindsets, with their merits and caveats, should be pivotal in various educational and training contexts. They should be considered as part of AI Literacy, as students of all ages need to develop a deliberate personal mindset and control over their decision to use AI. Training systems should consider the point in which skill development might be hindered by too early adoption of AI.

Examples to demonstrate the questions around the four mindsets and to discuss the practices derived from it will be presented from both an M.A course on Instructional Technologies, and high school program for using AI to prepare for graduation exams in Math and Language.

Keywords: AI Literacy, Generative AI, Critical Thinking, Human-AI Collaboration.

References

Allen, L. K., & Kendeou, P. (2024). ED-AI Lit: An Interdisciplinary framework for AI literacy in education. *Policy Insights from the Behavioral and Brain Sciences*, *11*(1), 3-10.

Chiu, T. K., Ahmad, Z., Ismailov, M., & Sanusi, I. T. (2024). What are artificial intelligence literacy and competency? A comprehensive framework to support them. *Computers and Education Open*, *6*, 100171.

Ding, A. C. E., Shi, L., Yang, H., & Choi, I. (2024). Enhancing teacher AI literacy and integration through different types of cases in teacher professional development. *Computers and Education Open*, *6*, 100178.

Spatola, N. (2024). The efficiency-accountability tradeoff in AI integration: Effects on human performance and over-reliance. *Computers in Human Behavior: Artificial Humans*, *2*(2), 100099.

Vasconcelos, H., Jörke, M., Grunde-McLaughlin, M., Gerstenberg, T., Bernstein, M. S., & Krishna, R. (2023). Explanations can reduce overreliance on ai systems during decision-making. *Proceedings of the ACM on Human-Computer Interaction*, *7*(CSCW1), 1-38.

Watkins, R., & Barak-Medina, E. (2024). AI's Influence on Human Creative Agency. *Creativity Research Journal*, 1-13.

Watkins, R., Barak-Medina, E., & Pugh, K. B. (2024, May 7). Is AI Hijacking Our Agency?. https://doi.org/10.31219/osf.io/8bpaq

Zhai, C., Wibowo, S., & Li, L. D. (2024). The effects of over-reliance on AI dialogue systems on students' cognitive abilities: a systematic review. *Smart Learning Environments*, *11*(1), 28.

Fostering AI Literacy in Higher Education: Lessons from Assessment Redesign

Nirmani Wijenayake[1]

[1]University of New South Wales, Sydney, Australia; b.wijenayakeg@unsw.edu.au

Correspondence: Nirmani Wijenayake: b.wijenayakeg@unsw.edu.au

Abstract:

The advent of generative AI in higher education has sparked considerable discourse on its potential and challenges (Selwyn, 2024). While these tools present opportunities for innovation, they also raise critical concerns about accuracy, ethical use, and equitable access. This research explores how students interact with generative AI tools during assessments, addressing the pressing need to understand these dynamics in the context of evolving educational policies and practices.

The study was conducted within a large general education science course, where students were allowed unrestricted use of AI tools for a 40% weighted assessment task. As part of this initiative, students provided reflective insights into their AI usage. These reflections revealed valuable data on their engagement, highlighting both benefits and challenges. The findings have informed a comprehensive redesign of assessment practices, aimed at fostering AI literacy and integrating critical engagement strategies into the curriculum.

Thematic analysis of student reflections identified key patterns in AI usage, perceived benefits, and challenges. Most students utilised AI for summarising information, sourcing references, and structuring their submissions. However, concerns about the reliability of AI-generated content led many to cross-reference outputs with traditional sources. These insights underscored the importance of balancing AI use with critical thinking and traditional research skills. Students also emphasised the need for clear guidance on effectively integrating AI tools into their academic work, highlighting a broader need for educator support and targeted pedagogical strategies.

The research contributes to ongoing discussions on transformative innovation through AI in education by providing actionable insights for assessment design. It underscores the role of educators in scaffolding AI usage to ensure equitable access and effective learning outcomes. This project has not only deepened understanding of students' interactions with AI but also driven significant revisions in assessment design, aligning them with the goals of fostering AI literacy, critical engagement, and academic integrity.

Keywords: Artificial intelligence, assessment, skill development, reflection, redesign

References

Selwyn, N. (2024). On the limits of artificial intelligence (AI) in education. *Nordic Journal of Pedagogy and Critique, 10(1)*, 3-14. https://doi.org/10.23865/ntpk.v10.6062

Integration of Generative AI (GenAI) Tools in Academic Learning: Analysis of Usage Patterns Among Undergraduate Students

Gila Kurtz[1], Nohar Raz Fogel[1], Hayley Weigelt-Marom[1], Oren Ben-Ahron[1], Omri Khana[1],

[1] Faculty of Instructional Technologies, HIT, Israel; gilaku@hit.ac.il

Correspondence: Gila Kurtz: gilaku@hit.ac.il

Abstract:

Generative artificial intelligence (GenAI) is rapidly entering academic curricula (Dempere et al., 2023; Kurtz et al., 2024), yet empirical evidence on how novices appropriate these tools across authentic design workflows remains scarce. This exploratory study examined GenAI usage patterns among 112 first-year undergraduate students in the Faculty of Instructional Technologies who collaborated on an integrated final project spanning three courses in user-interface (UI) design and web accessibility during the spring semester of 2024.

A post-project questionnaire captured tool choice, frequency of prompting, phase-specific purposes, and perceived value (1–5 Likert scale) across four canonical design phases: ideation, research, design specification, and asset creation. Descriptive statistics reveal that ChatGPT was the dominant platform, trailed by Google Gemini and Leonardo AI. Overall adoption followed a phase-dependent gradient: moderate uptake in research (45.5 %) and asset-creation phases (51.5 %), contrasted with lower engagement during ideation (21.5 %) and specification (27.3 %). Prompt activity exhibited a pronounced U-shaped trajectory—averaging 7.1 prompts in ideation, dipping to 5.1 and 4.1 in the subsequent phases, then rising to 7.4 during creation—suggesting an experiential learning curve characterized by early experimentation, mid-course efficiency consolidation, and renewed tactical prompting once concrete deliverables were in focus.

Concurrently, students' mean perceived value of GenAI increased monotonically from 3.6 (ideation) to 4.7 (creation), indicating that perceived utility intensified as proficiency and task-tool fit improved. Qualitative comments underscored three primary affordances: (a) rapid generation of conceptual stimuli (personas, mood boards), (b) iterative refinement of visual assets (illustrations, iconography), and (c) just-in-time explanations of accessibility heuristics. Notably, usage dipped in phases where course guidelines explicitly recommended canonical scholarly databases or instructor-provided templates, implying a regulatory effect of faculty scaffolding on GenAI engagement.

While the single-cohort context and self-report measures limit generalizability, the findings illuminate a phased adoption pattern that can inform instructional design. The study's findings highlight the evolving role of GenAI tools in academic projects, with students demonstrating increased proficiency and perceived value as they progress through different phases. Future research could explore the long-term impact of GenAI integration on learning outcomes and skill development in instructional technology programs. Additionally, investigating potential differences in GenAI usage patterns across various disciplines and academic levels could provide valuable insights for educators and policymakers. These insights contribute to a nascent evidence base on integrating GenAI into project-based learning and lay the groundwork for developing fine-grained pedagogical guidelines that balance creativity, efficacy, and ethical considerations.

Keywords: Generative AI, Learning Technologies, Higher Education, ChatGPT, UI Design

References

Dempere, J., Modugu, K., Hesham, A., & Ramasamy, L. K. (2023). The impact of ChatGPT on higher education. *Frontiers in Education*, 8, Article 1206936. https://doi.org/10.3389/feduc.2023.1206936

Kurtz, G., Amzalag, M., Shaked, N., Zaguri, Y., Kohen-Vacs, D., Gal, E., ... & Barak-Medina, E. (2024). Strategies for Integrating Generative AI into Higher Education: Navigating Challenges and Leveraging Opportunities. *Education Sciences*, *14*(5), 503.

Navigating Resistance: Understanding Student Reluctance to Experiment with AI in Higher Education

Lucy Gill-Simmen[1], Christiana Tsaousi[2]

[1] School of Business and Management, Royal Holloway University of London, UK; Lucy.Gill-Simmen@royalholloway.ac.uk
[2] Department of Communication and Marketing, Cyprus University of Technology, Cyprus; christiana.tsaousi@cut.ac.cy

Correspondence: Lucy Gill-Simmen: Lucy.Gill-Simmen@royalholloway.ac.uk

Abstract:

The integration of artificial intelligence (AI) in higher education has the potential to transform the learning experience, enhance pedagogical strategies and equip students with the digital competencies required in the modern workplace (Selwyn, 2019). However, student engagement with AI tools remains inconsistent, with a notable reluctance observed among Cypriot university students. This paper explores the theoretical underpinnings of this resistance and proposes a conceptual framework to explain students' reluctance to engage with AI-driven learning methods.

Traditional educational norms have long emphasised memorisation and structured learning, creating a rigid academic culture that discourages experimentation (Freire, 1970). Despite pedagogical advances advocating active learning, Cypriot students are reluctant to engage with AI tools, in part due to these entrenched academic traditions. This is in line with the principles of Davis' (1989) Technology Acceptance Model (TAM), which posits that perceived usefulness and perceived ease of use significantly influence technology adoption. Students often perceive AI as overly complex and unrelated to their immediate academic needs, thereby limiting their engagement (Lin & Chen, 2024). In addition, Dweck's (2006) concept of a fixed mindset plays a crucial role, as students who fear failure are less likely to experiment with unfamiliar technologies.

Cultural influences further contextualise this reluctance with uncertainty avoidance, suggesting that students from high uncertainty avoidance cultures prefer structured learning environments and resist ambiguity (Joy & Kolb, 2009). This is consistent with Cypriot students' preference for familiar, instructor-led approaches over open-ended experimentation.

Another critical factor influencing AI resistance is the lack of psychological safety in academic environments. Edmondson (1999) stresses the importance of fostering a culture that encourages risk-taking and learning from failure. If students fear judgment or academic penalties for making mistakes, they are less likely to explore AI-driven tools. This is compounded by the lack of a strong digital literacy framework, which leaves many students feeling unprepared to engage with AI technologies (Warschauer & Matuchniak, 2010).

Furthermore, confidence in digital skills affects students' willingness to engage with AI. Students with low digital self-efficacy are less motivated to experiment, which increases avoidance behaviours (Bandura, 1997). This also affects students' future employability, as employers expect graduates to have the necessary digital competencies to improve work-related tasks, which further emphasises the critical need to develop these competencies through education (Mukhamediev et al., 2022). In addition, Engeström (2001) helps to contextualise how broader socio-cultural structures, including rigid assessment-driven academic expectations, shape resistance to technological innovation in higher education.

To address these challenges, educators need to cultivate a culture of curiosity and experimentation. Strategies such as integrating AI literacy into the curriculum, creating psychologically safe learning environments and providing scaffolded learning experiences can help mitigate student reluctance (Jisc, 2022). By using insights from these theoretical perspectives, institutions can bridge the gap between AI innovation and student adoption, ensuring that graduates are equipped with the digital skills needed for the evolving workforce. Understanding and addressing student reluctance is essential to unlocking the full potential of AI in higher education and fostering a generation of adaptable, technologically fluent professionals.

This paper aims to contribute to the growing discourse on AI integration in education by identifying key barriers to student adoption and proposing strategies to foster greater engagement. By examining the intersection of psychological, cultural and pedagogical factors, we aim to provide educators and policymakers with actionable insights that can facilitate a more inclusive and effective approach to AI-driven learning. Ultimately, our goal is to bridge the gap between technological innovation and student confidence, ensuring that all learners are empowered to navigate and benefit from the digital transformation of education.

Keywords: AI in Higher Education; Student Reluctance; Digital Competencies; Psychological Safety and Technology

---

References

Bandura, A. (1997). *Self-efficacy: The exercise of control*. Freeman.

Davis, F. D. (1989). Perceived usefulness, perceived ease of use, and user acceptance of information technology. *MIS Quarterly*, 13(3), 319-340.

Dweck, C. S. (2006). *Mindset: The new psychology of success*. Random House.

Edmondson, A. (1999). Psychological safety and learning behavior in work teams. *Administrative Science Quarterly*, 44(2), 350-383.

Engeström, Y. (2001). Expansive learning at work: Toward an activity theoretical reconceptualization. *Journal of Education and Work*, 14(1), 133-156.

Freire, P. (2020). *Pedagogy of the oppressed*. In Toward a sociology of education (pp. 374-386). Routledge.

Jisc. (2023). AI in higher education: Opportunities and challenges. https://repository.jisc.ac.uk/8783/1/ai-in-tertiary-education-report-june-2022.pdf

Joy, S., & Kolb, D. A. (2009). Are there cultural differences in learning style? *International Journal of Intercultural Relations*, 33(1), 69-85.

Lin, H., & Chen, Q. (2024). Artificial intelligence (AI)-integrated educational applications and college students' creativity and academic emotions: Students and teachers' perceptions and attitudes. *BMC Psychology*, 12(1), 487.

Rogers, E. M., & Williams, D. (1983). *Diffusion of innovations*. The Free Press.

Selwyn, N. (2019). *Should robots replace teachers?: AI and the future of education*. John Wiley & Sons.

Warschauer, M., & Matuchniak, T. (2010). New technology and digital worlds: Analyzing evidence of equity in access, use, and outcomes. *Review of Research in Education*, 34(1), 179-225.

Mukhamediev, R.I.; Popova, Y.; Kuchin, Y.; et al. (2022) Review of Artificial Intelligence and Machine Learning Technologies: Classification, Restrictions, Opportunities and Challenges. *Mathematics*, 10, 2552.

Preparing for Work in the Age of Generative AI: How Higher Education Leaders Shape Institutional Resourcing Strategies to Prepare Students for AI-Driven Labour Markets

Patricia Mangeol[1], Josep Duart Maria[2], Àngels Fitó Bertran[3]

[1] Education & ICT Doctoral Programme, Universitat Oberta de Catalunya, Spain; pmangeol@uoc.edu
[2] Faculty of Psychology and Educational Sciences, Universitat Oberta de Catalunya, Spain; jduart@uoc.edu
[3] Faculty of Economics and Business, Universitat Oberta de Catalunya, Spain; afitob@uoc.edu

Correspondence: Patricia Mangeol: pmangeol@uoc.edu

Abstract:

The capabilities of generative artificial intelligence (AI) to perform complex tasks and its rapid adoption in society raise critical questions about the skills education systems should prioritize to prepare students for evolving labour markets. While research on generative AI impacts focuses both on pedagogy (Bhullar et al., 2024) and labour markets (Bick, Blandin & Deming, 2024), little attention has been given to how higher education institutions (HEIs) and their leaders respond strategically to AI-driven job market shifts.

This study aims to fill this gap by examining (i) how institutions and leaders respond to AI-driven labour markets, (ii) how they use resourcing strategies – both financial and human – as tools for transformation and (iii) the factors shaping leaders' decision-making and institutional strategy implementation.

Rooted in organizational sociology, the research examines how a balance of institutional structures and individual agency shapes leaders' resourcing strategies (Thornton et al., 2012). Further, it builds on other disciplinary lenses to guide the analysis: at a macro level, labour market economics helps conceptualize generative AI's current and potential labour market impacts (Webb, 2020). At a micro level, technology adoption frameworks help analyze individual perceptions of generative AI as an emerging technology (Venkatesh, 2012).

Methods include a systematic literature review, an online survey of leaders and a multiple-case study design to delve into institutional and leaders' decisions related to preparing students for AI-driven labour markets in three HEIs. Institutions will be selected to compose a comparable yet diverse sample.

- Similarity criteria: Institutions located in jurisdictions with comparable economic development, offering comprehensive education, with a stated focus on social mobility, labour market preparation and generative AI.
- Diversity criteria: Institutions from three regions – Europe, North America, and Asia – to account for economic, policy, and cultural differences, and at least one online institution to assess the role of intensive technology integration on AI strategies.

One of the case study institutions will be the Universitat Oberta de Catalunya, a fully online institution. Insights from preliminary interviews with leaders will be discussed, highlighting the potential of this research to contribute to organizational change theories and offer practical insights for HEI leaders navigating resourcing decisions in AI-driven labour markets.

Keywords: Generative Artificial Intelligence, Higher Education Leadership, Financial and Human Resources, Labour Markets Transformation, Institutional Logics, Technology Adoption

References

Bick, A., Blandin, A. and D. J. Deming, The Rapid Adoption of Generative AI Alexander, NBER Working Paper No. 32966 September 2024 JEL No. J24, O33.

Bhullar, PS., Joshi, M. and R. Chugh, R (2024), "ChatGPT in higher education: A synthesis of the literature and a future research agenda", Education and Information Technologies, Vol. 29, Iss. 16, 21501-21522.

Thornton, P. H., Ocasio, W., & Lounsbury, M. (2012). The institutional logics perspective: A new approach to culture, structure, and process. Oxford University Press.

Venkatesh, V., Morris, M. G., Davis, G. B., & Davis, F. D. (2003). User acceptance of information technology: Toward a unified view. MIS Quarterly, 27(3), 425–478.

Webb, M. (2020). The Impact of Artificial Intelligence on the Labor Market. SSRN Electronic Journal https://doi.org/10.2139/ssrn.3482150

University Students' Experiences with Generative AI: The Role of Critical Thinking and Technology Readiness

Vanessa Donadel[1], Marco Zuin[2], Simona Romani[3]

[1] Impresa e Management, Libera Università Internazionale degli Studi Sociali "Guido Carli", Italy; vdonadel@external.luiss.it
[2] Psicologia, Istituto Universitario Salesiano Venezia, Italy; m.zuin@iusve.it
[3] Impresa e Management, Libera Università Internazionale degli Studi Sociali "Guido Carli", Italy; sromani@luiss.it

Correspondence: Vanessa Donadel: vdonadel@external.luiss.it

Abstract:

The integration of Generative AI (GenAI) in higher education presents opportunities and challenges, shaping students' learning experiences, cognitive engagement, and productivity. This study examines how individual traits—Critical Thinking (CT), Growth Mindset (GM), Technology Readiness Index (TRI) dimensions (Optimism, Innovativeness, Discomfort, Insecurity)—influence students' perceptions of GenAI. Using a mixed-methods approach, data were collected from university students through qualitative responses to open-ended questions and standardized Likert-scale questionnaires measuring Critical Thinking, Growth Mindset, and Technology Readiness Index.

Thematic analysis identified four overarching themes in students' evaluations: Complementary Use of GenAI (Quality of Output; Creative Support & Learning), Efficiency and Productivity (Time-Saving; Use & Accessibility), AI Limitations (Error Detection; Technical Constraints), and Emotional-Social Impact (Ethical Concerns; Psychological Reactions).

Statistical analysis using Chi-square tests demonstrated significant associations between individual traits and students' evaluations of GenAI. Significant relationships emerged between Critical Thinking and Quality of Output ($\chi^2 = 8.41$, $p = 0.004$), Error Detection ($\chi^2 = 4.06$, $p = 0.044$), as well as Efficiency and Productivity ($\chi^2 = 4.56$, $p = 0.033$), indicating that individuals with higher CT levels exhibited greater scrutiny of AI-generated content, set higher expectations, and frequently identified inaccuracies, whereas those with lower CT levels demonstrated a more accepting attitude. Additionally, Optimism was significantly related to Error Detection ($\chi^2 = 5.58$, $p = 0.018$), with lower optimism levels correlating with reduced error identification. Discomfort was associated with Efficiency and Productivity ($\chi^2 = 8.59$, $p = 0.003$), as students with lower discomfort levels viewed AI as a useful productivity tool, while those with higher discomfort levels were hesitant to acknowledge its benefits.

To further explore these relationships, binary logistic regression models were employed using three dependent variables derived from qualitative coding: Quality & Precision of Output, Time-Saving, and Efficiency and Productivity. Independent variables included Critical Thinking, Growth Mindset, TRI dimensions, and gender. The regression model predicting Quality & Precision of Output ($R^2 = 0.264$, $\chi^2 = 15.6$, $p = 0.029$) revealed that higher CT levels were negatively associated with references to quality ($\beta = -0.2470$, $p = 0.032$), suggesting that students with strong critical thinking skills set higher expectations and identified more flaws in AI-generated content. Analysis of Time-Saving ($R^2 = 0.444$, $\chi^2 = 25.6$, $p < 0.001$) showed that Innovativeness ($\beta = -0.2248$, $p = 0.021$) negatively predicted efficiency mentions, as highly innovative students prioritized advanced functionalities over task optimization. Discomfort ($\beta = 0.2052$, $p = 0.026$) was positively associated with efficiency mentions, indicating that students with higher Discomfort focused on AI's immediate benefits, such as speed and task simplification. The model predicting Efficiency and Productivity ($R^2 = 0.441$, $\chi^2 = 22.5$, $p = 0.002$) found a positive association between Discomfort ($\beta = 0.3584$, $p = 0.011$) and efficiency mentions, while Insecurity ($\beta = -0.2173$, $p = 0.038$) had a negative effect, suggesting that students with high Discomfort tend to acknowledge AI's role in enhancing efficiency, whereas those with high Insecurity remained skeptical.

These findings provide insights for refining AI literacy programs, fostering critical engagement with AI-generated content, and optimizing AI integration in higher education.

Keywords: Generative Artificial Intelligence, Critical Thinking, Technology Readiness, Higher Education, Students

References

Sosu, E. M. (2013). The development and psychometric validation of a critical thinking disposition scale. *Thinking Skills and Creativity*, *9*, 107-119. 10.1016/j.tsc.2012.09.002

Parasuraman, A. (2000). Technology Readiness Index (TRI): A multiple-item scale to measure readiness to embrace new technologies. *Journal of Service Research*, *2*(4), 307-320. 10.1177/109467050024001

Dweck, C. S., (1999). *Self-theories: Their Role in Motivation, Personality, and Development* (1st ed.). Psychology Press.

Feeding the Beast: Anthropomorphic Metaphors for GenAI in Education

Carmen Vallis[1], Stephanie Wilson[2], Alison Casey[3]

[1] Business School, The University of Sydney, Australia; carmen.vallis@sydney.edu.au
[2] Business School, The University of Sydney, Australia; stephanie.wilson@sydney.edu.au
[3] Business School, The University of Sydney, Australia; alison.casey@sydney.edu.au

Correspondence: Carmen Vallis: carmen.vallis@sydney.edu.au

Abstract:

In educational settings, metaphors work on both conceptual and emotional levels, influencing practice, relationships and understanding (Cameron 2003; Cortazzi & Jin 2020). Metaphors also shape our understanding of GenAI's capabilities and limitations (Gupta et al. 2024). However, over-reliance on simplistic metaphors can be misleading (Cameron 2003; Fraser 2018). Anthropomorphic metaphors, for instance, falsely equate human and algorithmic capabilities (Kajava & Sawhney 2023; Bender 2024).

In this presentation, we discuss anthropomorphic metaphors generated in three workshops conducted at the University of Sydney to help teachers, students, and professional staff explore and make sense of GenAI in higher education (Vallis et al., 2024). Identifying conceptual similarities across workshop groups enabled us to identify patterns in how GenAI is understood and imagined across the educational community. Our analysis revealed that participants frequently anthropomorphised GenAI through role-based metaphors, a tendency documented elsewhere (Kajava & Sawhney 2023; Tlili et al. 2023; Bender 2024; Gupta et al. 2024). This diverse set of metaphors indicated complex perceptions of human-AI relationships in educational contexts, beyond their use as a cognitive tool.

Three distinct themes were identified in how participants conceptualise human-AI relationships: GenAI as helper, as learning partner, and as friend/foe. For example, ChatGPT was characterised as a learning *assistant*, a finding noted in other studies (Punar Özçelik & Yangın Ekşi 2024). Metaphors for the learning process, such as a *sparring partner,* suggested engaging learners in interactive dialogue and the critical evaluation of AI-generated responses (Walter 2024). Notable dualities surfaced in how participants conceptualised their relationship with GenAI. While some metaphors reflected a celebratory tone, many more foregrounded adversarial roles, from a *cheating assistant* to the unreliable *drunk reviewer*.

Participants also acknowledged that their 'relationship' with AI is different to a human one, and were cautious about the roles GenAI might play in education. Anthropomorphic metaphors, such as GenAI as both friend and foe, expressed this wary acceptance. This tension was variously described as a *double-edged sword,* a *friendly terminator* or a *frenemy,* conceptualizations also found in Derakshan and Ghiasvand (2024) and Wysel (2023). This ambivalence crystallised in the metaphor *feeding the beast.* Ironically, we sustain an insatiable system that could harm us, one that demands ever more attention, resources, and energy.

When a metaphor frames our understanding and attitudes without scrutiny, it constrains how we perceive and interact with technology. Anthropomorphising GenAI can over-attribute autonomy or intent, obscuring the ethical, social, and material dimensions of its development and use in education (Gupta 2024; Kajava & Sawhney 2023). Our study suggests that language and metaphors matter; they shape society's understanding and governance of technological systems. This tendency to anthropomorphise may diminish our humanity, reducing complex thinking and feeling to computer (Bender 2024). An awareness of this tension manifested in participants' attempts to position GenAI's capabilities relative to human cognition, as a machine with a *brain*, on a par with human thinking capabilities. Our work aims to problematize this persistent anthropomorphism of AI's capabilities and how we see ourselves in relation to technology.

Keywords: artificial intelligence, GenAI, metaphor, anthropomorphising, higher education

References

Bender, E. M. (2024). Resisting Dehumanization in the Age of "AI." *Current Directions in Psychological Science: A Journal of the American Psychological Society*, 33(2), 114–120. :10.1177/09637214231217286

Cameron, L. (2003). *Metaphor in educational discourse*. London & New York: Continuum.

Cortazzi, M., & Jin, L. (2020). Elicited metaphor analysis: researching teaching and learning. In: Ward MRM & Delamont S *Handbook of Qualitative Research in Education*. Cheltenham: Edward Elgar Publishing. pp. 488-505. :10.4337/9781788977159.00054

Fraser, R. E. (2018). The Ethics of Metaphor, *Ethics, 128*(4): 728–755. :10.1086/697448

Gupta, A., Atef, Y., Mills, A., & Bali, M. (2024). Assistant Parrot or Colonizing Loudspeaker? ChatGPT Metaphors for Developing Critical AI Literacies. *Open Praxis, 16*(1), 37-53. :10.55982/openpraxis.16.1.631

Kajava, K., & Sawhney, N. (2023). Language of algorithms: agency, metaphors, and deliberations in AI discourses. In: Lindgren, S., *Handbook of Critical Studies of Artificial Intelligence* Cheltenham: Edward Elgar Publishing. pp. 224–236. :10.4337/9781803928562.00025

Punar Özçelik, N., & Yangın Ekşi, G. (2024). Cultivating writing skills: the role of ChatGPT as a learning assistant—a case study. *Smart Learning Environments, 11*(10), 1-18. :10.1186/s40561-024-00296-8

Tlili, A., Shehata, B., Adarkwah, MA., Bozkurt, A., Hickey, DT., Huang, R., & Agyemang, B. (2023). What if the devil is my guardian angel: ChatGPT as a case study of using chatbots in education. *Smart Learning Environments, 10*(1). :10.1186/s40561-023-00237-x

Vallis, C., Wilson, S., & Casey, A. (2024). Generative AI: Beyond the binaries with metaphors. *ASCILITE Publications*, 590–595. https://doi.org/10.14742/apubs.2024.1408

Walter, Y. (2024). Embracing the future of Artificial Intelligence in the classroom: the relevance of AI literacy, prompt engineering, and critical thinking in modern education. *International Journal of Educational Technology in Higher Education, 21*(1): 15. :10.1186/s41239-024-00448-3

Wysel, M. (2023). Frenemies - Unleashing the Power of ChatGPT in Assessments. In: ASCILITE, Christchurch December 2023, pp. 614–618. :10.14742/apubs.2023.653

Exploring the Impact of Artificial Intelligence Training on University Faculty

Consuelo Garcia[1], Jose Sepúlveda[2]

[1] Faculty of Education, Valencia International University, Spain; mariaconsuelo.garcia@universidadviu.com
[2] School of Engineering, Science, and Technology, Valencia International University, Spain; joseramon.sepulveda@universidadviu.com

Correspondence: Consuelo Garcia: mariaconsuelo.garcia@universidadviu.com

Abstract:

The current technological revolution has placed Artificial Intelligence (AI) at the heart of the transformation of society and education. AI offers extraordinary potential for pedagogical innovation and academic research. However, to maximize the benefits of this technology, it is essential to provide adequate training to university faculty, enabling them to face AI challenges and opportunities. This study examines the impact of training in artificial intelligence on university faculty at an online institution. The primary objective was to train teachers to use AI tools and acquire the skills necessary for their effective application, enhancing both teaching and research efficiency. The training was a competency-based approach delivered through a combination of synchronous sessions and asynchronous materials, concluding with a practical assignment where participants presented evidence of using one or more of the AI tools covered in the program. The study involved a sample of 149 faculty members, of which 93 completed the training and 56 did not. The participants came from diverse academic backgrounds and exhibited varying levels of prior knowledge about AI. Three months after the program concluded, a survey was conducted to assess the frequency of AI usage and the specific purposes for which it was applied.

The results demonstrate a statistically significant association between training and increased frequency of AI usage, as evidenced by a Chi-squared test ($p = 0.002$). Faculty members who completed the training reported using AI tools more frequently than their untrained peers. Additionally, trained teachers showed a significantly higher propensity to use AI for research activities. However, no statistically significant differences were observed in the use of AI for teaching, content creation, or organization purposes between the two groups.

These findings align with existing literature emphasizing the importance of professional development in AI for educators. For instance, Mah and Groß (2024) highlight that faculty training programs significantly enhance self-efficacy and the adoption of AI tools in higher education. Similarly, Nguyen (2025) underscores the ethical and pedagogical benefits of integrating AI into academic practices, advocating for structured training to address challenges such as over-reliance and bias. Aubert et al. (2024) explore the interaction between university faculty and generative AI, emphasizing the need for critical and reflective approaches to its integration. Camacho et al. (2023) discuss the potential of AI in education while addressing the risks and ethical considerations associated with its use. Additionally, Zouhaier (2023) provides empirical evidence on the transformative impact of AI in higher education. Finally, Crompton and Burke (2023) stress the need of faculty training to bridge the gap between AI capabilities and practical application in educational settings.

The study demonstrates that AI training significantly increases faculty use of AI tools for research, enhancing academic productivity. However, the lack of impact on teaching, content creation, and organization highlights the need for future training to address these areas. These findings offer practical insights for universities to better integrate AI training for faculty.

Keywords: Artificial intelligence (AI), faculty training, usage frequency, research, Higher Education

References

Aubert, E., Gladkoff, L., Andreoli, S., Perillo, L., & Cherbavaz, M. C. (2024). Alquimia didáctica: la interacción de docentes universitarios con la Inteligencia Artificial Generativa. *TIES, Revista de Tecnología e Innovación en Educación Superior, (10)*, 37-60. :10.22201/dgtic.26832968e.2024.10.16

Camacho, M. U., Tambasco, P., Martínez, S., & Correa, M. G. (2023). El impacto de la Inteligencia Artificial en la educación. Riesgos y potencialidades de la IA en el aula. *RiiTE Revista interuniversitaria de investigación en Tecnología Educativa*, 41-57. :10.6018/riite.584501

Crompton, H., & Burke, D. (2023). Artificial intelligence in higher education: the state of the field. *International journal of educational technology in higher education, 20*(1), 22.: 10.1186/s41239-023-00392-8

Mah, D. K., & Groß, N. (2024). Artificial intelligence in higher education: exploring faculty use, self-efficacy, distinct profiles, and professional development needs. *International Journal of Educational Technology in Higher Education, 21*(1), 58. :10.1186/s41239-024-00490-1

Nguyen, K. V. (2025). The Use of Generative AI Tools in Higher Education: Ethical and Pedagogical Principles. *Journal of Academic Ethics*, 1-21. : 10.1007/s10805-025-09607-1

Zouhaier, S. (2023). The impact of artificial intelligence on higher education: An empirical study. *European Journal of Educational Sciences, 10*(1), 17-33.

How do Upper Secondary School English Language Teachers Use Generative AI to Create Materials? Preliminary Considerations from a Pilot Study

Maria Laura Ferroglio[1]

[1] PhD candidate. Department of Foreign Languages, Literatures and Modern Cultures, University of Turin, Italy. Department of Languages and Modern Cultures, University of Genoa, Italy. E-mail: marialaura.ferroglio@unito.it

Correspondence: marialaura.ferroglio@unito.it

Abstract:

Research on the use of Generative AI (GenAI) and its implications in education and teaching has proliferated in the past years (Crompton et al., 2024; Law, 2024). Advantages and drawbacks have been addressed, such as the potential to reduce teachers' workload and foster learner autonomy (Amonova et al., 2023; Barrot, 2024), These potentialities are counterbalanced by issues such as overreliance and content bias (Barrot, 2024; Binu, 2024; Cong-Lem et al., 2024; Ghafouri et al., 2024). One aspect that has been repeatedly highlighted in current research is how training and professional development are key to teachers' effective and responsible integration of GenAI in their practice (Allehyani & Algamdi, 2023; Crompton et al., 2024; Cong-Lem et al., 2024). While attempts have been made to explore teachers' acceptance of GenAI and their uses in higher education contexts (Dehghani & Mashhadi, 2024), limited empirical research has explored its hands-on use by English Language Teachers to create teaching materials or plan lessons (Dornburg & Davin, 2024, Evmenova et al., 2024; Ghafouri et al., 2024).

This paper is aimed at framing current issues in this evolving scenario by looking at current research perspectives and illustrating the preliminary findings from the author's progressing PhD research. The project investigates how Italian upper secondary teachers of English use GenAI to create lesson materials. A pilot study was conducted with a group of upper secondary English teachers in Turin, Italy, in autumn 2024 to introduce ChatGPT and ask it to design lesson materials which teachers partly or fully implemented in class. The two foci of the project are teachers' lived experiences of Gen-Ai use and their interaction with ChatGPT. In the pilot study, participants' perceptions and experiences were gathered through reflective questions, scripts of their dialogues with ChatGPT, and pre-and post-intervention focus groups. Key themes from these findings will be briefly presented and discussed in the presentation, which will include time for questions. Although the study has limitations which need addressing, findings already show how teachers gained more awareness of the tool's potential and of their training needs.

Keywords: Generative AI, English Language Teaching, Materials Design, Secondary Education

References

Allehyani, S. H., & Algamdi, M. A. (2023). Digital Competences: Early Childhood Teachers' Beliefs and Perceptions of ChatGPT Application in Teaching English as a Second Language (ESL). *International*

Journal of Learning, Teaching and Educational Research, 22(11), 343–363. https://doi.org/10.26803/ijlter.22.11.18

Amonova S., Juraeva G., & Khidoyatov M. (2023). Harnessing the Potential of Artificial Intelligence in Language Learning: Is AI Threat or Opportunity? *ACM International Conference Proceeding Series*, 292.0-297.0.

Barrot J.S. (2024). ChatGPT as a Language Learning Tool: An Emerging Technology Report. *Technology, Knowledge and Learning, 29*(2.0), 1151.0-1156.0.

Binu P.M. (2024). Affordances and Challenges of Integrating Artificial Intelligence into English Language Education: A Critical Analysis. *English Scholarship Beyond Borders, 10*(1.0), 34.0-51.0.

Cong-Lem N., Tran T.N., & Nguyen T.T. (2024). Academic integrity in the age of Generative AI: Perceptions and responses of Vietnamese EFL teachers. *Teaching English with Technology, 24*(1.0), 28.0-47.0.

Crompton H., Edmett A., Ichaporia N., & Burke D. (2024). AI and English language teaching: Affordances and challenges. *British Journal of Educational Technology, 55*(6), 2503-2529..

Dehghani, H., & Mashhadi, A. (2024). Exploring Iranian English as a foreign language teachers' acceptance of ChatGPT in English language teaching: Extending the technology acceptance model. *Education and Information Technologies, 29*(15), 19813-19834.

Dornburg, A., & Davin, K. J. (2024). ChatGPT in foreign language lesson plan creation: Trends, variability, and historical biases. *ReCALL,* 1-16.

Evmenova, A. S., Borup, J., & Shin, J. K. (2024). Harnessing the power of generative AI to support all learners. *TechTrends*, *68*(4), 820-831.

Ghafouri M., Hassaskhah J., & Mahdavi-Zafarghandi A. (2024). From virtual assistant to writing mentor: Exploring the impact of a ChatGPT-based writing instruction protocol on EFL teachers' self-efficacy and learners' writing skill. *Language Teaching Research, 1362.*

Law, L. (2024). Application of generative artificial intelligence (GenAI) in language teaching and learning: A scoping literature review. *Computers and Education Open*, 100174.

Control + Alt + Redesign: AI, Teaching, and the People Who Do Both

Danielle Maya Pratt[1], Devon Cadwell Bazata[2], Amanda Pacheco[3], Karen Haslett[4]

[1] Interdisciplinary Studies, University of Central Florida, United States of America; danielle.pratt@ucf.edu
[2] Interdisciplinary Studies, University of Central Florida, United States of America; devon.cadwellbazata@ucf.edu
[3] Interdisciplinary Studies, University of Central Florida, United States of America; amanda.pacheco@ucf.edu
[4] Interdisciplinary Studies, University of Central Florida, United States of America; karen.haslett@ucf.edu

Correspondence: Danielle Maya Pratt: danielle.pratt@ucf.edu

Abstract

What happens when a tight-knit faculty team takes a creative redesign approach to teaching with Artificial Intelligence (AI)? This paper chronicles our shared journey towards pedagogically sound integration, as we reimagined teaching within our integrative, interdisciplinary program serving over 675 students a year. Faced with students who have never opened ChatGPT or any kind of AI to those who write the code behind it, we designed a scaffolded AI literacy module that blends brain-based teaching approaches, humor, ethics, and hands-on exploration (even Skynet gets a mention). Course assignments were redesigned with a focus on practical application, transparent use, and student reflection, including adding a new AI Playground task. As we designed and redesigned, we listened to our students, drawing on survey data about student fears and hopes for the use of AI in the classroom, all while leaning into our collaborative model to keep things both human and flexible to the unique needs of our population.

In recent years, classroom conversations around AI often started with panic. Headlines focused on cheating, and our policies raced to catch up. But effective teaching is not built on discipline alone. Like Zawacki-Richter et al. (2019) point out, the educator's voice was often missing from early discussions on AI in education. We decided to change that by leading with design, not fear. Our teaching team works in a fully online, interdisciplinary program. We share a course template, group chat, and deep commitment to collaboration. This helped us move quickly when AI tools like ChatGPT became mainstream. Instead of banning them, we started redesigning around them. We launched an AI literacy module that uses approachable language, guided metacognition, and humor. It walks students through misconceptions, builds prompt engineering skills, and introduces ethical frameworks. The module ends with a playful, reflective assignment called the AI Playground, where students test a new AI use and share what they learn. These tasks are scaffolded to help everyone, from those first-time users to AI-savvy coders-feel like they can participate.

We found that transparency was key. When students know it is okay to experiment and that AI is not off-limits, they become better critical and creative thinkers. Recent research (Hubertz, Cadwell, & Pratt 1, 2025; Pacheco, 2025) show that students, especially those identifying as neurodiverse, found AI helped with brainstorming, organization, and focus. Pope and Nehmad (2023) emphasize how important it is to move beyond enforcement and toward ethical, open conversations around AI. We agree.

Ultimately, this is not just a paper about AI. It's a story about our journey, thoughtfully improving and updating our pedagogy. Teaching is still about people. Our job is to help students think critically, navigate complexity, and feel empowered to use today's tools to shape tomorrow. We believe deeply in the value of thinking. And we want students not only to think critically but to see AI as a powerful support, not a shortcut. Our pedagogy remains dynamic, relational, and human, but there is a seat at the table for our Skynet-adjacent friend, too.

Keywords: AI in higher education, instructional design, collaborative pedagogy, teaching innovation, student agency, faculty development

References

Cadwell Bazata, D., Hubertz, M., & Pratt, D.M. (2025, March 17). *Born digital, raised AI* [Conference presentation]. International Round Table Symposium, Harris Manchester College, University of Oxford, London, United Kingdom.

Pacheco, A. (2024). *Career exploration and student agency in AI-integrated classrooms* [Unpublished presentation slides].

Pratt, D.M. & Pacheco, A. (2024). *Helping students navigate career opportunities with AI: A tale of Bugs Bunny, Indiana Jones, and the learning brain.* Teaching Online Pedagogical Repository. https://topr.online.ucf.edu/helping-students-navigate-career-opportunities-with-ai-a-tale-of-bugs-bunny-indiana-jones-and-the-learning-brain/

Haslett, K., Pratt, D.M., & Pacheco, A. (2024). *AI-infused learning: Unlocking career potential*. Teaching Repository of AI-Infused Learning. https://stars.library.ucf.edu/traiil/10

Pope, J. C., & Nehmad, E. (2023). AI and academic integrity: A new frontier in higher education. *Journal of Learning and Technology*, 49(2), 45–59.

Zawacki-Richter, O., Marín, V. I., Bond, M., & Gouverneur, F. (2019). Systematic review of research on artificial intelligence applications in higher education – Where are the educators? *International Journal of Educational Technology in Higher Education*, 16(39). https://doi.org/10.1186/s41239-019-0171-0

Towards a Competency-Based Standard for Secondary Teacher Education in Ukraine: Insights from EU Models and Challenges for Post-War Reconstruction

Antonella Poce[1], Oleksandra Golovko[2],Inna Zabuzhanska[3], Renat Rizhniak[4]

[1] Department of History, Humanities and Society, University of Rome Tor Vergata, Italy; antonella.poce@uniroma2.eu
[2] Narva College, University of Tartu, Estonia; oleksandra.golovko@ut.ee
[3]Department of Foreign Languages, Vinnytsia Mykhailo Kotsiubynskyi State Pedagogical University, Ukraine; lartis.innazabuzhanska@gmail.com
[4] Department of Mathematics, Volodymyr Vynnychenko CUSU, Ukraine; rizhniak@gmail.com

Correspondence: Antonella Poce: antonella.poce@uniroma2.eu

Abstract:

Higher education plays a crucial role in shaping the future of secondary education, particularly in times of crisis and transformation. In Ukraine, the ongoing war has exacerbated existing challenges in teacher training, revealing significant gaps in competencies, pedagogical approaches, and professional readiness. This paper presents the preliminary findings of Work Package 2 (WP2) of a European project aimed at developing a Standard of Higher Education for BA students majoring in Secondary Education (Speciality 014) in Ukraine, with a focus on Ukrainian Language, Mathematics, and History.

Through desk research, stakeholder consultations, and comparative analysis of EU teacher education models, WP2 identifies critical disparities between Ukrainian and European teacher competencies. Findings highlight gaps in subject-specific skills, inclusive education practices, digital literacy, and psychological preparedness—all of which are crucial for teachers operating in a post-war context. The project will develop a Competency Framework encompassing integral, general, and professional competencies, as well as a proposed list of subject-specific competencies aligned with European standards (European Council, 2018).

Key discussion points include the need to reconceptualize teacher education programs in Ukraine, ensuring that future educators are equipped with the skills to support diverse learners, integrate digital technologies, and foster resilience in conflict-affected classrooms. The project draws on the Strategic Framework for European Cooperation in Education and Training 2021–2030 (European Council, 2021), emphasizing priorities such as improving the quality and inclusivity of education, as well as supporting digital and green transitions. The paper also reflects on findings from the PISA 2022 report, which highlights substantial learning losses among Ukrainian students due to war-related disruptions, underscoring the urgency of equipping teachers with new pedagogical strategies.

Additionally, the research considers insights from EU teacher training practices, particularly from countries such as Italy and Estonia, which have made significant progress in inclusive education and competency-based teacher preparation (OECD, 2004; Deluca, 2010). Aligning Ukrainian teacher education with EU policies on education quality assurance and lifelong learning is crucial to fostering a more integrated European Higher Education Area and ensuring the long-term sustainability of Ukraine's education system.

The paper concludes by addressing the implications for policy and curriculum reform, advocating for a structured approach to implementing competency-based teacher education in Ukraine. By leveraging EU expertise and best practices, the project contributes to the post-war recovery and modernization of Ukraine's education system in alignment with the Sustainable Development Goals (UNESCO, 2020).

Keywords: Teacher Competency Framework; Higher Education Standards; EU-Ukrainian Educational Alignment; Post-war Educational Resilience; Inclusive and Digital Pedagogies

References

Council of the European Union. (2018). Council Recommendation of 22 May 2018 on Key Competences for Lifelong Learning. Official Journal of the European Union, C 189, 1–13. https://eur-lex.europa.eu/legal-content/EN/TXT/?uri=CELEX%3A32018H0604(01)

European Commission. (2021). Towards the European Education Area and Beyond (2021-2030). Brussels.https://education.ec.europa.eu/document/towards-a-european-education-area-and-beyond-2021-2030

OECD. (2004). Equity in Education: Thematic Review. Organisation for Economic Co-operation and Development. https://www.oecd.org/education/school/29478741.pdf

OECD. (2023). PISA 2022 Results: Learning Losses and Educational Inequality. Organisation for Economic Co-operation and Development. https://www.oecd.org/pisa/

State Education Quality Service of Ukraine (SEQS). (2023). Impact of War on Education in Ukraine: Annual Report 2023. Kyiv, Ukraine.

UNESCO. (2020). International Taskforce on Teachers for Education 2030: Global Education Monitoring Report. United Nations Educational, Scientific and Cultural Organization. https://en.unesco.org/gem-report/

United Nations Ukraine. (2017). Sustainable Development Goals: Ukraine – National Report. United Nations. https://ukraine.un.org/en/2030-agenda

Ukrainian National Agency for Higher Education Quality Assurance (NAQA). (2021). Graduate Employment Monitoring Report. Kyiv, Ukraine.

Deluca, C. (2010). Inclusive Education in Italy: A Critical Analysis of Policy and Practice. International Journal of Inclusive Education, 14(5), 515–528. https://doi.org/10.1080/13603110802504598

Bridging the Competency Gap in Ukrainian Teacher Training: Developing a Skills Toolbox for Future Educators

Antonella Poce[1], Diana Andone[2], Olha Hurenko[3], Gemma Tur Ferrer[4]

[1] Department of History, Humanities and Society, University of Rome Tor Vergata, Italy; antonella.poce@uniroma2.eu
[2] ID / IFR and e-Learning Center (CeL), Polytechnic University of Timişoara, Romania; diana.andone@upt.ro
[3] Berdyansk State Pedagogical University, Ukraine; hurenkoolga75@gmail.com
[4] School of Education, University of the Balearic Islands, Spain; gemma.tur@uib.es

Correspondence: Antonella Poce: antonella.poce@uniroma2.eu

Abstract:

In the face of war-induced educational disruptions, the modernization of teacher training in Ukraine is crucial to ensuring the resilience of the national education system. This paper presents the preliminary approach of Work Package 3 (WP3) of a European project aimed at developing a competency-based skills toolbox for Ukrainian teacher education. The focus is on subject-matter, inclusive, psychological, information, and digital competences, essential for equipping future teachers with the skills required in a rapidly changing educational landscape.

WP3 adopts a multi-layered methodology, combining comparative research on EU best practices, internships in Spain on Teaching with Technology, and a study visit to Romania to examine teacher education models. A self-assessment exercise involving six Ukrainian HEIs and external stakeholders will map existing performance gaps in teacher training programs. Based on these findings, four core modules will be updated across three curricula, covering: Adaptive Teaching (subject-specific methodology for Mathematics, History, and Ukrainian Language and Literature); Inclusive Education Strategies (Pedagogy); Socio-emotional and Ethical Learning (Psychology); Digital Skills for Sustainable Education (ICT).

A key output of WP3 is the pilot course "Introduction to Educational Studies: Best EU Practice for Ukraine" (3 ECTS), designed to familiarize pre-service teachers with modern pedagogical paradigms. This course introduces barrier-free education, communication as a foundation for teaching, and the integration of pedagogical science and practice, aligning with EU educational priorities (European Council, 2021). The pilot phase will generate insights for refining content and delivery methods, ensuring alignment with European quality standards and lifelong learning frameworks (European Council, 2018).

Despite its potential, the initiative faces significant challenges, including adapting EU-based approaches to Ukraine's war-affected context, ensuring faculty readiness to implement new methodologies, and addressing infrastructural and digital disparities across institutions. Additionally, findings from PISA 2022 underscore the urgency of strengthening psychological and socio-emotional support for students, positioning teachers as key agents of educational recovery.

The paper concludes with a discussion on the policy and institutional implications of integrating the Competency Toolbox into Ukrainian teacher education. By piloting innovative curricula and drawing on EU expertise, WP3 aims to contribute to Ukraine's educational resilience and post-war reconstruction, ensuring that future teachers are equipped to meet the evolving needs of their students and society.

Keywords: Teacher Training Reform; Competency-Based Education; Digital and Inclusive Teaching; EU Best Practices in Pedagogy; Educational Resilience in Ukraine

References

Council of the European Union. (2018). Council Recommendation of 22 May 2018 on Key Competences for Lifelong Learning. Official Journal of the European Union, C 189, 1–13. https://eur-lex.europa.eu/legal-content/EN/TXT/?uri=CELEX%3A32018H0604(01)

European Commission. (2021). Towards the European Education Area and Beyond (2021-2030). Brussels.https://education.ec.europa.eu/document/towards-a-european-education-area-and-beyond-2021-2030

OECD. (2004). Equity in Education: Thematic Review. Organisation for Economic Co-operation and Development. https://www.oecd.org/education/school/29478741.pdf

OECD. (2023). PISA 2022 Results: Learning Losses and Educational Inequality. Organisation for Economic Co-operation and Development. https://www.oecd.org/pisa/

State Education Quality Service of Ukraine (SEQS). (2023). Impact of War on Education in Ukraine: Annual Report 2023. Kyiv, Ukraine.

UNESCO. (2020). International Taskforce on Teachers for Education 2030: Global Education Monitoring Report. United Nations Educational, Scientific and Cultural Organization. https://en.unesco.org/gem-report/

United Nations Ukraine. (2017). Sustainable Development Goals: Ukraine – National Report. United Nations. https://ukraine.un.org/en/2030-agenda

Ukrainian National Agency for Higher Education Quality Assurance (NAQA). (2021). Graduate Employment Monitoring Report. Kyiv, Ukraine.

Beyond the Classroom: Scaling Team-Based Learning Online Across Disciplines

Panos Vlachopoulos[1]

[1] Office of Academic Affairs , The American College of Greece ,Greece; pvlachopoulos@acg.edu

Correspondence: Panos Vlachopoulos: pvlachopoulos@acg.edu

Abstract:

As the demand for graduate employability skills continues to rise, universities emphasize integrating 21st-century competencies like critical thinking, problem-solving, communication, and teamwork into their curricula. One effective approach is Team-Based Learning (TBL), a structured, collaborative methodology designed to enhance student engagement and performance. TBL follows a structured process: the Individual Readiness Assurance Test (IRAT), where students complete a quiz individually to assess their understanding of preparatory materials; the Team Readiness Assurance Test (TRAT), in which students retake the same quiz collaboratively to deepen comprehension; an Appeals stage, where teams can challenge quiz answers and justify their reasoning; and Clarifications, where instructors address misconceptions before moving to Application Tasks, where teams apply knowledge to real-world problems. Additionally, increasing student-to-faculty ratios (Michaelson et al. 2014) drive the need for scalable collaborative learning approaches. However, research on TBL over the past decade calls for broader studies incorporating different disciplines, robust methodologies, and larger sample sizes (Haidet et al. 2014; Sisk 2011; Swanson et al. 2019).

The shift to online learning during and after the pandemic has accelerated the adoption of TBL in virtual environments, highlighting TBL's positive impact on student experience, engagement, and performance. Burton (2024) reported from a systematic review that TBL was equally as effective if carried out online or face-to-face, with no clear differences to outcomes related to satisfaction in online or traditional TBL approaches. However, most online TBL implementations are limited to health-related disciplines and rely on costly software such as InteDashboard or require self-hosting additional platforms like OpenTBL, posing financial and logistical challenges. No research has explored fully online (distance learning) TBL at the scale and disciplinary diversity of this study.

This study examines a large-scale, fully online TBL implementation with 1,000+ students across 12 Humanities and Social Sciences disciplines. Building on a previous study (author, 2021), it leverages Moodle's built-in tools to facilitate key TBL components, demonstrating how TBL can be executed without specialized software. The study details the design and execution of these stages, adapting Moodle to enhance interactive and collaborative learning.

The presentation will outline the methodology used to introduce TBL to a diverse student cohort, describe the development of each phase, and present student and faculty feedback on usability, engagement, and the perceived value of the approach in an online setting.

Additionally, this study explores the potential of Artificial Intelligence (AI) in enhancing online TBL, an approach that has only seen limited implementation in this team work methodology to date (see Vaughman, 2024). It examines how AI can aid in developing IRAT and TRAT assessments—an approach already trialed by the authors—and plans for AI-driven chatbots to support online clarification sessions. The emerging findings, subject to further analysis, contribute to discussions on scaling and broadening access to TBL, offering insights into its effective implementation using widely available learning management systems.

Our findings provide valuable practical implications for academics and learning designers seeking to implement structured collaborative learning methodologies that enhance student engagement, learning experiences, and teamwork while improving overall performance.

Keywords: Team-Based Learning, Skills, Online Learning, AI

References

Burton, R., Kellett, U., Mansah, M., & Sriram, D. (2024). A systematic review of online team based learning approaches in health professional education. *Nurse Education Today* 138, 106156. https://doi.org/10.1016/j.nedt.2024.106156

Haidet, P., Kubitz, K., & McCormack, W. T. (2014). Analysis of the team-based learning literature: TBL comes of age. *Journal on Excellence in College Teaching 25(3&4)*, 303-333.

Michaelsen, L. K., Davidson, N., & Major, C. H. (2014). Team-based learning practices and principles in comparison with cooperative learning and problem-based learning. *Journal on Excellence in College Teaching 25(3&4),* 57-84

Sisk, R. J. (2011). Team-based learning: Systematic research review. *Journal of Nursing Education 50,* 665-669

Swanson, E., McCulley, L., Osman, D. J., Lewis, N. S., & Solis, M. (2019). The effect of team-based learning on content knowledge: A meta-analysis. *Active Learning in Higher Education 20(1),* 39–50.

Vaughans, A., Belle, N., & Kayalackakom, T. (2024). Leveraging ai and team-based learning to enhance remediation and reduce faculty workload in medical education, edulearn24 Proceedings, pp. 4896-4899. http://doi.org/10.21125/edulearn.2024.1203

Vlachopoulos, P., K. Jan, S., & Buckton, R. (2021). A case for Team-Based Learning as an effective collaborative learning methodology in higher education. *College Teaching, 69*(2), 69-77. https://doi.org/10.1080/87567555.2020.1816889

"I'm Very Scared Right Now". Supporting Educators to Engage with Generative AI

Denise Mac Giolla Ri[1], Geraldine McDermott[2]

[1] Centre for Pedagogical Innovation and Development, Technological University of the Shannon, Ireland; denise.macgiollari@tus.ie
[2] Centre for Pedagogical Innovation and Development, Technological University of the Shannon, Ireland; geraldine.mcdermott@tus.ie

Correspondence: Denise Mac Giolla Ri: denisemacgiollari@tus.ie

Abstract:

The disruptive nature of Generative Artificial Intelligence has called into question teaching and learning approaches across higher education, forcing educators to redefine their role within education.
This presentation shares the experiences of one Irish higher education institution, which has adopted a multifaceted approach to tackling the "wicked problem of Generative Artificial Intelligence" (Banville et al., 2024, p.3), that includes a focus on Universal Design, Academic Integrity and AI literacy.
Acknowledging the potential of Artificial Intelligence (AI) to "level the playing field" (McDermott & O'Donoghue, 2024) and make higher education more inclusive and equitable, this presentation shares practical suggestions for embedding AI within teaching and learning practices, underpinned by Universal Design.
Similarly, as educators are charged with assuring the validity of their e-assessment strategies (Gundu, 2024), this presentation explores steps they can take through thoughtful assessment design, to ensure students are evidencing their learning and are committed to academic integrity.
However, in order to support students to avoid 'efficiency blindness'[1] and understand the value of the learning process, educators need to engage with AI tools and understand the associated challenges and risks. Through a variety of approaches, this Irish university has put in place a range of initiatives to increase AI literacy amongst its teaching and research community, which extends to its international partners.
Finally, as the authors acknowledge the fear that exists for many educators, they offer a call to action, reaffirming the added value of the human educator in preparing students to live and work in an increasingly volatile world.

1. Term coined by one of the authors to explain the process of reaching a learning goal without going through the "messy" (Derby-Talbot, 2023) process of learning.

Keywords: AI literacy, academic integrity, higher education

References

Banville, M., Byrd, A., Gupta, A., Johnson, G. P., Robertshaw, J., & Woods, C. (2024). On Fishbowls, Student Personas, and the Wicked Problem of Generative Artificial Intelligence. In *Proceedings of the Computers & Writing Conference* (p. 4).

Derby-Talbot, R. (2023). Learning that Matters is Messy: Experiments Revealing Hidden Potential in Higher Education. *Turning Toward Being: The Journal of Ontological Inquiry in Education*, *1*(1), 5.

Gundu, T. (2024). Strategies for e-Assessments in the Era of Generative Artificial Intelligence. *Electronic Journal of e-Learning*, *22*(7), 40-50.

McDermott, G., & O'Donoghue, C. (2024). Levelling the Playing Field: Using Artificial Intelligence to Make the Learning Experience More Accessible. *All Ireland Journal of Higher Education*, *16*(2).

Disciplinary Differences in Pedagogical AI Competences of Higher Education Teachers

László Horváth[1]

[1] Institute of Education, ELTE Eötvös Loránd University, Budapest, Hungary; horvath.laszlo@ppk.elte.hu

Correspondence: László Horváth: horvath.laszlo@ppk.elte.hu

Project no. 146998 has been implemented with the support provided by the National Research, Development and Innovation Fund of Hungary, financed under the OTKA FK funding scheme.

Abstract:

The emergence of generative artificial intelligence tools presented new opportunities and challenges for (higher) education and prompted various responses from different stakeholders (Zawacki-Richter et al., 2019). Concerns are raised regarding ethical, data privacy issues (Abdurohman, 2025), academic integrity and algorithmic bias (Zhao, 2025). The widespread adoption of AI in higher education is still limited, with lack of evidence on its pedagogical impact (O'Dea & O'Dea, 2023). To effectively navigate the AI era, higher education teachers must develop their competencies in using AI to support teaching and learning (Muttaqin, 2022). Existing frameworks provide foundation for digital competences (e.g. DigCompEdu (Redecker & Punie, 2017; AI-TPACK (Ning et al, 2024))) but they do not sufficiently capture the pedagogical dimensions of AI integration in higher education. Therefore, the aim of our study is to develop and validate such a tool.

We have developed our scale based on the DigCompEdu instrument, focusing on pedagogical use of AI in higher education context and included it in a university-wide needs assessment survey focusing on AI use conducted in one large comprehensive university in Hungary. After data-cleaning, the database consists of 610 respondents (~16.8% response rate) covering a wide range of disciplines. 52.6% of respondents are female, 53.9% do not have any formal pedagogical background. 14.9% of respondents are younger than 30, 47.5% are between 31-50, while 37.7% are over 51 years old. Randomly splitting the sample, we conducted an EFA on one part and validated the results on the other half with a CFA approach using jamovi. The results confirmed a 4-factor solution: AI-Supported Professional and Collaborative Work (ω=0.869); AI-Enhanced Student Engagement and Learning Support (ω=0.896); AI-Driven Personalization and Assessment (ω=0.875); Developing Students' AI Literacy and Responsible AI Use (ω=0.829). The AICompEdu model fits the data adequately and the reliability statistics of the scales (McDonald's omega) is also acceptable (χ2(58)=279; p<.001; CFI=0.962; TLI=0.948; SRMR=0.038; RMSEA=0.079). Descriptive statistics suggest that respondents lack pedagogical AI competences in general (mean values smaller than 3 on a scale of 6), the lowest being personalization and assessment (M=1.58; SD=1.04). Inspecting disciplinary differences, we found significant differences between different faculties using non-parametric variance analysis (Kruskal-Wallis). The pairwise comparisons (Dwass-Steel-Critchlow-Fligner) highlighted patterns indicating that the IT, business, and education and psychology faculties scoring significantly higher in all competence domains compared to other faculties (law, special needs education, humanities, social sciences, natural sciences).

Exploring the factor-structure of the AICompEdu and underlying individual differences will help us better understand patterns in pedagogically-aware use of AI in higher education setting. Furthermore, we intend to use the results to assess needs of professional development and support for the ethical and transparent use of AI in higher education.

Keywords: AI literacy, DigCompEdu, AICompEdu, disciplinary differences

References

Abdurohman, N. R. (2025). Artificial intelligence in higher education: Opportunities and *challenges. Eurasian Science Review An International Peer-Reviewed Multidisciplinary Journal,* 2(Special Issue), 1683–1695. https://doi.org/10.63034/esr-334

Muttaqin, I. (2022). Necessary to increase teacher competency in facing the Artificial Intelligence era. *Al-Hayat: Journal of Islamic Education, 6*(2), 549. https://doi.org/10.35723/ajie.v6i2.460

Ning, Y., Zhang, C., Xu, B., Zhou, Y., & Wijaya, T. T. (2024). Teachers' AI-TPACK: Exploring the relationship between knowledge elements. *Sustainability, 16*(3), 978. https://doi.org/10.3390/su16030978

O'Dea, X., & O'Dea, M. (2023). Is Artificial Intelligence Really the Next Big Thing in Learning and Teaching in Higher Education? A Conceptual Paper. *Journal of University Teaching & Learning Practice, 20*(5). https://doi.org/10.53761/1.20.5.05

Redecker, C., & Punie, Y. (2017). *European framework for the digital competence of educators*. Publications Office of the European Union.

Zawacki-Richter, O., Marín, V.I., Bond, M. et al. (2019). Systematic review of research on artificial intelligence applications in higher education – where are the educators?. *International Journal of Educational Technology in Higher Education, 16*(39). https://doi.org/10.1186/s41239-019-0171-0

Zhao, C. (2025). AI-assisted assessment in higher education: A systematic review. *Journal of Educational Technology and Innovation, 6*(4). https://doi.org/10.61414/jeti.v6i4.209

POSTER ABSTRACTS

Comparing University Alliance Member Responses to Generative AI

Leigh Graves Wolf[1], Sasa Tkalcan[2], Ana Belén Sánchez Prieto[3], Alexa Gallo[4], Alexandra Tzortzi[4]

[1] University College Dublin, Ireland; leigh.wolf@ucd.ie
[2] University of Helsinki, Finland; sasa.tkalcan@helsinki.fi
[3]Complutense University of Madrid, Spain; anabelsa@ucm.es
[4]Paris 1 Panthéon-Sorbonne, France; alexa.gallo@univ-paris1.fr, Alexandra.Tzortzi@univ-paris1.fr

Correspondence: Leigh Graves Wolf, leigh.wolf@ucd.ie

Abstract:

This poster examines the institutional responses to Generative AI (GenAI) across universities within a large European University alliance. The poster maps institutional policies and guidelines, strategic approaches to AI integration in teaching and learning, methods for maintaining academic integrity, and support mechanisms for staff and students. By visualising these varied responses within different cultural and institutional contexts, we provide insights into how European universities are adapting to AI-driven educational change. This work offers valuable perspectives for policymakers and educators developing GenAI integration strategies, while demonstrating the importance of cross-institutional networks in addressing shared educational challenges.

Keywords: Higher Education, Policy, European Collaboration

This poster will examine how European universities within the Una Europa alliance are responding to and engaging with Generative Artificial Intelligence (GenAI) in their educational environments. Through the collaborative work of the Educational Design and Technology working group, we have gathered data on institutional approaches, policies, and implementation strategies across our network.

European university alliances serve as a fertile ground for cross-institutional collaboration and knowledge exchange (Pinheiro et al., 2023). The Educational Design and Technology working group has been actively sharing practices and policies around GenAI integration, providing unique insights into how different institutions are adapting to this technological shift. Our poster will utilise visual timelines and comparative frameworks to illustrate these diverse institutional approaches, highlighting both commonalities and distinctive features in how each university is responding to AI-driven educational change.

While supranational bodies and national organizations have begun developing preliminary frameworks and guidelines for AI in education (European Commission, 2023; Miao & Holmes, 2023), the current landscape is characterized by varied institutional responses and implementation strategies. Our visualization will map these differences, examining how distinct cultural contexts and institutional values have shaped approaches to GenAI integration across the alliance.

The poster will focus on the following dimensions:

- Institutional policies and guidelines
- Strategic approaches to AI integration in teaching and learning
- Methods for maintaining academic integrity

- Support mechanisms for staff and students

This work contributes to the broader discourse on ethical and responsible AI use in education. By mapping the diverse approaches within our alliance, we provide valuable insights for other institutions navigating similar challenges. The poster will showcase both the challenges and opportunities in integrating AI into higher education, offering practical insights for policymakers, educators and researchers working to develop effective strategies for AI integration across European institutions.

References

Pinheiro, R., Gänzle, S., Klenk, T., & Trondal, J. (2023). Unpacking strategic alliances in European higher education. *Tertiary Education and Management*, 29(3), 213-228.

European Commission. (February 15, 2023.) *European University Association (EUA) urges higher education sector to adapt to AI impact*. https://euraxess.ec.europa.eu/worldwide/asean/news/european-university-association-eua-urges-higher-education-sector-adapt-ai

Miao, F. & Holmes, W. (2023) Guidance for generative AI in education and research. UNESCO. https://unesdoc.unesco.org/ark:/48223/pf0000386693

Navigating Online Higher Education: First-Year Students' Motivations, Challenges, and Support Strategies

Hanne Kristin Dypedal[1], Per Ivar Kjærgård[2]

[1] Department of digitalization, NLA University College, Norway; handyp@nla.no
[2] Department of Teacher Education, NLA University College, Norway; pk@nla.no

Correspondence: Hanne Kristin Dypedal, handyp@nla.no

Abstract:

This poster presentation addresses how young adults who choose online education as their first encounter with higher education experience motivations and academic support strategies during their first year of study in higher education. Online education has become increasingly prevalent in recent years, with a growing number of students opting for online programs. Over the past decade, Norwegian higher education institutions have observed a notable surge in the number of students aged 15-25 enrolling in online programs. National education statistics reveal a steady year-on-year growth in this demographic, with particularly pronounced increases between 2019 and 2021 (*Database for Statistikk Om Høyere Utdanning - DBH*, n.d.).

Through qualitative research, utilizing semi-structured interviews with three students aged 19-21 years old. The study employed thematic analysis informed by the methodological guidelines described by Braun and Clarke (2006). Participants were strategically selected based on their enrollment in their first online higher education course, providing rich insights into their experiences and expectations.

Participants primarily viewed online studies as a pathway to qualify for further education, strategically using these courses to improve their academic grades. Additionally, students perceived online courses to enhance their career opportunities. Interestingly, students uniformly described their online academic year as a type of "gap year," highlighting their expectation of manageable workload and personal freedom. Together, these considerations were important factors influencing their decision to pursue online studies.

Beyond academic and career considerations, flexibility emerged as a key factor influencing students' experiences and decisions regarding online education. When students elaborate on flexibility, they emphasize the ability to balance academic pursuits alongside work, leisure, and varying family commitments, while also acknowledging that succeeding as an online student requires a high degree of self-regulation. Additionally, the extensive flexibility in online studies created challenges in coordinating suitable times for collaborative activities, as students navigated diverse schedules due to employment, leisure activities, and varying family situations. Despite studying online, informants emphasized that social learning and interaction were significant for their educational experience, prompting them to prefer campus-based studies for their future academic endeavors.

Regarding academic activities and support systems, students predominantly relied on digital technologies, including AI tools and search engines like Google. Teachers ranked notably lower in perceived importance for academic and personal support, with students describing teachers as a "last resort" when encountering academic or practical challenges. However, all informants emphasized the teacher's significance within the study context, describing teacher communication as both important and valuable in their daily academic lives.

These findings underscore critical shifts in the role of traditional educators in online higher education, highlighting students' growing reliance on technology-driven resources for academic success and personal management, yet also pointing to continued appreciation for interpersonal communication with teachers and peers (Lysitsa & Mavroeidis, 2024).

Keywords: Online education, AI, support, first-year students

References

Braun, V., & Clarke, V. (2006). Using thematic analysis in psychology. *Qualitative Research in Psychology*, *3*(2), 77–101. https://doi.org/10.1191/1478088706qp063oa

Database for statistikk om høyere utdanning—DBH. (n.d.). Retrieved March 14, 2025, from https://dbh.hkdir.no/tall-og-statistikk/

Lysitsa, E., & Mavroeidis, I. (2024). Critical factors affecting student satisfaction in a distance learning environment. *European Journal of Open, Distance and E-Learning*, *26*(1), 1–23. https://doi.org/10.2478/eurodl-2023-0014

Developing Cognitive Competences in Preschool Age Children Using Educational Innovations

Nijole Ciuciulkiene[1], Ilona Tandzegolskiene-Bielaglove[2] , Viktorija Ceponyte[3]

[1] Education Academy, Vytautas Magnus University, Lithuania; nijole.ciuciulkiene@vdu.lt
[2] Education Academy, Vytautas Magnus University, Lithuania; Ilona.tandzegolskiene-bielaglove@vdu.lt
[3]Viktorija Ceponyte, Vytautas Magnus University, Lithuania; Viktorija.ceponyte@vdu.lt

Correspondence: Nijole Ciuciulkiene; nijole.ciuciulkiene@vdu.lt

Abstract:

Educators are looking for innovative measures to awaken the basic needs of children's cognition. The most effective educational method today is the integration of educational technologies into the educational process to develop the cognitive competence of preschool children. Educational innovations in Lithuania are regarded not only as a tool helping to ensure the continuity of the educational process (Daukšienė, Trepulė et al., 2021; Korhonen et al., 2023), but also as providing pupils' involvement and differentiating their educational content. Danniels and Pyle (2020) state that smart technologies, such as tablets, computers, interactive whiteboards, and floors, also play an important role in developing children's cognitive abilities. During educational activities, voice, video recordings, games, artificial intelligence tools, or other innovative methods are used to convey the desired information, to create more effective adaptation possibilities to the needs of different children, individualizing the learning process, promoting children's creativity, critical thinking, gaining new experiences, and discovering interesting solutions, thus developing cognitive competence. After analyzing Barrichello and Morano, 2020; Danniels and Pyle (2020); Foti (2020); Alqhtani et al. (2021), it is noticeable that researchers emphasize the emergence of educational innovations, summarize their purpose and nature.

Methodology. The research is conducted using a quantitative strategy. In the quantitative study, data were collected using a structured online questionnaire. Statistical data processing was performed using the SPSS program, and correlation and analytical analysis were selected. The Chi-square criterion was calculated, and Pearson's statistical relationship was searched. The deductive strategy of quantitative (statistical) research was applied (hypotheses are formed, research is conducted to test the hypotheses - data are analyzed - conclusions are formed). During the quantitative study, it was found how often and what educational innovations are used by preschool teachers to develop pupils' cognitive competence. The results obtained during the survey revealed that preschool educators differently assess the benefits of educational innovations and the frequency of their application for the development of children's cognitive competence. Most educators use educational innovations at least once a week or more often. Senior teachers and experts apply innovations more often than other educators with the qualification category. However, no statistically significant relationship was found between the perception of the importance of educational innovations and the frequency of their use. It was observed that mixed methods, combining traditional and innovative methods, are most often used. The study also revealed that most educators notice progress in children's cognitive competence when applying innovations, but expert educators tend to indicate only minimal progress. Nevertheless, it could be taken for granted that educational innovations help children develop cognitive competence. Although seniority, age and education have a certain influence, the main factor that determines the integration of educational innovation into the educational process is the views of the teachers in which they follow the cognitive activities.

The use of educational innovations and the choice of tools depend on the educator's competence, work experience and education. In the opinion of teachers, the most important educational innovations in the educational process are interactive, smart boards, educational apps and sensory tables, as well as smart toys and robots. Preschool educators use these tools to encourage active exploration and participation in the cognitive process. Although most educators actively apply advanced technologies, it is still noticeable that there are teachers who tend to stick to traditional methods due to a lack of competence to integrate educational innovations. The quantitative research confirmed the hypotheses put forward, which allow us to state that the constant application of educational innovations contributes to the development of cognitive competence; therefore, it is necessary to create appropriate conditions for the implementation of these innovations in preschool educational institutions.

This study analyzed how preschool teachers evaluate technological innovations, what innovative teaching methods and tools, in the opinion of teachers, form good practices that allow integrating educational technological innovations into the educational process in order to develop the cognitive competence of preschool children; what educational innovations are the most effective for developing children's cognitive competence.

The aim of this research is *to* reveal how the cognitive competence of preschoolers might be effectively developed while applying educational innovations.

Keywords: Cognitive Competences, Educational innovations, Preschool Age

References

Alqhtani, W. M., Alhajri, B. M., Alotibi, W. N., & Barsom, R. M. M. (2021). The reality of the distance learning experience during the corona pandemic from the point of view of kindergarten teachers. *Review of International Geographical Education Online*, *11*(7), 1768–1783

Barrichello, A., Morano, R. S., Feldmann, P. R., & Jacomossi, R. R. (2020). The importance of education in the context of innovation and competitiveness of nations. *International Journal of Education Economics and Development*, *11*(2), 204–224.

Danniels, E., Pyle, A., & DeLuca, C. (2020). The role of technology in supporting classroom assessment in play-based kindergarten. *Teaching and Teacher Education*, *88*.

Daukšienė, E., Trepulė, E., & Naujokaitienė, J. (2021). Kokybiško nuotolinio ugdymo link: mokyklų pirmosios išmoktos pamokos COVID-19 pandemijos metu. *Pedagogy Studies/Pedagogika*, *142*(2).

Foti, P. (2020). Research in distance learning in Greek kindergarten schools during the pandemic of COVID-19: Possibilities, dilemmas, limitations. *European Journal of Open Education and E-learning Studies*, *5*(1).

Korhonen, T., Salo, L., Laakso, N., Seitamaa, A., Sormunen, K., Kukkonen, M., & Forsström, H. (2023). Finnish teachers as adopters of educational innovation: Perceptions of programming as a new part of the curriculum. *Computer Science Education*, *33*(1), 94–116.

The Development of Preschool Educators' Digital Competence while applying the Multisensory Environments

Nijole Ciuciulkiene[1], Rasa Didziuliene[2], Birute Sciukiene[3]

[1] Vytautas Magnus University, Lithuania; nijole.ciuciulkiene@vdu.lt
[2] Vytautas Magnus University, Lithuania; rasa.didziuliene@vdu.lt
[3] Vytautas Magnus University, Lithuania; birute.sciukiene@vdu.lt

Correspondence: Nijole Ciuciulkiene: nijole.ciuciulkiene@vdu.lt and Rasa Didziuliene: rasa.didziuliene@vdu.lt

Abstract:

Technological advances and the availability of innovations create opportunities for teachers to apply a lot of digital tools in the educational process. No wonder that multisensory technologies are quite popular in preschool institutions (Solichah & Fardana, 2024). Multisensory education includes teaching through hearing and speaking, seeing and perceiving, touching, tasting, moving and doing (Garzotto et al.,2020; Volpe & Gori, 2019). For example, in order to improve early literacy skills, the following forms of multisensory programs can be used: 1) visual (e.g., drawing, interpreting the meaning of read words/sentences, playing with alphabet cards, reading words or sentences correctly, and reading labels on food and toy packages); 2) auditory (e.g., singing, reading storybooks, mentioning letter sounds, spelling syllables, language activities, speeches and stories); 3) kinesthetics (e.g., children's word division into syllables using media strips, writing, clapping, marching, dancing, and drama); and 4) tactile (e.g., writing a word with your index finger on a flannel/fabric) (Solichah & Fardana, 2024).

In multisensory environments, children are more likely to calm down, concentrate, and focus more easily. Teachers note that education that takes place in different spaces, using different stimuli, provides children with significantly more benefits than education that takes place only in classrooms (Juel, 2015). Multisensory environments are also designed for exploration, because there you can find many tools that the child can touch, smell, and observe, i.e. different textures, smells, and images are revealed. Multisensory environments offer an excellent opportunity to teach children to sort, count and measure various objects, learn colours, recognize shapes, smells and properties of objects. It is important to emphasize that this activity promotes the development of social, communicative, cognitive, artistic and physical abilities and skills. It is important to understand that it is not enough to simply have access to newly created digital tools, and perhaps it is even more important, to develop teachers' digital competence, which plays a decisive role in successfully implementing the principles of inclusive education in pedagogical practice (Mykyteichuk et al., 2022).

Teachers who are interested in the changing educational process and methods will more often seek to introduce digital tools into the educational process and create innovative environments using interactive technologies (Jinghong & Sanmugam, 2025). One of such technologies is multisensory environments. Teachers who include multisensory environments in the educational process can reorient themselves more quickly to the changing educational process (Solichah & Fardana, 2024). It is precisely on the efforts of teachers, their love for their work and their desire to help children and make the educational process successful that the creation of multisensory environments depends. In conclusion, the development of digital competence provides pre-school teachers with digital literacy skills for effective and efficient work with children, ensuring their needs.

Methodology. A qualitative research strategy was applied. The effective application of the multisensory environment in the educational process promotes the inclusion of children, but it is important to find out how educators create and apply these environments in the education of preschoolers, forming competencies for inclusion (Volpe & Gori, 2019). Data collection methods: to conduct semi-structured interviews with pre-school educators with experience in multisensory teaching and learning. The data obtained were analysed through inductive qualitative content analysis (Mayring, 2014). For the implementation of semi-structured interviews, 17 key questions were prepared (Ciuciulkienė at al., 2023). The answers were recorded and subsequently transcribed. Transcriptions were analysed by two independent researchers, combining the main ideas and regularities into subcategories, categories and topics.

This study analysed how the improvement of the digital competence of pre-school educators could influence the more effective application of multisensory environments in the educational process.

The aim of this research is to reveal the development of digital competence of preschool teachers by involving multisensory environments in the educational process.

Keywords: Digital Competence; Preschool Educators; Multisensory Environments.

References

Ciuciulkiene, N., Tandzegolskiene-Bielaglove, I., & Culadiene, M. (2023). Phenomenon-based learning in teaching a foreign language: Experiences of Lithuanian teachers. *Social Sciences, 12*(12), 670.

Garzotto, F., Beccaluva, E., Gianotti, M., & Riccardi, F. (2020). Interactive multisensory environments for primary school children. *In Proceedings of the 2020 CHI Conference on Human Factors in Computing Systems* (pp. 1-12).

Jinghong, Z., & Sanmugam, M. (2025). Strategies for Bridging the Digital Divide in Inclusive Education Through Multisensory Learning and Emerging Technologies. *Fostering Inclusive Education With AI and Emerging Technologies,* 207-232.

Mayring, P. (2014). *Qualitative content analysis: theoretical foundation, basic procedures and software solution*.

Mykyteichuk, K., Perepeliuk, I., Perkhun, L., Bondarenko, Y., Yakovleva, S., & Sydoruk, I. (2022). Future Teacher Training for Work in the Inclusive Education Framework. *Revista Romaneasca Pentru Educatie Multidimensionala, 14*(2), 244-256.

Solichah, N., & Fardana, N. A. (2024). Exploring multisensory programs as early literacy interventions: a scoping review. *International Journal of Evaluation and Research in Education (IJERE), 13*(5), 3411-3418.

Volpe, G., & Gori, M. (2019). Multisensory interactive technologies for primary education: From science to technology. *Frontiers in psychology, 10*, 1076.

The Impact of the Teacher's Digital Competence in Strengthening Leadership in the Classroom

Rasa Didziuliene[1], Salomeja Karaseviciute[2], Elena Trepule[3], Edita Balzariene[4]

[1] Vytautas Magnus University, Lithuania; rasa.didziuliene@vdu.lt
[2]Mykolas Romeris University, Sudovian Academy, Lithuania; salomeja.karaseviciute@mruni.eu
[3]Vytautas Magnus University, Lithuania; elena.trepule@vdu.lt
[4] Kaunas School of Applied Arts, Lithuania; edita.balzariene@ktdm.lt

Correspondence: Salomėja Karaseviciute

Abstract:

Digital transformation, as one of the priority areas of the education sector, requires the active involvement of educators (Lucas et al., 2021). The involvement of an educator as a leader in the classroom helps to create innovative learning environments and effectively implement digital change (Hunzicker, 2017). Digital technologies are currently seen as an opportunity to transform educational and pedagogical processes, aligning education with the needs of the digital society. The pedagogical potential of digital resources challenges the educational process, promotes its transformation and innovation (Navaridas-Nalda at al., 2020). The study focuses on the teacher as a leader who captures the importance of digital competence in the educational process. General prime digital competence is a set of knowledge, skills, approaches needed to use digital technologies to solve problems, manage information, collaborate, create and share content, create and share knowledge efficiently, critically, creatively, independently, flexibly, ethically and reflect work, leisure, learning, consumption and empowerment (Ferrari, 2012). A teacher's digital competence can be described as the ability to use digital technologies in a professional context: pedagogical- didactic solutions and impact on learning strategies and digital student formation (Krumsvik, 2011). The pioneers of the idea of teacher leadership, Andrews and Crowther (2002) were the first to propose to transform educational leadership into teacher leadership. Teacher leadership is more a position or a way of thinking and being than a set of behaviour. When creating his leadership in the classroom, the teacher must discover his strengths in areas of digital competence, be interested in innovation, share knowledge and experience with students and colleagues (Hunzicker, 2017; Falloon, 2020). Leading teachers are individuals who lead not only in the classroom but also outside the classroom, individually or collectively influence their colleagues, improve teaching and learning practices, taking advantage of skate literacy (Bradley-Levine, 2017). Even though teachers do not have a formal description of their functions, the essence of their activities consists in creating an environment based on mutual trust, promoting cooperation between colleagues, sharing experiences, solving learning and teaching problems, enabling digital competence.

Methodology. A qualitative research strategy was applied. In the professional activity of the educator, digital competence is increasingly important, which determines his leadership in the classroom, ensuring a smooth and effective process in the classroom (Falloon, 2020). Using a semi-structured interview, the aim was to find out the experience, situation and exploratory process of using digital technologies by informants in the lessons, revealing the impact of the teacher's digital competence in strengthening his leadership in the classroom. For data collection, a semi-structured interview is used, which is applied as a deep analysis of the object of research to study the impact of the teacher's digital technology leadership in the classroom. The data obtained were analysed through inductive qualitative content analysis (Mayring, 2014). The study involved 10 informants. During the study, 14 interviews were conducted in 2 stages. The answers were recorded and subsequently transcribed, combining the main ideas and regularities into subcategories, categories and topics.

Research problem question: How do teachers, taking a leading position in the classroom, contribute to changes in professional performance by strengthening digital competence?

The purpose of this study is to reveal the impact of a teacher's digital competence in strengthening leadership in the classroom.

The results of the study showed that the ability of teachers to create a clear vision and goals of digital transformation in the educational process is closely related to the strengthening of their digital competence. It can be assumed that the effect of teacher leadership in the classroom is manifested through roles - the teacher is not only a student counsellor, but also a guide who pays great attention to digital literacy, contributes to changes in professional activity, and safely and effectively applies digital technologies and innovative methods in the classroom.

Keywords: Digital Competence; Teacher's Leadership.

References

Bradley-Levine, J. (2018). Advocacy as a practice of critical teacher leadership. *International Journal of Teacher Leadership, 9*(1), 47-62.

Clarke, V., & Braun, V. (2013). Teaching thematic analysis: Overcoming challenges and developing strategies for effective learning. *The psychologist, 26*(2). Crowther (2002)

Ferrari, A. (2012). *Digital competence in practice: An analysis of frameworks* (Vol. 10, p. 82116). Luxembourg: Publications Office of the European Union.

Falloon, G. (2020). From digital literacy to digital competence: the teacher digital competency (TDC) framework. *Education Tech Research Dev.* Doi:10.1007/s11423-020-09767-4.

Hunzicker, J. (2017). From teacher-to-teacher leader: A conceptual model. *International journal of teacher leadership, 8*(2), 1-27.

Krumsvik, R. J. (2011). Digital competence in the Norwegian teacher education and schools. *Högre utbildning, 1*(1), 39-51.

Lucas, M., Bem-Haja, P., Siddiq, F., Moreira, A., & Redecker, C. (2021). The relation between in-service teachers' digital competence and personal and contextual factors: What matters most?. Computers & Education, 160, 104052.

Mayring, P. (2014). Qualitative content analysis: theoretical foundation, basic procedures and software solution.

Navaridas-Nalda, F., Clavel-San Emeterio, M., Fernández-Ortiz, R., & Arias-Oliva, M. (2020). The strategic influence of school principal leadership in the digital transformation of schools. *Computers in Human Behaviour, 112*, 106481.

Solichah, N., & Fardana, N. A. (2024). Exploring multisensory programs as early literacy interventions: a scoping review. *International Journal of Evaluation and Research in Education (IJERE), 13*(5), 3411-3418.

Enhancing Soft Skills in Healthcare: Digital Learning Approach with Micro-Credentials

Estela Daukšienė[1], Indrė Oleškevičienė[2], Otčenášková Tereza[3], Marek Zanker[4], Martina Husáková[5], Ilja Tachecí[6], José Blas Pagador Carrasco[7], Luisa Fernanda Sánchez Peralta[8], Nina Pereza[9]

[1] Education Academy, Vytautas Magnus University, Lithuania; estela.dauksiene@vdu.lt
[2] Education Academy, Vytautas Magnus University, Lithuania; indre.oleskeviciene@vdu.lt
[3] Faculty of Informatics and Management, University of Hradec Kralove, Czech Republic; tereza.otcenaskova@uhk.cz
[4] Faculty of Informatics and Management, University of Hradec Kralove, Czech Republic; marek.zanker@uhk.cz
[5] Faculty of Informatics and Management, University of Hradec Kralove, Czech Republic; martina.husakova.2@uhk.cz
[6] Faculty of Medicine in Hradec Králové, Charles University, Czech Republic; tachecii@lfhk.cuni.cz
[7] Jesus Usón Minimally Invasive Surgery Centre (CCMIJU), Spain; jbpagador@ccmijesususon.com
[8] Jesus Usón Minimally Invasive Surgery Centre (CCMIJU), Spain; lfsanchez@ccmijesususon.com
[9] Faculty of Medicine, University of Rijeka, Croatia; nina.pereza@medri.uniri.hr

Correspondence: Estela Dauksiene: estela.dauksiene@vdu.lt

Abstract:

Despite their critical role in patient care and teamwork, soft skills are often underemphasised in healthcare training and education. Erasmus + project MISS4Health addresses this gap with an innovative digital education approach. This initiative offers a modular Massive Open Online Course (MOOC) leading to micro-credentials, providing structured, tailored training for healthcare professionals.

Keywords: soft skills, healthcare, MOOC, micro-credentials

Summary

The main objective of Erasmus+ KA2 project MISS4Health: Micro-credentials in Soft Skills for Healthcare Professionals and Students (2023-1-CZ01-KA220-HED-000159335) is to improve transversal competencies of healthcare professionals, focusing on the development of their soft skills. Thus, an interactive modular Massive Open Online Course (MOOC) leading to micro-credentials that certify their skills is constructed. The modular MOOC development includes curricular design, interactive content creation, micro-credentials' design and initial MOOC piloting with healthcare specialists and medical students. The double loop validation is planned to assure the overall quality of the MOOC, as well as its embedded real-life examples.

A modular MOOC is constructed from 5 modules, which are interrelated but may also be piloted as stand-alone self-directed learning online courses. Each module focuses on the single-skill development, together representing key soft skills necessary in daily clinical practice. The five modules include: communication, decision-making, leadership, situational awareness, and teamwork. Incorporating modern digital tools—such as multimedia content and serious games— ensures learner engagement and practical application. The implemented self-assessment tools and feedback mechanisms also ensure personalised learning for selected skill development. The embedded micro-credentials help with further skill recognition as they are structured following the recommendations of the EU Council Recommendations (2022) on the micro-credential mandatory elements, their descriptors and principles for the micro-credential design and implementation (EU Council, 2022)

Disclaimer: The project is funded by the European Union. The created project results, views and opinions expressed are however those of the author(s) only and do not necessarily reflect those of the European Union. Neither the European Union can be held responsible for them.

References

EU Council. (2022). COUNCIL RECOMMENDATION of 16 June 2022 on a European approach to micro-credentials for lifelong learning and employability (2022/C 243/02; Official Journal of the European Union, pp. 10–22). https://eur-lex.europa.eu/legal-content/EN/TXT/PDF/?uri=CELEX:32022H0627(02)

Digitally Signed Credentials – Smart Motivation with Stackability

Daiva Urmonienė[1], Indrė Oleškevičienė[2]

[1] Lithuanian Association of Distance and e-Learning (LieDM), Lithuania; daiva.urmoniene@vdu.lt
[2] Lithuanian Association of Distance and e-Learning (LieDM), Lithuania; indre.oleskevieiene@vdu.lt

Correspondence: Indrė Oleškevičienė: indre.oleskevieiene@vdu.lt

Abstract

The Digitally Signed Credentials – Smart Motivation with Stackability (DISCO SMS) project, funded by the European Commission's Erasmus+ program. The aim of the project to enhance education and training by focusing on soft skills recognition by creating methodology that combines them with Open Badge technology. It proposes a trainer and VET teacher training course that utilizes gamification techniques using digital open badges to recognize and reward these soft skills in a visible, transferable, and multilingual manner, supporting learners in a diverse social and professional environment.

DISCO SMS aims to pave the way for a more interconnected and standardized system of digital credentials in European education, enhancing the processes of issuing, exchanging, and recognizing achievements. By prioritizing soft skills recognition through gamification and open badges, this initiative aligns with the evolving demands of both educators and employers, ensuring learners are well-prepared to proceed in their careers and beyond.

Keywords: Digital open badges, gamification, soft skills, educators

Summary

Education should not solely focus on academic achievement but also on nurturing well-rounded individuals capable of navigating various social and professional contexts. By valuing and recognizing soft skills, educators can support students and learners to be better equipped to thrive in diverse environments. Many employers prioritize soft skills alongside technical expertise when hiring, recognizing their significance in fostering a collaborative and dynamic work environment. By emphasizing these skills in education, students are better positioned to meet the expectations of prospective employers and proceed in their careers (Caron, 2021).

Teacher training in soft skills recognition and gamification offers numerous benefits, enhancing educators' pedagogical skills and creating a dynamic educational atmosphere conducive to student success and personal growth. Additionally, such training empowers teachers to personalize their awarding schemas to meet the diverse needs and motivational styles of their students, leading to improved comprehension and retention of course material.

The target audiences of DISCO SMS project are:

- Teachers and Trainers: Includes educators from Vocational Education and Training (VET) systems, secondary schools, and adult education.
- Students and Adult Learners: Focuses on the direct beneficiaries of training and learning programs.
- Institutional Management: Involves administrators and decision-makers within educational institutions.

- IT Developers and Support Personnel: Includes technical teams responsible for developing and maintaining educational IT solutions.

Expected DISCO SMS project result: A 30-hour online course and downloadable trainers' and teachers' guidebook with 3 modules on gamification, on how to recognize soft skills, and on interoperability and stackability, including scenarios covering all educational sectors, in English, Hungarian, Latvian, Spanish, Greek, Lithuanian, designed to allow for self-learning. The material is supported with a running and operational OB 2.1 compatible Displayer certified portal with enhanced stackability functions and services.

A core innovation of this initiative is the introduction of stackable digital badges through the DISCO PLAYER (DcP from now on) portal. These badges will include standardized, multilingual metadata, marking a significant step toward a unified European approach to issuing and exchanging digital credentials in VET and HE. This system will ensure that credentials are automatically recognized and integrated across organizations using 'Meta-badges.'

The DISCO SMS project will create digital repositories for students, enabling them to display and earn endorsements for their Open Badges. These repositories will streamline the recognition and validation of achievements across diverse educational platforms. By providing universally available recognition markers, digital badges can help democratize career advancement opportunities in the scientific community, thereby supporting the recognition of soft skills in a more equitable manner.

Acknowledgments

The project "Digitally Signed Credentials – Smart Motivation with Stackability (DISCO SMS)" has been funded within the framework of Erasmus+ programme KA220-VET - Cooperation partnerships in vocational education and training (KA220-VET).

References

Caron, B., R. (2021). Open Science Badges Are Coming—And the New Nobel. Retrieved from https://doi.org/10.21428/8bbb7f85.908cd829

QualityLink: a new Interoperable Architecture for Exchanging Quality Data on Learning Opportunities

Colin Tück[1], Tiago Simões[2], Jochen Ehrenreich[3], Estela Daukšienė[4], Elena Trepulė[5], Arantza Mongelos Garcia[6]

[1] Knowledge Innovation Centre (KIC), colin@knowledgeinnovation.eu
[2] European University Foundation (EUF), tiago.simoes@uni-foundation.eu
[3] DHBW, jochen.ehrenreich@heilbronn.dhbw.de
[4] EDEN DLE, estela.dauksiene@vdu.lt
[5] EDEN DLE, elena.trepule@vdu.lt
[6] Mondragon University, amongelos@mondragon.edu

Correspondence: Colin Tück: colin@knowledgeinnovation.eu

Abstract:

The QualityLink project focuses on aggregating basic descriptions and quality indicators on learning opportunities leading to micro-credentials. Currently, such data is often hidden completely or not published in interoperable formats. With the increasingly diverse landscape of learning opportunities, both potential learners and other stakeholders, such as employers or recognition officers, need reliable and open data to inform their choices and decisions.

The project proposed a technical architecture that allows higher education institutions and other data providers to easily publish relevant data using existing widespread data standards (e.g. ELM, OOAPI, Edu-API, OCCAPI). Through a standardised data discovery mechanism, this data can then be aggregated Europe-wide. The QualityLink will test the proposed technical specifications and launch a pilot data portal.

Keywords: micro-credentials, quality, indicators, interoperability, data

Summary

The QualityLink project focuses on aggregating basic descriptions and quality indicators on learning opportunities leading to micro-credentials. A comprehensive inventory of possible quality indicators has been created by the project consortium. Work is currently underway to prioritise the relevance and importance of different indicators for potential learners and other stakeholders.

Currently, such data is often hidden completely or not published in interoperable formats. With the increasingly diverse landscape of learning opportunities, both potential learners and other stakeholders, such as employers or recognition officers, need reliable and open data to inform their choices and decisions. The QualityLink project aims to integrate data from three types of sources:

1. **Education providers** themselves may provide trusted data on their own learning opportunities;

2. **Authoritative sources** (such as DEQAR, ETER or national authorities) may provide trusted data on various providers' learning opportunities;

3. **Other data sources** (such as ranking providers, rating portals, etc.) may provide specific data on existing learning opportunities.

The project has proposed a technical architecture that allows higher education institutions and other data providers to easily publish relevant data using existing wide-spread data standards. The poster illustrates the proposed architecture, including the following main components:

- **Unique course identifier**: aims to harmonise approaches to identifying and tracking learning opportunities regardless of data standard used;

- **Data source discovery**: uses existing registries (e.g. DEQAR or the EWP registry) to enable recognised higher education institutions to publish their data without a need for manual registration or onboarding;

- **Data exchange**: standardises a the data formats in which education providers and others can make data available for aggregation and addresses issues such as incremental transport;

- **Ontology**: extends the European Learning Model (ELM) and its application profile for Learning Opportunities and Qualifications (LOQ) to cover all quality indicators from the inventory.

The proposed architecture allows to publish data using ELM, the Open Education API (OOAPI), the Edu-API or the Open Course Catalogue API (OCCAPI) interchangeably. The QualityLink will test the proposed technical specifications and launch a pilot data portal. All higher education institutions are invited to participate in testing and make their data available for aggregation.

More information: https://quality-link.eu/

This project has been funded with support from the European Commission. This publication reflects the views only of the authors, and the Commission cannot be held responsible for any use which may be made of the information contained therein.

References

1EdTech (no year). Edu-API. https://www.1edtech.org/standards/edu-api

EU Council. (2022). COUNCIL RECOMMENDATION of 16 June 2022 on a European approach to micro credentials for lifelong learning and employability (2022/C 243/02; Official Journal of the European Union, pp. 10–22). https://eur-lex.europa.eu/legal-content/EN/TXT/PDF/?uri=CELEX:32022H0627(02)

European Commission (no year). European Learning Model Browser. https://europa.eu/europass/elm-browser/index.html

European University Foundation (no year). Open Course Catalogue API (1.0.0-beta5). https://occapi.uni-foundation.eu/

QualityLink project (2025). Technical Specifications: Public Consultation. https://quality-link.eu/technical-specs/

Simões, T. & Tück, C. (2025). Quality Data Exchange Architecture: QualityLink report. https://quality-link.eu/project-outputs/concept-paper/

SURF (no year). Open Education API. https://openonderwijsapi.nl/#/

Trepulė, E., Čepauskiene, R., Braun, C. & Tück, C. (2024). Quality Domains and Indicators: QualityLink report. https://quality-link.eu/quality-domains-and-indicators/

Tück, C., Simões, T. & Ehrenreich, J. (2025). Feasibility Analysis of Indicators: QualityLink report. https://quality-link.eu/project-outputs/feasibility-analysis/

In the Sandbox with GenAI: Faculty Practices and Reflections

Leigh Graves Wolf[1], Geraldine O'Neill[2]

[1] UCD Teaching & Learning, University College Dublin, Ireland; leigh.wolf@ucd.ie
[2] UCD Teaching & Learning, University College Dublin, Ireland; geraldine.m.oneill@ucd.ie

Correspondence: Leigh Graves Wolf, leigh.wolf@ucd.ie

Abstract:

This poster explores a 'sandbox' approach to faculty development in generative AI (GenAI) implementation within University College Dublin's Professional Teaching Qualification Programme. Students in a module on assessment were offered three options for incorporating GenAI in their own final assessment: *no use of GenAI to produce a critical reflection, GenAI as the author of a critical reflection, and GenAI as a 'thought partner' for critical reflection*. The findings demonstrate the value of protected spaces for faculty to explore emerging technologies, offering a transferable model for faculty development programs grappling with GenAI integration in higher education.

Keywords: Generative AI, Faculty Development, Assessment, Higher Education

In software development, sandboxes serve as protected testing environments where developers can experiment, fail, and learn without risk to live systems. This same principle is essential for faculty development, particularly when exploring and supporting them to play with emerging technologies (Proyer's, 2014). As generative artificial intelligence (GenAI) transforms higher education, faculty require similar protected spaces to experiment with and critically evaluate these tools

While discussions about GenAI continue to dominate discourse in academic circles, many faculty members remain hesitant to engage with these tools in practice. This hesitation stems from various concerns: ethical implications, academic integrity, and uncertainty about effective implementation (Kizilcec, 2024). To address this hesitancy, this poster explores a 'sandbox' initiative within a Professional Teaching Qualification Programme at a European research-intensive university, where faculty were encouraged to experiment with GenAI in a structured, low-stakes environment initially and then allowed to choose whether to use it in a more high-stakes assessment.

In the Spring of 2024, 32 faculty in a module on assessment in higher education were presented with three options for integrating GenAI into their final assessment: *no use of GenAI to produce a critical reflection, GenAI as the author of a critical reflection, and GenAI as a 'thought partner' for critical reflection*. Faculty were also scaffolded in the process with a technical session encouraging them to 'play' with GenAI, learning some of the rules of the game by using an 'Evaluating AI Text' rubric (University of British Columbia, 2023.). In addition, in-class discussions and associated video resources explored the rationale for the use of GenAi in these different options. This allowed staff the option to 'play' with GenAI, linking with some of Proyer's (2014) functions of adult play, i.e. mastery orientation, creativity, coping strategies, and coping with situations. This poster shares both the process and product of this exploration (n=17 study participants), providing a visual of a 'moment in time' where faculty were provided an opportunity to explore what GenAI means to themselves and their discipline.

This poster will offer transferable examples for faculty development programs seeking to address the challenges and opportunities presented by GenAI in higher education. It will share the examples and tensions that arose in the explorations and will provide a model to consider for implementation in parallel faculty development programmes. The poster will provide pragmatic and research-informed resources for faculty and educational developers and will include links to resources for attendees interested in implementing similar initiatives at their institutions, including assessment rubrics, assignment templates, and guidance for creating supportive spaces for staff to explore and play with GenAI.

Note: Ethical approval was granted for this study by the University Human Research Ethics Committee

References

Kizilcec, R. F. (2024). To advance AI use in education, focus on understanding educators. *International Journal of Artificial Intelligence in Education*, 34(1), 12-19. http://dx.doi.org/10.1007/s40593-023-00351-4

Proyer, R. T. (2014). Perceived functions of playfulness in adults: Does it mobilize you at work, rest, and when 17 being with others? *European Review of Applied Psychology / Revue Européenne de Psychologie Appliquée,* 64(5), 241 – 250. https://doi.org/10/1016/j.erap.2014.06.011

University of British Columbia (2023) *Evaluating AI text.* https://learningdesignviews.educ.ubc.ca/evaluating-ai-text/

Innovative Teaching and Assessment in Biomechanics: Leveraging GenAI to Empower Students for Enhanced Learning

Kathleen Shorter[1], Amanda Benson[2]

[1] School of Health Sciences, Swinburne University of Technology, Australia; kshorter@swin.edu.au
[2] School of Health Sciences, Swinburne University of Technology, Australia; abenson@swin.edu.au

Correspondence: Kathleen Shorter kshorter@swin.edu.au

Abstract:

AI is transforming the educational landscape, and the rapid development of Generative AI (GenAI) poses both opportunities and challenges for learning, teaching and assessment (Tertiary Education Quality and Standards Agency, 2024). There is sometimes a disconnect between industry and emerging workforce expectations of graduates and the speed of adaptations in emerging curriculum areas in higher education. Within exercise and sport science, computer coding, digital literacy skills, including GenAI, are some of the recent and emerging integrations (Bruce et al., 2022; Exercise and Sports Science Australia, 2024; World Economic Forum, 2025). However, only 8% of academic teaching staff reported integrating AI as a teaching tool (McDonald et al., 2024). Embracing GenAI in learning and teaching, underpinned by constructivist theory (Savery & Duffy, 1995), enables the application of GenAI as an educational tool for students with no or limited prior knowledge or experience in computer programming. In this context, it can be used as a mechanism to empower students and enable them to gain familiarity with coding environments to increase the complexity of contextual learning. Additionally, it enables critical thinking about ethical use of GenAI to ensure compliance with professional standards, such as, privacy and data management (Exercise and Sports Science Australia, 2024); expected skills of work-ready graduates (World Economic Forum, 2025).

We present a case study of how a traditional lab-based biomechanics curriculum was reimagined to problem-based learning (Savery & Duffy, 1995) where students were assessed on their application of biomechanical methods in the design and validation of an instrumented biofeedback device to address the needs of a stakeholder. The project teams used an exploratory process to determine what would assist them, with students encouraged to use GenAI as a tool to assist with the coding required to complete the assessment task. This enabled students to learn and apply biomechanical concepts (the learning outcomes of the unit) whilst also developing future work and lifelong skills such as collaboration and critical thinking as part of the inter-section between people and technology working together (World Economic Forum, 2025).

Keywords: Generative AI, enhanced learning, assessment, biomechanics, industry brief, digital transformation

Summary

This poster outlines the process of how Generative AI (GenAI) was used to transform traditional biomechanics laboratory classes for undergraduate students, who will graduate as Exercise Scientists, to enable industry-relevant projects for students with no or limited coding experience. It showcases the project brief teaching materials and how they encourage students to utilize GenAI as a tool in the development of their product; incorporating prototype validation and refinement through the application of biomechanical knowledge and skills before developing a video-based pitch for a specific audience. The project demonstrates the collaboration of people and technology working together to develop a technology-based solution whilst also fostering collaboration, critical thinking, ethical and data management skills to prepare students for the future of work and the development of lifelong learning skills. Future work will also enable us to develop an understanding from the student's perspective.

References

Bruce, L., Bellesini, K., Aisbett, B., Drinkwater, E. J., & Kremer, P. (2022). A profile of the skills, attributes, development, and employment opportunities for sport scientists in Australia. *Journal of science and medicine in sport*, *25*(5), 419-424.

Exercise and Sports Science Australia (2024) *Digital Practice Standards.* https://www.essa.org.au/Common/Uploaded%20files/Standards/digital-practice-standards.pdf

McDonald, P., Hay, S., Cathcart, A., & Feldman, A. (2024). Apostles, Agnostics and Atheists: Engagement with Generative AI by Australian University Staff. QUT Centre for Decent Work and Industry, Brisbane, Qld.

Savery, J. R., & Duffy, T. M. (1995). Problem Based Learning: An Instructional Model and Its Constructivist Framework. Educational Technology, 35(5), 31–38.

Tertiary Education Quality and Standards Agency (2024). *Generative AI strategies: Emerging practice toolkit.* https://www.teqsa.gov.au/sites/default/files/2024-11/Gen-AI-strategies-emerging-practice-toolkit.pdf

World Economic Forum (2025). *The future of jobs report 2025.* https://reports.weforum.org/docs/WEF_Future_of_Jobs_Report_2025.pdf

The PDC Ladder for Teacher Education: A Three-Tiered Framework for Digital Competence Integration

Sigrun Lindaas Norhagen[1]

[1]Department of Teacher Education, NLA University College, Norway; sigrun.norhagen@nla.no

Correspondence: Sigrun Lindaas Norhagen: sigrun.norhagen@nla.no

Abstract:

This poster showcases a novel three-level framework, the PDC Ladder for Teacher Education (TE), designed to scaffold teacher educators in implementing Professional Digital Competence in teacher education programs (Norhagen et al., 2024). Although existing research recognizes the difficulties associated with integrating digital competence into teacher education curricula, there remains a gap in practical implementation models. Our framework addresses this gap by presenting a hierarchical structure that explicitly connects the metacognitive aspects of teaching with technology integration, highlighting the distinct responsibilities of teacher educators beyond those of teachers. Whereas teachers are expected to incorporate technology into their practice, teacher educators must also explicitly model and articulate the pedagogical reasoning behind these choices, fostering student teachers' ability to critically engage with and apply digital competence in their own teaching.

Keywords: Professional Digital Competence, Teacher Educator, Second-order teacher, Digital Skills Framework, Technology Integration, Teacher Education Framework

Teacher educators face a unique challenge in their dual role: they must both teach student teachers and prepare these students to teach pupils. This duality extends to all aspects of their work, including the integration of Professional Digital Competence (PDC). Although teachers are responsible for developing and applying PDC in their teaching, teacher educators must also explicitly model and articulate their pedagogical reasoning, ensuring that student teachers not only use digital tools effectively as student teachers but also critically reflect on their role in fostering digital competence for primary school students.

To address these challenges, we introduce the PDC Ladder for Teacher Education (TE), a structured framework designed to help teacher educators navigate their dual role in fostering Professional Digital Competence. This model emphasizes the necessity of explicit modeling and pedagogical transparency, ensuring that student teachers not only acquire digital skills but also develop a critical awareness of how and why digital tools are integrated into teaching. By distinguishing the responsibilities at different levels of teacher education, the framework supports teacher educators in making informed decisions about their own digital practices while guiding student teachers toward reflective and strategic technology use in their future classrooms.

The PDC Ladder comprises three interconnected levels: the foundational level, which addresses pupils' digital skills in primary school; the intermediate level, which focuses on teachers' professional digital competence; and the top level, which emphasizes teacher educators' meta-cognitive role. Using Starkey's PDC model (2019) as an example for the intermediate level, we demonstrate how teacher educators can effectively model and communicate three key dimensions of the teacher: managing the digital learning environment, dimensions of integration of technology into teaching practices (including teaching children using technology) and the professional work of being a teacher.

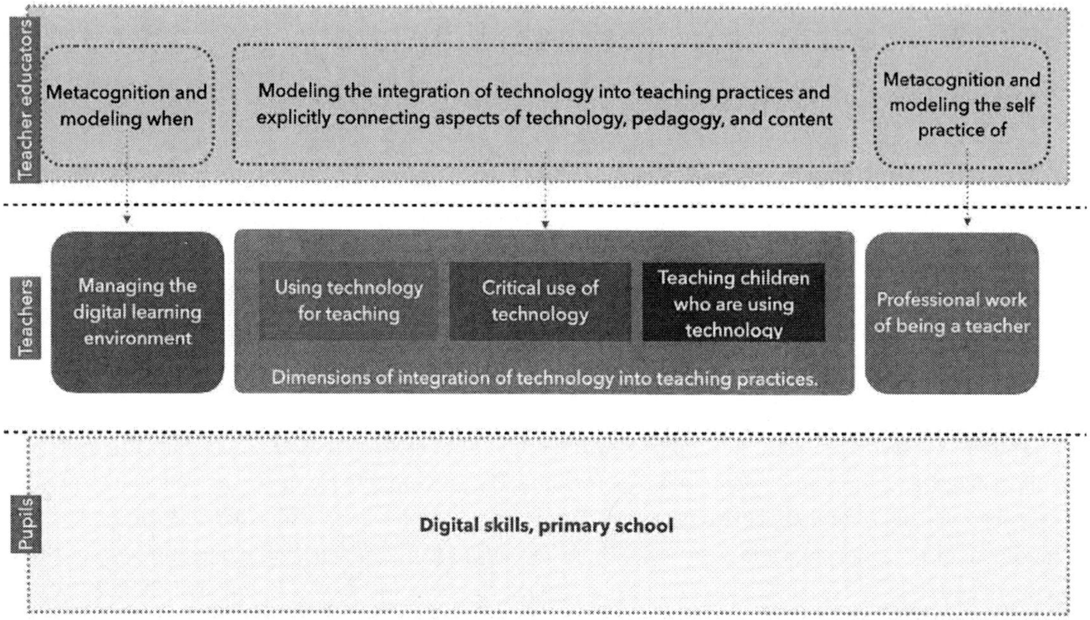

The framework's distinctive feature lies in its explicit separation of concerns across the three levels while maintaining clear connections between them. This poster specifically focuses on how the model supports teacher educators in differentiating and addressing what needs to be taught at each level all while remaining cognizant of the interconnections between levels. By emphasizing both metacognition and explicit modeling at the teacher educator level, the framework offers a practical tool for understanding and implementing the dual role of teaching both with and about digital competence (Uerz et al., 2018), addressing a critical gap in teacher education practice. By offering a structured yet flexible approach, the PDC Ladder provides teacher educators with a concrete tool to guide the development of Professional Digital Competence at all levels, ensuring a cohesive and comprehensive integration of technology in teacher education.

References

Norhagen, S. L., Krumsvik, R. J., & Røkenes, F. M. (2024). Developing professional digital competence in Norwegian teacher education: a scoping review. Frontiers in Education, 9, 2.

Starkey, L. (2019). A review of research exploring teacher preparation for the digital age. *Cambridge Journal of Education*, *50*(1), 37-56.

Uerz, D., Volman, M., & Kral, M. (2018). Teacher educators' competences in fostering student teachers' proficiency in teaching and learning with technology: An overview of relevant research literature. *Teaching and Teacher Education*, *70*, 12-23.

Turning Theory into Practice: A Quality Survey for Diverse Online Learners

Astri-Birgitte Grimenæs[1], Hanne Kristin Dypedal[2]

[1] Unit for Educational Quality, NLA University college, Norway; astgri@nla.no
[2] Department of digitalization, NLA University college, Norway; handyp@nla.no

Correspondence: Hanne Kristin Dypedal: handyp@nla.no

Abstract:

This poster aims to demonstrate how research-based frameworks can be used to systematically evaluate online course quality and identify areas for development. In recent years, online education has experienced significant growth in Norway (Norwegian Directorate for Higher Education and Skills, 2022, p. 35). As advisors on educational quality and online studies at a university college experiencing significant growth in online education, it has been essential to gain a deeper understanding of this emerging student group. This poster presents the results of a project at NLA University College, where we developed a survey applying a research-based framework to systematically evaluate students' experiences in online programs, with the aim of informing strategic course development and quality enhancement. Understanding the needs and experiences of this diverse student body is essential for ensuring high-quality, engaging online courses.

The survey was inspired by Garrels and Zemliansky (2022), whose work identifies three key pillars for successful online learning: student-active learning, user-centered structure, and social interaction. Building on this framework, a survey was developed and distributed to our online students across 16 different study programs during autumn 2024. A total of 143 students consented to participate, providing insights into their perceptions of course quality and their individual learning experiences. The dataset was analyzed to identify patterns across demographic groups, such as age, time since previous studies, and study program.

Our findings reveal notable differences in student satisfaction. Younger students (under 22 years) report lower levels of satisfaction, particularly concerning social interaction and opportunities for active learning. In contrast, students over the age of 36 rate their experiences more positively, highlighting well-structured courses with clear learning objectives.

Social interaction emerges as the area with the most potential for improvement at the university college, particularly for younger and full-time students. However, positive correlations were identified between students' use of support services (such as library and IT assistance) and higher ratings of both social interaction and course structure. Furthermore, respectful and supportive communication from instructors was strongly linked to students' overall satisfaction, suggesting that communication quality plays a central role in fostering a positive online learning environment.

While the dataset is not sufficient to draw general conclusions about all online students and study programs, the findings provide a valuable foundation for further internal investigations into how individual programs can be developed. Additionally, this survey serves as a starting point for the development of a research-based questionnaire focused on evaluating the quality of online education. By integrating student feedback into strategic planning and course design, the project provides practical insights for institutions seeking to tailor online education to the needs of diverse student populations.

Keywords: Education quality, online learning, course design, student satisfaction, student feedback

Summary

This poster aims to demonstrate how research-based frameworks can be used to systematically evaluate online course quality and identify areas for development. By integrating student feedback into strategic planning and course design, the project provides practical insights for institutions seeking to develop their online study portfolio and gain new insights.

References

Garrels, V., & Zemliansky, P. (2022). Improving Student Engagement in Online Courses through Interactive and User-Centered Course Design: Practical Strategies. *Nordic Journal of Digital Literacy*, 17(2), 112-122.

Norwegian Directorate for Higher Education and Skills. (2022). *Higher Education Condition Report 2021–2022. Norwegian Ministry of Education and Research*. https://hkdir.no/rapporter-undersokelser-og-statistikk/tilstandsrapport-for-hoyere-utdanning-2022

Six Online Student Personas

Hanne Kristin Dypedal[1]

[1] Department of digitalization, NLA University College, Norway; handyp@nla.no

Correspondence: Hanne Kristin Dypedal@nla.no

Abstract:

As the diversity of online student populations continues to grow, understanding who these learners are becomes increasingly important for designing effective and supportive online education. This poster presents a project conducted at a Norwegian university college, aiming to identify and illustrate the characteristics of online students through the development of six representative personas. These personas serve as a practical tool for educators to better understand their student groups and adapt course design and support services accordingly. Personas serve as composite archetypes based on real user behaviors and motivations, enabling a deeper understanding of their goals in specific contexts (Cooper & Reimann, 2003, p. 55). This approach allows for a more targeted design of online education that aligns with diverse student needs.

The project analyzed 230 self-introduction posts from online students across several programs, using qualitative content analysis with inductive coding to identify key traits such as age, previous study experience, motivations, and study habits. Through thematic grouping, six personas were developed: "First-Time Student Finn," "Ambitious Alice," " Lifelong Learner Laura," "Paternity Leave Peter," "Career-Changer Caleb," and "Grown-up Grace." Each persona captures distinct motivations and learning strategies, providing insight into the varied needs of online learners.

To refine the personas, all posts were reanalyzed, and adjustments were made to better represent the identified groups. Descriptive statistics were applied to quantify the distribution of personas across different study programs, visualized through pie charts to give an overview of student composition. This approach allows the institution to reflect on whether certain programs attract a broad spectrum of learners or are dominated by specific student types, which can inform strategic pedagogical adjustments.

For dissemination, the personas were brought to life through short, animated videos created using AI-assisted tools. Each video presents a persona describing their motivation for studying online and sharing personal study strategies. QR codes linking to these videos are included on the poster, along with key descriptors for each persona.

This project demonstrates how persona methodology, combined with qualitative analysis, can provide actionable insights into online student populations. By presenting the findings in an accessible and engaging format, the personas have become a valuable resource for educators seeking to tailor their courses to diverse learner needs, even within the constraints of a busy academic environment.

Keywords: Online studies, instructional design, student personas, student motivation, education quality

Summary

This poster presentation provides an example of how personas can be used to support the development and enhancement of online education, tailored to diverse student groups. By constructing representative personas based on qualitative analysis, educators and institutions can gain deeper insights into the motivations, study habits, and needs of online learners, facilitating more informed pedagogical and structural adjustments.

References

Cooper, A. & Reimann, R. (2003). About Face 2.0. *The essentials of Interaction Design.* Wiley Publishing, inc. Retrieved from https://cs.uwaterloo.ca/~jianzhao/cs449-649/files/personas-and-goals.pdf

Fostering a Sustainable Future: Innovation and Education Management in Vocational Education and Training

Ugne Supranaviciene [1], Genute Gedviliene[2], Lina Vaitkute[3]

[1] Education academy, Vytautas Magnus University, Mykolas Romeris PhD student, Lithuania; ug.supranaviciene@stud.mru.eu
[2] Education academy, Vytautas Magnus University, Lithuania; genute.gedviliene@vdu.lt
[3] Education academy, Vytautas Magnus University, Lithuania; lina.vaitkute@vdu.lt

Correspondence: Ugne Supranaviciene: ugne.supranaviciene@vdu.lt

Abstract:

Relevance. Vocational Education and Training plays a crucial role in preparing individuals for a rapidly changing world, and integrating sustainability into VET curricula is essential for fostering a future-oriented workforce aligned with global sustainable development goals (Franco et al., 2018). This abstract proposes a framework for enhancing sustainability in VET through innovation, effective education management, and a structured skills development approach. The framework encompasses different aspects. Curriculum innovation: integrating sustainability principles and practices into VET programs across diverse sectors, such as building and construction, and the energy sector. This includes incorporating the economical and resource-conserving use of materials and addressing skills gaps related to sustainability. Technology integration: leveraging new technologies like 3D modeling and virtual reality (Maričić et al., 2019) to create immersive learning experiences that promote sustainable practices. Mobile and flexible technologies can also enhance workplace learning in VET (Ng & Lam, 2018). Innovative pedagogical approaches: promoting blended learning approaches (Samuel, 2023) that combine theoretical knowledge with practical skills and real-world applications. Encouraging project-based learning and cooperative learning (Zhang, 2012) to foster critical thinking, problem-solving, and collaboration skills related to sustainability. Drawing upon principles of adult learning, the framework emphasizes personalized learning approaches that recognize prior knowledge, ensure relevance to real-world scenarios, and cater to diverse learning styles, as well as building soft skills (Gedvilienė et al., n.d.). Skills development matrix: development of a skills development matrix, which identifies key sustainability competencies, learning objectives, and assessment methods for each VET program. This matrix ensures a systematic approach to skills development and enables the tracking of learner progress. This component helps to ensure a skills match between the skills offered and the skills demanded in the labor market. Education management for sustainability: implementing management practices that support the integration of sustainability into all aspects of VET institutions (Vakaliuk et al., 2021). This includes fostering an innovative culture (None, n.d.), providing professional development opportunities for educators, and establishing partnerships with industry and community stakeholders. Addressing soft skills: developing soft skills of teachers, such as communication, teamwork, critical thinking, and digital literacy (Gedvilienė et al., n.d.; Uskova & others, 2022), to enable them to effectively deliver sustainability-focused VET programs. This should include components that are directly applicable to educators' job satisfaction (Gedvilienė et al., n.d.). Regional development: recognizing the importance of regional planning in achieving sustainability (Veckalne & Tambovceva, 2022) and tailoring VET programs to meet the specific needs of local communities and industries.

By embracing innovation, implementing effective education management strategies, and utilizing a skills development matrix, VET institutions can equip learners with the knowledge, skills, and values needed to contribute to a more sustainable future. This abstract calls for further research and collaboration to develop and implement sustainable VET practices that address the evolving challenges of the 21st century.

Methodology. Quantitate method applied. The research performed in compliance with the main principles of ethics: benevolence, insights and express their opinion; honesty. The research respondents were 119 employees in construction organisations from different countries (Germany, Lithuania, Spain, The Netherlands, Finland, and Italy). The research based on the following methodological dispositions: transformative learning and experiential learning theory. Research was conducted in two stages: 1) research into required interdisciplinary competencies, identifying the importance of digital literacy and its relations with interdisciplinary competences development 2) research into the sustainable interdisciplinary competencies development.

This paper will present what conditions are needed for a VET learner to develop sustainability competencies in the interdisciplinary context in the construction sector and how it is related to technological innovations. What prerequisites are needed to ensure sustainable interdisciplinary competencies development?
The aim of this paper is to reveal sustainability importance in developing interdisciplinary competencies in the construction sector.

Keywords: Adult education, personalized learning, skills development, soft skills, sustainability, vocational education and training.

References

Gedvilienė, G., Tūtlys, V., Mičiulienė, R., et al. (Gedvilienė et al., n.d.). *Soft skills training model for pedagogues, promoting job satsfacton, responding to the needs of educatonal processes in the context of LLL.*

Franco, I. B., Saitô, O., Vaughter, P., et al. (Franco et al., 2018). Higher education for sustainable development: actioning the global goals in policy, curriculum and practice. *Sustainability Science, 14,* 1631–1642.

Maričić, S., Mrša Haber, I., Radolović, D., et al. (Maričić et al., 2019). The Emerging Role of New Technologies in Vocational Education.

McGrath, S., & Powell, L. (McGrath & Powell, 2016). Skills for sustainable development: Transforming vocational education and training beyond 2015.

Ng, R. Y.-K., & Lam, R. Y. S. (Ng & Lam, 2018). Using Mobile and Flexible Technologies to Enhance Workplace Learning in Vocational Education and Training.

Vakaliuk, T. A., Novitska, I., Verbovsky, I., et al. (Vakaliuk et al., 2021). Management of educational institutions with inclusive education based on innovative technologies.

Veckalne, R., & Tambovceva, T. (Veckalne & Tambovceva, 2022). SUSTAINABLE REGIONAL DEVELOPMENT PLANNING. *Baltic Journal of Regional Development, 1,* 94–104.

Zhang, A. (Zhang, 2012). Cooperative Learning and Soft Skills Training in an IT Course. *2022 7th International Conference on Social Sciences and Economic Development.*